HISTORY *of* the Present

A JOURNAL OF CRITICAL HISTORY

Reproductive Racial Capitalism

JENNIFER L. MORGAN AND ALYS EVE WEINBAUM, SPECIAL ISSUE EDITORS

Volume 14 ▪ Number 1 ▪ April 2024

T0335248

Jennifer L. Morgan and Alys Eve Weinbaum

Introduction
Reproductive Racial Capitalism

ABSTRACT This essay introduces the special issue with a critique of Cedric Robinson's heuristic, "racial capitalism," and a discussion of our titular intervention: "reproductive racial capitalism." The essay is necessarily grounded in the reproductive crisis of the present day. It centers the histories and afterlives of hereditary racial slavery and the radical contestations and refusals of its logics. Overall, it argues that contemporary racial capitalism is always already reproductive. Reproductive labor and the experiences of conception, gestation, parturition, and childrearing are the heart and engine of both slave racial capitalism and contemporary forms of reproductive racial capitalism. They are also the sites from which reproductive racial capitalism and its exploitative conditions were contested under slavery, are being challenged in the present moment, and yet might be altogether refused in the future.

KEYWORDS slavery, human reproduction, racial capitalism, feminism, Marxism

We cannot consider the question of the relationship of race to reproduction, or the relationship of both race and reproduction to capitalism, isolated from our current reproductive crisis. The June 2022 United States Supreme Court ruling in *Dobbs v. Jackson Women's Health Organization* is the context in which we write this introduction and meditate on the connections across the contributions that are included in this special issue on *reproductive racial capitalism*. In its ruling, the court rescinded the bodily autonomy of pregnant persons and pitted them against their fetuses. As the feminist legal scholar Dorothy Roberts illustrated over two decades ago, it is hereditary racial slavery that first inserts the idea of a maternal/fetal conflict into the reproductive cultures and politics that shape the Atlantic world. As we argue in this introduction, hereditary racial slavery subsequently places the battle over reproduction at the heart of modern racial capitalism. Mobilizing the disturbingly iconic image of a hole dug in the ground for a pregnant woman to lay her belly in while being flogged, Roberts graphically crystallized the conflict on which

HISTORY of the PRESENT ▪ A Journal of Critical History ▪ 14:1 ▪ April 2024
DOI 10.1215/21599785-10898330 © 2024 Duke University Press

slavery's foundational ideological and material logics rest (39–41). Here we argue that it is from this conflict that the commercial imperatives of modern racial capitalism emerge and henceforth shape the social and economic organization of race, gender, and sexuality in slavery and in what Christina Sharpe has influentially metaphorized as its wake (Sharpe).

In placing the pregnant belly of the enslaved woman in a hole in the ground while flogging the woman's body, the slave owners' interest in financial futurity wrenches reproductive labor and kinship away from her. Her exposed back is lashed while her belly and her fetus—the objectified "flesh" that the slave owner treats as his property (Spillers)—lay beneath the earth, supposedly protected. As the enslaved woman endures this specifically reproductive torture, violence that comes on top of all the myriad violations to which she has already been subjected prior to this moment, her futurity is reshaped. She comprehends the profound limits imposed on her capacity to situate a potential child in her future, to identify herself as a mother in relation to the life gestating in her body, and she senses the looming impossibility that steals labor from her womb and potential kinship from the world. As Hortense Spillers has written, under slavery "the captive female" emerges as both "mother and mother-dispossessed" (80). As Saidiya Hartman has observed, building on Spillers and others (Morgan, *Laboring Women*; Weinbaum, "Gendering"), under slavery the birth canal becomes a middle passage ("Belly" 169).

The notion that a person's reproductive processes and children are the human biological commodities on which the entire system of hereditary slavery relies, and that the commodification of reproduction and its living products together negate kinship, are the twinned logics that are set in motion by what Walter Johnson has called "slave racial capitalism" ("To Remake" 14). Here we both specify and expand on Johnson's concept by introducing the new term *reproductive racial capitalism*. Our term resonates with concepts like slave racial capitalism and colonial racial capitalism (Koshy et al.) insofar as it too attempts to add to and at once reveal something new about the workings of racial capitalism. Specifically, reproductive racial capitalism is capitalism that is inclusive of slave racial capitalism and colonial racial capitalism but is not restricted to either. Like both, it is at once a pervasive form of racial capitalism and a specific vantage point on racial capitalism. What it underscores above all is that all forms of racial capitalism are predicated on ongoing reproductive extraction, dispossession, and accumulation. Reproductive racial capitalism is, in our view, most visible in hereditary racial slavery, but it is also, we argue, alive and well today. As we elaborate below, just as all capitalism ought to be regarded as racial capitalism, we propose that all racial capitalism ought to be regarded as reproductive. Our new term captures this *reproductive* truth and attempts to bring it to light.

In advancing an argument about reproductive racial capitalism, we build on arguments that Jennifer L. Morgan (*Laboring Women*, *"Partus Sequitur Ventrem," Reckoning*, "Reproductive Rights") and Alys Eve Weinbaum (*Wayward Reproductions*, "Gendering," *Afterlife*, "Reproducing Racial Capitalism," "Slave Episteme," "Ungendering") have each advanced elsewhere about the importance of studying reproduction in both slavery (Morgan, *Laboring Women*) and in the subsequent decades that constitute its afterlife (Weinbaum, *Afterlife*). We also build on a rich tradition of work by feminist scholars of reproductive dispossession in past and present, including contributions that have been made by many of those whose work is included in this special issue (Briggs, Johnson, Solinger, Turner, Vertommen). While we cannot speak for all contributors, at least for the two of us, slavery is not simply one among many important examples of reproductive racial capitalism. Rather, we regard slavery as both exceptional and exemplary because it is underpinned materially, decisively, and so incredibly visibly (when we choose to see it thus) by reproductive extraction, dispossession, and accumulation. Indeed, we regard reproduction in slavery as *the* paradigm case, as an ür-text, and as an episteme that must be studied if we are to understand how and why reproductive racial capitalism works and is able to continue to expand. This is because in our view it is only when we center reproduction in slavery that it becomes possible to come to a full account of reproductive racial capitalism at both its inception and as it unfurls across time.

Reproductive exploitation fueled Atlantic slavery. And, as enslaved women and men pushed back against slavery regimes, reproductive contestation was part and parcel of the many forms of opposition that they mobilized. Because the legacies of slavery live on in both the material and ideological organization of reproductive racial capitalism today, it is imperative that we learn to track both the forms of exploitation and the forms of refusal that continue to power it. A full and historically accurate account of racial capitalism must center reproduction in slavery and keep it in view. While not all contributions to this special issue are principally focused on slavery, all share a common interest in the constitutive relationship between reproduction and racial capitalism, and all in one way or another explore the refusal of reproductive racial capitalism—albeit through analysis of historically and geospatially distinct events, spaces, and places.

How did enslaved women reconcile the world-changing conflict established between their reproductive bodies and the fetuses growing within their wombs with their efforts to protect their most intimate bodily experiences, their potential children, their existing families, and the larger communities to which they belonged from the violence of hereditary racial slavery? The archives of slavery yield any number of stories regarding the efforts that enslaved women made as they sought to wrest pregnancy or children from the maws of slavery. Their actions stand as testimony not to the existence of an ahistorical idea about the power of mother love; rather, they reveal to us the extent to which slavery fundamentally transformed all aspects of human reproduction—including procreation, conception, gestation, parturition, and childrearing—into a multifaceted experience that was and remains saturated with economic conflicts and contradictions. Women's resistant actions also testify to their desire to challenge or altogether refuse the logics of an emerging global marketplace predicated on the use of the reproductive body and its products as both an economic engine of valuable commodities and as a source of raw materials.

We begin from the conceit that enslaved women simply could not have been ignorant of the demands that hereditary racial slavery placed on them. Indeed, from the vantage point of reproductive racial capitalism, procreation, conception, gestation, parturition, and childrearing together constitute *the* crucial reproductive sites from which enslaved women built their understanding of their situation, and thus the sites from which scholars must build our understanding of the Black radical tradition. This scholarship traces a genealogy of women's complex challenge to the extraction and exploitation of their reproductive capacities, and it is thus what we must learn from as we attempt to catalyze an insurgent response to ongoing reproductive dispossession. It is from this vantage point that we understand the actions of enslaved women to remove their reproductive potential and children from the account books of slave owners as acts of contestation that straddled the social and affective space of kinship, and at once imagined refusal of the material violence of reproductive racial capitalism.[1]

Our resolutely and unapologetically feminist understanding of the Black radical tradition as inclusive of women's reproductive insurgency has only really begun to take hold in recent years, mainly in the work of scholars focused on reproduction in slavery and in that of a handful of scholars focused on reproduction in contemporary racial capitalism. The latter have sought to theorize the "enslaving" dynamics of reproductive dispossession as these have been recalibrated across time and forwarded into the present. In this special issue, we have gathered the work of a number of these scholars together to situate an extended and collaborative rumination on the ways in which reproductive racial capitalism develops from and then moves beyond the period of hereditary racial slavery alongside an extended account of specific ways that reproductive racial capitalism was contested, challenged, and refused beginning in the slave past and extending into the present moment. Indeed, as implicit and explicit dialogue among contributors to the present issue makes apparent, the essays collected here are the product of an intensive series of exchanges that took place in workshops held remotely in 2021 and 2022 in which contributors and interlocutors focused on reproductive cultures and politics across time and place so as to map reproduction's travels in slavery and beyond.

The scholarship on reproduction and racial capitalism that we allude to above (and which includes our own) has been adjacent to and at times has intersected with the veritable boom over the past two decades in scholarship coincident with the republication of political scientist Cedric Robinson's *Black Marxism: The Making of the Black Radical Tradition*. As a range of scholars, situated across the disciplines, have sought to understand exactly how capitalism works, to theorize its mechanism, and, above all, to review its history and the history of resistance to it through an expressly racial lens, they have found Robinson's concept of racial capitalism especially instructive. Racial capitalism allows for consideration of the constitutive nature of racializing processes, racial formations, racial projects, and racialized geographies in capitalism's global expansion. By following Robinson's lead, scholars have been able to develop fascinating arguments about the periodization of the history of capitalism that center slavery and colonialism rather than viewing these ongoing systems of accumulation as singular precapitalist events (Baptist; Beckert; Johnson, *River*; Smallwood). They have also sought to reconceptualize how the process that Marx and Engels labeled "so-called primitive accumulation" not only existed at capitalism's inception but also persists into the present. Not least, those who have built on Robinson's work have offered richly detailed studies of how a variety of racialisms have been and continue to be mobilized within and among nations to make capitalism go (Day; Haley; Jung; Lowe).

Although many of Robinson's central insights about how racial capitalism works and how Black Marxists lay the groundwork for its theorization have been taken up, we find it notable that scholars have tended to pay less attention to Robinson's primary reason for urging us to contribute to the ongoing theorization of racial capitalism and to understand its *longue durée* in the first place. Namely, so that we might learn from both the individual and collective struggles against racial capitalism that have taken place in the past as we figure out how to struggle against racial capitalism in the present. For us it is therefore important to pause and to emphasize that there are two parts of Robinson's project that we take heed of here: (1) that which offers scholars ways to rethink the racializing processes, racial formations, and racialized geographies that make capitalism go, and (2) that which proffers concrete examples of refusal that enable understanding of the complex forms of opposition to racial capitalism that have taken place in the past and might yet take place in the future. In short, with this issue we seek to expand on the most truly radical aspects of *Black Marxism*. To this end, contributions included here take up existing discussions about how racial capitalism works by advancing an understanding of its reproductive mechanism, and they explore how racial capitalism has been and may yet be refused at the site of reproduction. At stake in bringing these two parts of the project together, in our view, is what we know today as reproductive justice. As Loretta Ross and Rickie Solinger explain, reproductive justice always includes three crucial pieces: "(1) The right to *not* have a child; (2) the right to *have* a child; and (3) the right to parent children in safe and healthy environments" (9). In our reading, reproductive justice is by necessity a feminist, anti-capitalist, and anti-racist theory and praxis that pursues truly substantive reproductive freedom and sexual autonomy for everyone regardless of race or gender.

In recalibrating how we discern and make meaning of the forms of refusal of racial capitalism that have existed in the past, Robinson sought to attend to challenges to capitalist hegemony that have too often been overlooked by traditional analyses that focus exclusively (and thus myopically) on organized social movements, overt manifestations of class consciousness, and expression of political solidarities that assume that all historical actors must be conscious of their belonging within insurgent groups in order to act and in so doing make meaningful individual contributions to larger collective struggles for freedom. What remains missing from *Black Marxism* is express attention to the ways in which racial capitalism mobilizes the language of the body, intimacy, sexuality, and specific racialized and gendered identities. Consequently, *Black Marxism* is largely silent on the ways in which racial capitalism creates sites of contestation, challenge, and refusal that are corporeal, intimate, and complexly lived by individuals who most often do not recognize themselves as members of organized social movements or of large self-conscious collectivities.

Our choice to center slavery and its afterlife in discussions of the relationship of reproduction to racial capitalism requires further explanation of how we understand both slavery and reproduction. In Robinson's work and in that of other Black Marxist scholars, the history of Atlantic slavery is, of course, a key concern. Building on readings of what W. E. B. Du Bois and C. L. R. James (among others) wrote about the international slave trade,

Robinson advanced an argument for recognizing Atlantic slavery as an early capitalist formation and for the interconnectedness of Atlantic slavery with both contemporaneous and ongoing processes of colonization, settler colonialism, empire building, and Indigenous genocide. However, even as Robinson recognized the importance of slavery to capitalism's global expansion, in our reading we acknowledge that Robinson did not treat the *reproductive* exploitation, extraction, and accumulation that fueled and thus ultimately enabled racial capitalist expansion. In this way, Robinson leaves out of his story of racial capitalism a discussion of the visceral and biological engine that made racial capitalism go, namely, the human sexual and reproductive labor that was first performed by enslaved women over several centuries and subsequently performed by a range of laborers both paid and unremunerated. In this issue we center questions of reproduction, sex, and motherhood in slavery, and treat the enduring impact of specifically enslaved forms of reproduction, sex, and motherhood on what Weinbaum (*Afterlife*) has elsewhere called "the afterlife of reproductive slavery." Our goal in doing so is not only to add to the existing scholarship that has taught us that all capitalism is racial capitalism but also to demonstrate that reproduction is racial capitalism's condition of possibility in both the past and present.

Treating racial capitalism from the vantage point of reproduction is an expressly feminist undertaking that builds on the work of a range of feminist scholars who have come before us. From the scholarship on reproduction in slavery we know that women navigated newly shaped identities as they confronted and responded to the foundational logics of reproductive racial capitalism in the Americas and the Caribbean, even if *reproductive racial capitalism* has not heretofore been the language that the scholarship on enslaved women has employed. In the New World, enslaved women were forced to consider their implication in the embodied violence on which the economies of Atlantic slavery depended, and thus we must comprehend their efforts either to avoid making kin or to mount and maintain relationships of kin that were denied them as efforts to dislodge the stranglehold of reproductive racial capitalism. As richly detailed studies demonstrate, enslaved women's efforts are nothing less than an open invitation to consider the highly conflicted relationship that existed among reproduction, motherhood, kinship, and racial capitalism. Likewise, from emergent scholarship on the reproductive afterlife of slavery, we know that slavery's racializing and sexualizing logics persist in the present, even as they continue to be recalibrated in specific locations and markets. From this scholarship, especially that which focuses on the plight of reproductive laborers in contemporary capitalism— here we are thinking of surrogates, egg vendors, creators of stem cells and of babies —we learn that as people sell reproductive labor and products and navigate newly shaped identities as participants in a global marketplace, they both confront and respond to the foundational logics of reproductive racial capitalism. Indeed, contemporary reproductive laborers, like enslaved women before them, both acquiesce to and challenge their dispossession and disposability and in so doing express forms of insurgency and refusal of reproductive racial capitalism that have yet to be carefully studied. In sum, whether in the past or the present, when feminist scholars have focused on the range of reproductive activities in which human beings are necessarily engaged as they reproduce our world, they have made it clear that human reproduction is not a singular, isolatable issue or activity that can be simply incorporated into existing theories of racial capitalism. Rather, reproduction must be placed front and center so that it can do the work of fundamentally reorienting our study of racial capitalism and the long and ongoing history of its contestation.

The concept of reproduction with which we are working may not be common sense and thus may require further amplification. To be clear, we do not intend to treat reproduction as an economic abstraction, or as the name for a generalizable process that enables the maintenance of the relations of production (this is, by contrast, precisely what Marxist theory has already done so well). Instead, we mobilize the concept of reproduction in a narrower sense that we believe, perhaps paradoxically, widens existing theoretical frameworks and historical methodologies. We treat reproduction first and foremost as a bodily process, as a vital individual experience, and therefore as a visceral, biological, and highly intimate object of study. It is visceral because it is felt in the body and precedes mental processing; it is biological because it involves the body as a technology of production; and it is intimate because it happens inside individuals and involves their most private physiological and psychological sensations. In slavery, reproduction involves direct participation in the reproduction of chattel. In slavery's wake, it involves direct participation in the reproduction of a range of commodities ranging from gestational labor to eggs, stem cells, and children.

To summarize and underscore the two principal arguments that we seek to advance by coining and using the titular concept, reproductive racial capitalism: (1) Reproductive labor and the experiences of conception, gestation, parturition, and childrearing are the heart and engine of both slave racial capitalism and contemporary forms of reproductive racial capitalism. (2) They are also, by necessity, the sites from which reproductive racial capitalism and its exploitative conditions have been contested in the past, are being challenged in the present, and might yet be refused in future.

To an extent, our focus on reproductive racial capitalism involves drawing on the long legacy of Marxist and socialist feminist theory generated over many decades that stretches back to early critiques of traditional Marxism that were initiated by nineteenth-century communist, socialist, and anarchist women (think of Emma Goldman, Alexandra Kollontai, and Rosa Luxemburg, among so many others), forwards to the Marxist and socialist feminists of the twentieth century (there are simply too many to list here, but we nonetheless begin by noting some of those most dear to us, including Claudia Jones, Silvia Federici, Maria Mies, Michele Barrett, Lise Vogel, Angela Davis, and the Combahee River Collective), and advances into the present by way of social reproduction theory (here we are thinking especially of *Feminism for the 99%* by Cinzia Arruzza, Tithi Bhattacharya, and Nancy Fraser, as well as work included in *Social Reproduction Theory*, edited by Bhattacharya).[2] In short, there is nothing particularly new in our calling attention to the many ways in which reproduction and its links to maternity, sexual intimacy, and women's care work have been associated with exploitation, extraction, dispossession, and accumulation throughout history. Prior Marxist and socialist feminist theorists have set up the terms for and have already made profound contributions to a collective and ongoing political discussion and struggle that centers women's reproduction of workers, women's sexual labor, women's unremunerated labor in the private realm, and the "feminization" that characterizes the degradation of labor in globalization—in sum, all that women and supposedly "feminized" laborers contributed and continue to contribute each day to the reproduction of capitalism across time. As important to the present issue as is Marxist and socialist feminist work, is feminist scholarship on slavery. Here we are engaged with the watershed contributions that began to appear in the 1970s, including essays by Angela Davis and foundational studies by Darlene Clark Hine and Deborah Gray White. As the historical study of slavery expanded to encompass scholarship on the Caribbean and thus to include works by Lucille Mair, Hilary McD. Beckles, and Barbara Bush, among others, it clarified that analysis of both gender and sexuality must reside at the center of studies of the Black Atlantic writ large. On these groundbreaking interventions stand a growing body of historical studies of gender and sexuality under slavery that began to appear in the 2010s and 2020s. These are exemplified in books by contributors to this issue, including Johnson and Morgan, and in scholarship by participants in the workshops that culminated in this issue, such as Diana Paton, Shauna Sweeney, and Sasha Turner.

The intimate bodily process of reproduction in slavery and beyond opens up a space of possibility for those who are reproducers, and too for those who accumulate reproductive labor and its products. Under slavery, the explicit accumulation of reproduction and its products was rationalized by those who sought ongoing commodification of human beings. That specific and foundational notion of human bodily objectification is one that has been simultaneously extended and reworked in the aftermath of slavery such that it shapes new relationships to human reproduction that are manifest in the present moment. These new relationships include population control through mass sterilization, forced abortion, or, conversely, forced pregnancy. They also include the creation of markets in artificial reproductive technologies (or ARTs), surrogate labor, and the raw materials used in both surrogacy and assisted reproduction, including eggs, sperm, and frozen embryos. These new relationships inform state intervention, increasingly in the form of criminalization, into access to reproductive health care, including surgical and medical or pill-based abortion.

In turn, the refusal to relinquish reproduction and kinship to the vagaries and violence of the market, the rejection of the attribution of pathology to Black family life and to impoverished family life, the reshaping of kinship and ideas of relationality, and the rise of the reproductive justice movement in the United States and related movements abroad together marshal a substantive challenge to reproductive racial capitalism, and signal to us the existence of both national and international insurgency against the forms of reproductive extraction, exploitation, dispossession, and accumulation that began in slavery and that persist to this day. Scholars of racial capitalism who follow in Robinson's footsteps identify the effort to invalidate terms of relationality among the dispossessed and exploited around the globe as the driving force of racial capitalism. They argue that violent destruction of relationships (among human beings, between human beings and animals, and between all living beings and planet earth) constitutes *the* edifice on which racial capitalism rests (Melamed 78–80; Byrd et al.). Reclamation of relationality constitutes a response to this ongoing violence and destruction of ties that might otherwise bind. Here we build on this argument by regarding the efforts of pregnant persons and their allies to maintain and reshape reproduction, kinship, and other forms of relationality in the face of reproductive racial capitalism's need to appropriate and enclose reproduction as insurgency. This form of insurgency lies at the heart of what we learn when we center reproduction, when we critically reexamine and then re-narrate the dominant story of capitalism.

It is because we treat reproduction as intimate, bodily, biological, and visceral that many of the articles included in this issue treat mothers and motherhood, both enslaved and supposedly free. This noted, contributors do so neither to reify motherhood as the centerpiece of feminist inquiry, nor to uncritically consolidate the equation of motherhood and femaleness that was set in place during slavery. Rather, contributors home in on mothers and motherhood in order to elaborate the stakes of reproductive racial capitalism as they have been historically experienced by those individuals who have been tasked with reproduction or who have elected to participate in kin making despite the negation of their status as mothers. What this means on a practical level is that some contributors to this issue treat "motherhood" as a contentious category that can be reasonably placed in quotation marks, parsed, and scrutinized (see Solinger, Vertommen, and Weinbaum), while others treat motherhood as a historical given, as an identity that was important to enslaved women and thus as an experience that affords specific forms of knowledge about the lives of individual historical actors that would otherwise be marginalized or altogether lost. Indeed, in some essays collected here (see Ashby and Johnson, Knapp, and Zhang) it is only as mothers that individuals become visible in the historical archive and capable of articulating their humanity and value to those who would deny it.

In following Robinson's lead, we argue not only for recognition of the centrality of reproduction to racial capitalism (and thus for express study of *reproductive racial capitalism*) but also for recognition of reproduction as the principal site and stake when racial capitalism is contested, challenged, or radically refused by those whose reproductive labor and products are exploited, extracted, and dispossessed. In different ways, all contributors advance what we identify above as the largely neglected aspirational and liberatory part of Robinson's project. In so doing, each makes an important methodological contribution either implicitly or explicitly. By employing new analytical practices, each contribution instructs readers, sometimes by way of historical example or case study, in how to examine cultural texts in order to locate and foreground reproductive content and thus in how to analyze the reproductive texture of racial capitalism and the myriad responses to it. This noted, contributions to this issue can be roughly divided into two groups: those that principally though not exclusively examine the reproductive mechanism of racial capitalist extraction and accumulation (Weinbaum, Vertommen, Briggs, and Solinger), and those that principally, though not exclusively, explore contestation and refusal of it (Johnson and Ashby, Knapp, and Zhang).

Overall, in bringing together a group of overlapping and at once diverse contributions on reproductive extraction, exploitation, dispossession, accumulation, and the myriad forms of contestation and refusal, we hope to leave readers with a number of overarching questions about reproductive racial capitalism. Among the most pressing: how does centering reproduction in slavery and in its wake force a rethinking of the dialectic of history? We know that from the vantage point of reproductive racial capitalism the distinction between the oppressed and the oppressor must not only be racialized, it must also be gendered and sexualized. Put otherwise, in centering reproductive racial capitalism, we seek to make it clear that we must not only move beyond the focus on historical actors and the conflagrations and insurgencies that have concerned both traditional historians and traditional Marxists and Marxist feminists. When reproduction in slavery is taken as the starting point, we can no longer tell the story of capitalism as a story about a conflict between the proletariat and the bourgeoisie, or even as a story about a gendered and sexualized conflict between oppressed and oppressors. Instead, we must think about the role played by individuals and groups in reproductive labor, extraction, exploitation, dispossession, and accumulation—and consider how this relationship might organize the relations of (re)production as well as responses to it. Relatedly, when reproductive racial capitalism in the present moment is understood to be constitutively intertwined with reproduction in slavery, conventional ways of treating the gendered organization of productive versus reproductive labor and the distinctions between free and unfree labor are revealed to be far too rigid. Indeed, the usual categories of analysis become insufficient, and new ideas about the nature of what it means to labor and to be a laborer emerge.

In sum, when we center reproductive racial capitalism as we do here, procreation, conception, gestation, parturition, and childrearing quickly become the principal sites and stakes of historical struggles for hegemony. As a consequence, additional queries about the dialect of history proliferate: How does a focus on reproductive racial capitalism compel our reconceptualization of the conflicts and contradictions that drive historical change? How might a focus on expressly reproductive conflicts and contractions compel us to think in broader historical strokes than we tend to do and thus to re-periodize capitalism in fresh ways? How might a focus on reproductive labor require us to rethink the relationship between gender and labor, public and private, paid and unpaid work? Reproduction is a universal and omni-historical practice, and yet it has been experienced and treated in distinct ways by individuals, collectivities, capitalists, and nation-states as it has moved across time. How can we learn to track reproductive labor's change and understand the historical antecedents to its ongoing transformation? At the very least, to contend with the salient facts and the questions raised, we argue here that the study of reproductive racial capitalism allows us to deepen our engagement with histories of capitalism before and after European industrialization—indeed, we are suggesting that it affords a nearly complete reorientation to the question of historical periodization that in turn will no doubt catalyze new understandings of historical continuity and rupture, and lead to the creation of new analytical categories, hermeneutics, and heuristic devices.

For scholars of slavery, in particular, the proposed focus on reproduction demands a radical rethinking of many of the categories that have long defined the discipline. Studies that concern processes of creolization, the emergence of Afro-Caribbean and Afro-American identities in relationship to and in tension with the African past, for example, must treat reproductive practices and impediments as key nodes of engagement. The experiences of maroon communities, runaways or those who harbor them, those planning and participating in insurrection or rebellion—all these spaces of contestation of racial capitalism have for the most part been understood as ones in which women were marginal at best. By considering reproduction as a problem space that, in turn, generates the contestation of enslavement, new ways of understanding oppositional ideology and praxis emerge. Regarding enslaved women's contributions to struggle not merely as social historical evidence of the importance of Black community to the enslaved but also as revolutionary allows us to reconsider not only which historical actors we ought to focus on but also which historical acts and events. It is through a focus on reproduction, in other words, that new capacities for theorizing enslaved opposition emerge.

For scholars of reproduction in the current moment, continuities exist with slavery that ought to compel deep concern. One such continuity is shaped by the existence of a multibillion-dollar transnational market in reproductive labor and products, including surrogate labor, human eggs, stem cells, and babies. Another continuity is found in the relentless devaluing of Black women's reproductive health in the contemporary United States to the extent that today maternal and infant mortality among Black women and children occur at rates that outpace that of white women and children by 400 percent and 200 percent, respectively. Similar statistics reveal related inequalities for all women of color (Miller, Kliff, and Buchanan; Villarosa). Exploration of reproductive racial capitalism in the past and present allows for attention to how reproduction in slavery serves as an important historical backdrop to both current forms of reproductive extraction and dispossession, and to current forms of reproductive contestation and refusal. In the context of the recent Supreme Court ruling in *Dobbs*, which overturned the decision in *Roe v. Wade* that held sway for fifty years, an exploration of slavery as context is especially revealing. As we suggested in the opening to this essay, the justices' arguments in *Dobbs* eerily echo arguments that were made in support of slavery. They allow us to apprehend the persistence of ideas about the reproductive body of the enslaved and about human beings as property that first took root in the Middle Passage and on New World plantations. Whereas the conflict in slavery was between the enslaved woman and her enslaver and manifests as a struggle for control over the reproductive body and its products, the conflict today is poised as one between the mother and the state and is manifest as a struggle over control of the maternal body and the embryo or fetus (both of which are mistakenly referred to as "the child" by anti-abortionists). We see the justices' arguments as specifically curtailing the freedoms that were enshrined in both the Thirteenth and Fourteenth Amendments to the Constitution. *Dobbs* hinged on overt rejection, by the conservative justices, of the claim that the Fourteenth Amendment protects women's access to abortion. The court, however, did not expressly consider the fact that a forced pregnancy amounts to involuntary servitude and that the Thirteenth Amendment's freedoms entail the right of enslaved women to refuse to relinquish reproductive control over their own bodies so as to exit involuntary servitude (Goodwin). As concerning as the court's failure to recognize the necessary connection between human freedom and bodily autonomy is the court's consolidation of an ideology that centers the life of the conceptus over that of the woman in arguments against abortion. This ideology replays the misplaced concerns of nineteenth-century abolitionists whose primary sense of moral outrage took aim at the sinful taint of slavery on white people, rather than at the racism and racial hierarchies that powered the economic system of slavery (Greenidge). Mobilizing the identity of the savior dehumanizes the pregnant person through their reduction to a non-rights-bearing entity. And it simultaneously elevates the conceptus—like the suffering white slave owner—as a "person" who is deserving of legal protection, even that afforded by citizenship.

Issues that can be surfaced through analysis of *Dobbs* are clearly rooted in slavery, the practice of slave reproduction, and in the ideas about the reproductive body that have been passed forward in time out of slavery. The *Dobbs* decision thus reminds us—even urges us—to investigate the antecedents for what amount to "enslaved" and "enslaving" thinking about reproduction, the pregnant person, the womb, the conceptus, the possibilities of kinship, and the negation of the reproductive body's autonomy. Elsewhere, we have named this persistence "the slave episteme" (Weinbaum, *Afterlife*) and "the DNA of the nation" (Livingston and Morgan). Just as we need to see the ongoing material and ideological work of slavery in the *Dobbs* decision, so too, we must learn to recognize how the protest against *Dobbs* now underway constitutes insurgency against reproductive racial capitalism. Such protests reveal the persistence of forms of specifically reproductive contestation that were pervasive in the context of forced reproduction in slavery. Here we are thinking about the long history of enslaved women regulating their own fertility through abstinence, emmenagogues, abortifacients, and self-managed abortions (Schiebinger; Schwartz; Fett; Latimer). We are also thinking about the ways in which a radical politics of *abolition feminism* remains to be realized.[3] We have seen the perverse impact of the form of liberal abolitionism that was prevalent in the nineteenth century that used women's reproductive capacities to hijack the control of formerly enslaved women's reproductive labor beyond formal Emancipation (Turner). We have seen the end of the slave trade without seeing the end of slavery (Sharpe; Hartman, *Lose*). We have seen former slaveowners explicitly building a system of extractive labor based on women's reproduction after 1807. Likewise, in the present, we can clearly see, if we are willing to think outside the box about the meaning of substantive reproductive freedom, that liberal ideas of "the right to privacy" have not and will not suffice to protect the basic human right to control one's body.

For us, a politics of abolition feminism that is committed to a truly radical form of reproductive justice will need to learn from both prior failures of liberal abolition and recent failures of a liberal pro-choice movement that takes the right to privacy as its horizon.[4] Can we be so bold as to suggest that all pregnant people deserve health care and bodily autonomy, the material resources to have or not to have a child, and the myriad forms of material and social support that enable personal decision-making? Is it possible that in our current conjuncture we might yet learn from the histories of enslaved women who yearned for, and sometimes radically appropriated, an insurgent reproductive future? Can we learn from historically contextualizing the present reproductive crisis that we find ourselves in today? Can we turn to history to turn the present crisis into an opportunity to create substantive reproductive freedom? ▧

Jennifer L. Morgan is professor of history in the Department of Social and Cultural Analysis and the Department of History at New York University. She is the author of *Reckoning with Slavery: Gender, Kinship, and Capitalism in the Early Black Atlantic* (2021), which won the Mary Nickliss Prize in Women's and/or Gender History from the Organization of American Historians and the Frederick Douglass Prize awarded by the Gilder Lehrman Center for the Study of Slavery, Resistance, and Abolition at Yale University; and of *Laboring Women: Gender and Reproduction in the Making of New World Slavery* (2004).

Alys Eve Weinbaum is professor of English in the Department of English and adjunct professor in Gender, Women, and Sexuality Studies at the University of Washington, Seattle. She is author of *The Afterlife of Reproductive Slavery: Biocapitalism and Black Feminism's Philosophy of History* (2019), which won the Sarah A. Whaley Book Prize for groundbreaking scholarship on women and labor from the National Women's Studies Association (NWSA), and an honorable mention for the Gloria Anzaldúa Book Prize for transnational scholarship in Women's Studies also from the NWSA; and of *Wayward Reproductions: Genealogies of Race and Nation in Transatlantic Modern Thought* (2004).

NOTES

1   Throughout we seek to indicate through careful word choice that we have absorbed the critique of "resistance" (Johnson, "On Agency," "To Remake") and therefore move toward the language of contestation, challenge, refusal, and insurgency. Our general preference is to use *contestation* for discussions of the enslaved, to use *challenge* when considering the present moment, and to reserve *refusal* for discussion of "freedom dreams" (Kelley) of a future yet to come in which racial capitalism is rejected *tout court*. Of course when referring to the work of other scholars we use their preferred language.

2   On early Marxist feminists see Boyce Davies and Hemmings; on the Marxism of Combahee see Taylor.

3   The term is elaborated in great detail by Davis et al.

4   Our thinking on the problem of holding out liberal rights as the sole horizon of justice is indebted to Melamed and Reddy; Lowe.

WORKS CITED

Arruzza, Cinzia, Tithi Bhattacharya, and Nancy Fraser. *Feminism for the 99%: A Manifesto.* London: Verso, 2019.

Baptist, Edward E. *The Half Has Never Been Told: Slavery and the Making of American Capitalism.* New York: Basic Books, 2014.

Barrett, Michele. *Women's Oppression Today.* London: Verso Books, 1988.

Beckert, Sven. *Empire of Cotton: A Global History.* New York: Vintage Books, 2014.

Beckles, Hilary McD. *Natural Rebels: A Social History of Enslaved Black Women in Barbados.* New Brunswick, NJ: Rutgers University Press, 1997.

Bhattacharya, Tithi, ed. *Social Reproduction Theory: Remapping Class, Recentering Oppression.* London: Pluto, 2017.

Boyce Davies, Carole. *Left of Karl Marx: The Political Life of Black Communist Claudia Jones.* Durham, NC: Duke University Press, 2008.

Bush, Barbara. *Slave Women in Caribbean Society: 1650–1838.* Bloomington: Indiana University Press, 1990.

Byrd, Jodi A., Alyosha Goldstein, Jodi Melamed, and Chandan Reddy. "Predatory Value: Economies of Dispossession and Disturbed Relationalities." *Social Text* 36, no. 2 (2018): 1–18. https://doi.org/10.1215/01642472-4362325.

Davis, Angela Y. "Reflections on the Black Woman's Role in the Community of Slaves." *Massachusetts Review* 13, nos. 1–2 (1972): 81–100. https://doi.org/10.1080/00064246.1981.11414214.

Davis, Angela Y. *Women, Race, and Class*. New York: PM, 2012.

Davis, Angela Y., Gina Dent, Erica R. Meiners, and Beth Richie. *Abolition. Feminism. Now.* Chicago, IL: Haymarket Books, 2022.

Day, Iyko. *Alien Capital: Asian Racialization and the Logic of Settler Colonial Capitalism*. Durham, NC: Duke University Press, 2016.

Federici, Silvia. *Revolution at Point Zero: Housework, Reproduction, and Feminist Struggle*. Oakland, CA: PM, 2012.

Fett, Sharla. *Working Cures: Healing, Health, and Power on Southern Slave Plantations*. Chapel Hill: University of North Carolina Press, 2002.

Goodwin, Michele. "No, Justice Alito, Reproductive Justice Is in the Constitution." *New York Times*, June 26, 2022. https://www.nytimes.com/2022/06/26/opinion/justice-alito-reproductive-justice-constitution-abortion.html.

Greenidge, Kerri K. *The Grimkes: The Legacy of Slavery in an American Family*. New York: Liveright, 2023.

Haley, Sarah. *No Mercy Here: Gender, Punishment, and the Making of Jim Crow Modernity*. Chapel Hill: University of North Carolina Press, 2016.

Hartman, Saidiya. "The Belly of the World: A Note on Black Women's Labors." *Souls* 18, no. 1 (2016): 166–73. https://doi.org/10.1080/10999949.2016.1162596.

Hartman, Saidiya. *Lose Your Mother: A Journey along the Atlantic Slave Route*. New York: Farrar, Straus and Giroux, 2007.

Hemmings, Clare. *Considering Emma Goldman: Feminist Political Ambivalence and the Imaginative Archive*. Durham, NC: Duke University Press, 2018.

Hine, Darlene Clark. "Female Slave Resistance: The Economics of Sex." *Western Journal of Black Studies* 3, no. 2 (1979): 123–27.

Johnson, Jessica Marie. *Wicked Flesh: Black Women, Intimacy, and Freedom in the Atlantic World*. Philadelphia: University of Pennsylvania Press, 2020.

Johnson, Walter. "On Agency." *Journal of Social History* 37, no. 1 (2003): 113–24. https://doi.org/10.1353/jsh.2003.0143.

Johnson, Walter. *River of Dark Dreams: Slavery and Empire in the Cotton Kingdom*. Cambridge, MA: Harvard University Press, 2013.

Johnson, Walter. "To Remake the World: Slavery, Racial Capitalism, and Justice." *Boston Review*, no. 1 (2017): 11–32. https://www.proquest.com/magazines/remake-world-slavery-racial-capitalism-justice/docview/2203038906/se-2.

Jung, Moon Ho. *Coolies and Cane: Race, Labor, and Sugar in the Age of Emancipation*. Baltimore, MD: Johns Hopkins University Press, 2006.

Kelley, Robin D. G. *Freedom Dreams: The Black Radical Imagination*. Boston: Beacon, 2002.

Koshy, Susan, Lisa Marie Cacho, Jodi A. Byrd, and Brian Jordan Jefferson, eds. *Colonial Racial Capitalism*. Durham, NC: Duke University Press, 2022.

Koshy, Susan, Lisa Marie Cacho, Jodi A. Byrd, and Brian Jordan Jefferson. Introduction to Koshy, Cacho, Byrd, and Jefferson 1–30.

Latimer, Heather. "Abortion Regulation and the Afterlife of Reproductive Slavery; or, A Call to Make Abortion Natural Again." *Feminist Studies* 48, no. 2 (2022): 342–66. https://doi.org/10.1353/fem.2022.0030.

Livingston, Julie, and Jennifer L. Morgan. "Reproductive Dispossession: A Long History of Outrage." In *Exterminate All the Brutes*, edited by Hazel Carby and Raoul Peck. New York: Random House, forthcoming.

Lowe, Lisa. *The Intimacies of Four Continents.* Durham, NC: Duke University Press, 2017.

Mair, Lucille. "A Historical Study of Women in Jamaica from 1655–1844." PhD diss., University of the West Indies, 1974.

Melamed, Jodi. "Racial Capitalism." *Critical Ethnic Studies* 1, no. 1 (2015): 76–85. http://doi.org/10.5749/jcritethnstud.1.1.0076.

Melamed, Jodi, and Chandan Reddy. "Using Liberal Rights to Enforce Racial Capitalism." *Items: Insights from the Social Sciences*, July 20, 2019. https://items.ssrc.org/race-capitalism/using-liberal-rights-to-enforce-racial-capitalism/.

Mies, Maria. *Patriarchy and Accumulation on a World Scale: Women in the International Division of Labor.* London: Zed, 1986.

Miller, Claire Cain, Sarah Kliff, and Larry Buchanan. "Childbirth Is Deadlier for Black Families Even When They're Rich, Study Finds." *New York Times*, February 19, 2023. https://www.proquest.com/newspapers/childbirth-is-deadlier-black-families-even-when/docview/2777802000/se-2.

Morgan, Jennifer. *Laboring Women: Reproduction and Gender in New World Slavery.* Philadelphia: University of Pennsylvania Press, 2004.

Morgan, Jennifer. "*Partus Sequitur Ventrem*: Law, Race, and Reproduction in Colonial Slavery." *Small Axe*, no. 55 (2018): 1–17. https://doi.org/10.1215/07990537-4378888.

Morgan, Jennifer. *Reckoning with Slavery: Gender, Kinship, and Capitalism in the Early Black Atlantic.* Durham, NC: Duke University Press, 2021.

Morgan, Jennifer. "Reproductive Rights, Slavery, and Dobbs v Jackson." *Black Perspectives*, The African American Intellectual History Society, August 2, 2022. https://www.aaihs.org/reproductive-rights-slavery-and-dobbs-v-jackson/.

Paton, Diana. "Gender History, Global History, and Atlantic Slavery." *American Historical Review* 127, no. 2 (2022): 726–56. https://doi.org/10.1093/ahr/rhac156.

Roberts, Dorothy. *Killing the Black Body: Race, Reproduction, and the Meaning of Liberty.* New York: Pantheon, 1997.

Robinson, Cedric J. *Black Marxism: The Making of the Black Radical Tradition.* Chapel Hill: University of North Carolina Press, 2000.

Ross, Loretta J., and Rickie Solinger. *Reproductive Justice: An Introduction.* Berkeley: University of California Press, 2017.

Schiebinger, Londa. "Agnotology and Exotic Abortifacients: The Cultural Production of Ignorance in the Eighteenth-Century Atlantic World." *Proceedings of the American Philosophical Society* 149, no. 3 (2005): 316–43. https://www.jstor.org/stable/4598938.

Schwartz, Marie Jenkins. *Birthing a Slave: Motherhood and Medicine in the Antebellum South.* Cambridge, MA: Harvard University Press, 2006.

Sharpe, Christina. *In the Wake: On Blackness and Being.* Durham, NC: Duke University Press, 2016.

Smallwood, Stephanie. *Saltwater Slavery: A Middle Passage from African to American Diaspora.* Cambridge, MA: Harvard University Press, 2007.

Spillers, Hortense. "Mama's Baby, Papa's Maybe: An American Grammar Book." *Diacritics* 17, no. 2 (1987): 65–81.

Sweeney, Shauna. "Gendering Racial Capitalism and the Black Heretical Tradition." In *Histories of Racial Capitalism*, edited by Destin Jenkins and Justin Leroy, 58–84. New York: Columbia University Press, 2021.

Taylor, Keeanga-Yamahtta. *How We Get Free: Black Feminism and the Combahee River Collective*. Chicago, IL: Haymarket Books, 2017.

Turner, Sasha. *Contested Bodies: Pregnancy, Childbearing, and Slavery in Jamaica*. Philadelphia: University of Pennsylvania Press, 2017.

Villarosa, Linda. "Why America's Black Mothers and Babies Are in a Life-or-Death Crisis." *New York Times*, April 11, 2018. https://www.nytimes.com/2018/04/11/magazine/black-mothers-babies-death-maternal-mortality.html.

Vogel, Lise. *Marxism and the Oppression of Women: Towards a Unitary Theory*. New Brunswick, NJ: Rutgers University Press, 1983.

Weinbaum, Alys Eve. *The Afterlife of Reproductive Slavery: Biocapitalism and Black Feminism's Philosophy of History*. Durham, NC: Duke University Press, 2019.

Weinbaum, Alys Eve. "Gendering the General Strike: W. E. B. Du Bois's *Black Reconstruction* and Black Feminism's 'Propaganda of History.'" *South Atlantic Quarterly* 112, no. 3 (2013): 437–64.

Weinbaum, Alys Eve. "Reproducing Racial Capitalism." *Boston Review Forum* 44, no. 2 (2019): 85–96.

Weinbaum, Alys Eve. "The Slave Episteme in Biocapitalism." *Catalyst: Feminism, Theory, Technoscience* 8, no. 1 (2022): 1–25. https://catalystjournal.org/index.php/catalyst/article/view/35232.

Weinbaum, Alys Eve. "Ungendering Intersectionality and Reproductive Justice: Returning to Hortense Spillers's 'Mama's Baby, Papa's Maybe.'" In *The Routledge Companion to Intersectionalities*, edited by Jennifer Nash and Samantha Pinto, 45–56. New York: Routledge, 2023.

Weinbaum, Alys Eve. *Wayward Reproductions: Genealogies of Race and Reproduction in Transatlantic Modern Thought*. Durham, NC: Duke University Press, 2004.

White, Deborah Gray. *Ar'n't I a Woman? Female Slaves in the Plantation South*. New York: Norton, 1985.

Alys Eve Weinbaum

Hortense Spillers and the Ungendering of (Re)productive Racial Capitalism

ABSTRACT This article theorizes the reproductive dimensions of racial capitalism. It begins by bringing into conversation Black Marxist theories of racial capitalism and Marxist feminist theories of social and biological reproduction proffered by Cedric Robinson and Silvia Federici respectively. It demonstrates that since its inception, racial capitalism has depended on processes of *racialized (re)productive accumulation* that are ongoing but not yet fully theorized. At the center of the essay is a close reading of Hortense Spillers's 1987 contribution "Mama's Baby, Papa's Maybe: An American Grammar Book." Though Spillers is not generally regarded as either a Black Marxist or a Marxist feminist, the essay argues that she ought to be recognized as a theorist of racialized (re)productive accumulation—a process that begins aboard the slave ship, persists on the plantation, and endures into the present. Racialized (re)productive accumulation exploited *she* whom Spillers often denotes as "the captive female," and, also, paradoxically, *ungendered* her. Ultimately, through examination of the process of ungendering in Atlantic slavery, the essay suggests that Spillers opens up new ways to think about the history of racial capitalism, (re)productive dispossession, and the possibility of its refusal. The article concludes by considering how Spillers's complex insights about the process of ungendering might yet be mobilized to secure truly substantive forms of reproductive justice.

KEYWORDS Hortense Spillers, racial capitalism, slavery, primitive accumulation, reproductive justice

The concept of *racial capitalism*, first advanced by political scientist Cedric J. Robinson in 1983, has since the 2000 republication of his *Black Marxism: The Making of the Black Radical Tradition* taken on new life. Over the past two decades racial capitalism has come to function as a heuristic device that is of aid to scholars who treat the constitutive racializing processes that initially fueled and that continue to shape global capitalist expansion. Especially in the fields of American history and American studies, adaptation of Robinson's heuristic has sparked scholarship on the evolving forms of

HISTORY of the PRESENT ▪ A Journal of Critical History ▪ 14:1 ▪ April 2024
DOI 10.1215/21599785-10898341 © 2024 Duke University Press

anti-Black dispossession that characterized slavery and colonialism (Baptist; Beckert; Fuentes; Johnson, *River*; Johnson, *Wicked*; Morgan, *Reckoning*; Paugh; Smallwood; Sweeney) and animate the afterlife of both formations (Day; Haley; Jung; Lowe; Vergès). In some intellectual genealogies (including Robinson's own), theorization of racial capitalism is attributed *avant la lettre* to W. E. B. Du Bois, C. L. R. James, and other Black radicals who followed in their footsteps (Robinson focuses on Richard Wright and Eric Williams, for instance). Such thinkers center slavery and colonialism when narrating the emergence of modern capitalism, even though they do not employ the conceptual terminology that Robinson would subsequently develop. More recently, historian Walter Johnson has offered a related but expanded term: *slave racial capitalism* (Johnson, *River* 6). With the addition of *slave*, Johnson eschews arguments that Atlantic slavery is either feudal or precapitalist, advancing instead an argument that slavery is constitutive of both American and global capitalism.

In Marxist feminist scholarship—which ought to be but has rarely been in direct dialogue with the abovementioned work on racial capitalism—reproductive labor is cast as intertwined with productive labor. Marxist feminists in the 1970s and 1980s (Federici, *Revolution*; James; Eisenstein; Barrett; Mies; Vogel) and contemporary social reproduction theorists (Bhattacharya; Arruzza, Bhattacharya, and Fraser) maintain, albeit differently, that the labor force simply would not exist without the ongoing exploitation of reproductive labor—both the biological labor involved in reproducing laborers and the domestic and care work that are either hyper-exploited or entirely unremunerated because these forms of labor take place in the home, in private (Boris and Parreñas). Without the biological reproduction of workers and the social reproduction of the relations of production, Marxist and socialist feminists both past and present argue that capitalism, as we know it, ceases to exist.

Building on these insights, scholarship on human reproduction (here I include my own and that by feminist science and technology scholars who have shaped the discussion of reproductive technologies) suggests that today there exist forms of in vivo reproductive labor and products that are directly commodified and therefore enter global circuits of exchange alongside traditional forms of productive labor and its products (Almeling; Deomampo; Dickenson; Cooper; Cooper and Waldby; Franklin; Twine; Waldby; Weinbaum, *Afterlife*; "Reproducing"). Gestational or surrogate labor, eggs, stem cells derived from umbilical cord blood, and so-called designer babies stand out among a quickly expanding array of commodities that are currently for sale around the globe.

The contemporary transnational exchange of reproductive labor and products challenges existing distinctions between production and reproduction. To describe the current form of capitalism in which human biological life itself is for sale, the descriptive term *biocapitalism* is useful.[1] In my reading, the prefacing *bio* ought to remind us (though, unfortunately, this is not always what it is used to do) that gestational labor, eggs, stem cells, and babies (and too, a range of additional bodily products such as organs and blood) are routinely bought and sold, and that reproductive labor and its products are continuously dispossessed, extracted, and accumulated. Existence of global markets in reproductive labor and its products compels me to advance a second semantic shift, one I began to employ in the 1990s and continue to find useful (Weinbaum, "Marx"). By placing parentheses around the prefacing *re* in *(re)production*, I call attention to the transit of reproduction into what was previously regarded as territory belonging exclusively to production and productive labor. In this way I signal (re)productive labor's actual domain in the past (under slavery) and in the present (under biocapitalism) and highlight the evolving array of (re)productive commodities that are for sale transnationally.

In the present article one of my principal aims is to bring together the two areas of scholarly inquiry that I have briefly sketched above: (1) that which recognizes that capitalism is rooted in *racialized* extraction and dispossession and therefore ought to be understood as always already *racial* capitalism; and (2) that which demonstrates that *(re)productive* labor and products are central to capitalist expansion, which therefore ought to be recognized as both racial capitalist and biocapitalist.[2] In bringing these two scholarly inquiries together, I demonstrate that racial capitalism is subtended by various forms of what I will henceforth call *racialized (re)productive accumulation*. Racialized (re)productive accumulation is most robustly manifest in Atlantic slavery, specifically in the practice of forced sex and (re)production or so-called slave breeding that sustained slavery over three centuries, and especially after the 1807 closure of the transatlantic slave trade and the turn to intensified interstate slave trafficking.[3] Once successfully harnessed, (re)productive labor was used to create not only an enslaved labor force but also vast empires built on trade in sugar, cotton, and tobacco. Although racialized (re)productive accumulation enabled capitalist expansion, it has seldom been considered alongside other forms of what Marx famously labeled "so-called primitive accumulation."[4] One of my main arguments is that it clearly ought to be. Racialized (re)productive accumulation is part and parcel of racial capitalism. It was a key feature of what Laura Briggs (in this issue) insightfully labels "the pre-accumulation process," it perpetuated slave racial capitalism over several centuries, and it continues to power both racial capitalist and biocapitalist accumulation and expansion into the present. The Italian Marxist feminist Silvia Federici's now iconoclastic treatise, *Caliban and the Witch: Women, the Body, and Primitive Accumulation*, offers a provocative story of capitalism's origins that provides important groundwork for the present argument about racialized (re)productive accumulation. Through a richly detailed historical narrative based on a variety of archives, Federici demonstrates the intensive dispossession of women's reproductive bodies and labor power beginning in the fifteenth century, and explores the violent destruction of what she calls the "reproductive commons" in the sixteenth and seventeenth centuries.[5] By centering the enclosure of reproductive bodies and the dispossession and extraction of sexual and reproductive labor across the medieval and early modern periods in Europe and its emerging colonies, Federici radically reconceptualizes the traditional Marxist story of capitalism's inception. Mirroring and at the same time filling in gaps in the Marxist account of so-called primitive accumulation, Federici shows readers that capitalism required enclosure of women's sexuality and wombs to get going, and that it is unsustainable without continuous sexual and (re)productive extraction and dispossession. Privatization of women's sexuality and wombs reached a dramatic apex in the sixteenth and seventeenth centuries. This was most palpable in the demonization and destruction of witches and a host of witchy women who individually and sometimes collectively refused their subjection to processes of reproductive enclosure over the *longue durée* that Marx described with uncanny accuracy, but without the feminist sensibility that might have rendered his words prescient, as a protracted "bloody birth." Such witches, scolds, gossips, vagabonds, healers, midwives, and farmers of the commons were subjected in shocking numbers to torture and murder by drowning, fire, dismemberment, and other ruthless means.

I find *Caliban and the Witch* gripping for several of the same reasons as *Black Marxism*. It, too, offers nuanced engagement with traditional Marxism and audaciously matches *Capital*'s epic sweep. It boldly contests dominant Marxist pieties about the evolution of contemporary capitalism out of a feudal or premodern world. And yet, for present purposes I also find Federici's blind spots illuminating. Most significantly, Federici only incidentally treats the racialization of the reproductive violence about which she writes. In situating processes of racialization solely in the contexts of European colonialism and slavery, and in thus viewing racialization as a function of European contact with non-Europeans, Federici replicates rather than interrogates Marx's analytical myopia. This is the same myopia that is roundly critiqued by Robinson and by those who have built on his insights. As Robinson explains, although Marx correctly recognized that intra-European social distinctions (such as those marking out the Irish and the Slavs) created the social divisions that rationalized the initial identification and exploitation of laboring populations, he failed to recognize these divisions as not only racialized in character but also as subject to processes of continuous recalibration. As Robinson observes, Marx failed to see that *all* forms of capitalist accumulation, past and present, depend on processes that racialize the distinctions between the exploited and the exploiters—distinctions that must be continuously reinvented over time and across geographies to enable capitalist expansion. To put a fine point on it, processes of racialization are neither exclusive to colonization and slavery, nor are they incidental by-products of the meeting of phenotypically distinct populations. Rather, race is invented and mobilized to rationalize the social and economic hierarchies that power racial capitalism globally and across time (Robinson, chaps. 1 and 2). Even though Federici includes in *Caliban* a chapter on conquest and slavery in South America, she does not regard processes of racialization as constitutive to capitalist expansion. The upshot: Federici's story of reproductive enclosure lacks an account of the imbrication of reproduction and racialization (what I elsewhere describe as "the race/reproduction bind" [*Wayward*, chap. 1]) wherever and whenever (re)productive enclosure, dispossession, and accumulation occur.

It is for the above reasons that when theorizing racialized (re)productive accumulation I have found it necessary to construct a supplementary relationship between Federici's and Robinson's theories. In doing so, I offer correctives to the work of each: I add an account of a specifically *(re)productive* form of accumulation to Black Marxist scholarship on racial capitalism such as Robinson's. And I add an account of *racialization* to Marxist feminist scholarship on biological and social reproduction such as Federici's. In elaborating these correctives, I lean on watershed feminist histories of slavery that began to appear in the 1980s (Beckles; Bush; White; Hine, "Female," "Rape") and that have been richly expanded over the last three decades (Berry; Camp; Morgan, *Laboring*; Paugh; Turner; among others). These histories focus on sex, reproduction, motherhood, and kinship in slavery, and decisively demonstrate that what I am calling racialized (re)productive accumulation constituted *the* engine of slave racial capitalism, especially in the nineteenth century. While feminist histories of slavery mainly treat enslaved women's resistance, in the present article, rather than examine women's historical agency, I instead analyze the role played by a process of *ungendering* in rationalizing and therefore enabling the materialization of an economic system dependent on racialized (re)productive accumulation. I focus my work in this way not because I believe that theorizing racialized (re)productive accumulation is somehow more important than telling the story of women's resistance to enslavement. Rather, I focus thus because the process of ungendering in slavery that I elaborate here has not yet been fully treated in existing work on slave racial capitalism, or, more generally, in histories of racial capitalism.

In accounting for the process of ungendering in slavery, I seek to advance a theory of racial capitalism that recognizes its dependence on the abstracting and dehumanizing calculations that enable the exchange relationship that drives all forms of capitalism. At the same time, I seek to open our collective imagination about the forms of revolt that refuse to stop at what Hortense Spillers refers to as "the gender question" (more on this "question" shortly), and that therefore attend to the *possibility* that Spillers imagines inheres in the historically violent unhinging of gender and reproduction. Overall, through focus on the process of ungendering in slavery, I hope to do three things: (1) Expand on existing discussions about the relationship between capitalism and slavery; (2) offer an expressly (re)productive account of racial capitalism in past and present; and (3) follow Spillers in speculating about what might yet lie beyond the reach of racial capitalism and the processes of racialized (re)productive accumulation that subtend it.

Ungendering (Re)production

As readers will have surmised from my title and what I have observed thus far, the ideas about ungendering that I engage with here emerge from a reading of Spillers's watershed 1987 article, "Mama's Baby, Papa's Maybe: An American Grammar Book." While Spillers is often considered a key contributor to Black feminism, in building my analysis of racialized (re)productive accumulation out of a reading of Spillers's ideas about the process of ungendering, I suggest that Spillers ought to be included within the pantheon of Black radical thinkers that Robinson dubbed Black Marxist. Spillers's theorization of ungendering in slavery and beyond raises interlinked and heretofore unexamined questions about the relationship of racial capitalism to the long history of (re)productive extraction, dispossession, and accumulation.[6] These include questions about the ungendering of (re)productive labor performed by she whom Spillers refers to throughout her article as "the captive female," [7] questions about the stamp of a process that was begun in Atlantic slavery on the forms of (re)productive accumulation that continue to fuel racial capitalism (and by extension biocapitalism) in the present, and, not least, questions about the liberatory possibility that inheres in the process of ungendering—a process that Spillers casts as both violent and simultaneously open to radical reappropriation.

For some readers the idea of ungendered (re)production may feel counterintuitive and thus present a potential stumbling block. In vivo creation of eggs, in utero creation of embryos and their gestation, and the labor of parturition are conventionally viewed as activities performed by female bodies. And yet treating (re)production as a process of ungendering makes good sense when Spillers's formulations are situated not only within the history of Atlantic slavery but also within Spillers's moment of writing and publication. During the 1980s (re)productive labor, for the first time since Emancipation, was being actively dispossessed, extracted, and accumulated. Whereas in slavery, accumulation of racialized (re)productive labor and products was organized by enslavers, slave traders, and New World planters seeking to turn a profit, in the 1980s (re)production began to be organized by those seeking a "cure" for the "problem" of infertility; by those hoping to (re)produce genetically related offspring in wombs not their own; by gay, lesbian, and queer individuals and couples desiring to create kin; and, not least, by individuals and corporations involved in brokering the sale of gestational surrogacy, the necessary raw materials (ova, sperm, and embryos), and a range of required technologies including genetic screening and selection, cryopreservation of gametes and embryos, artificial insemination, and in vitro fertilization that together enable fulfillment of consumer desires.[8]

According to histories of reproductive technological development, assisted reproduction technologies (or ARTs) began to be used in human reproduction after initial development for use in the breeding of domestic animals (Franklin). By the early 1990s surrogacy was becoming increasingly common in the United States and elsewhere (Markens; Jacobson; Spar; Twine). By the start of the new millennium (and therefore coincident with renewed interest in Robinson's theory of racial capitalism), paid gestational surrogacy had become a highly visible practice, one frequently represented and commented on in popular media. Complex and at once sensational legal cases resulting from breached surrogate contracts were discussed by TV pundits, and surrogacy was routinely treated in fiction and film (Latimer, *Reproductive*; Weinbaum, *Afterlife*). The pervasive use of surrogate labor over the past two decades has sparked development of transnational markets in a range of related commodities (Almeling; Cooper; Cooper and Waldby; Deomampo; Rudrappa; Thompson; Waldby; Weinbaum, "Reproducing," *Afterlife*).[9] Today ova, sperm, embryos, genetic testing and selection, stem cells and stem cell banking, and, not least, "designer babies" can be purchased globally. Indeed, what some describe as "global fertility chains" bind our world (Nahman, Parry, and Vertommen), enabling a coordinated transnational response to international consumer demand for the (re)production of genetically related offspring and the hyper-exploitation of (re)productive laborers.

Significantly, many of the same ARTs that were referred to as "new" in the 1980s are today becoming not only common but banal. ARTs are thus being used in divergent ways, both to shore up hegemonic kinship structures and social identities (Mamo; Smietana, Thompson, and Twine; Thompson), and, albeit far more rarely, to challenge them. Given the swift technological development that has taken place over little more than three decades, it is retrospectively evident that during the period in which Spillers wrote "Mama's Baby, Papa's Maybe," ARTs were already beginning to enable both a historically significant consolidation of the gendered organization of kin making, and pointing toward the possibility of untethering gender from (re)production. As Spillers appears to have realized, the ARTs that had begun to appear held out the potential to give rise to "the different social subjects" (80) whom she optimistically heralded as emergent in her article's final paragraphs—the same paragraphs that have been regarded as both cryptic and radical by readers, especially those invested in feminist, queer, and trans studies and politics.

While Spillers argues that the process of ungendering impacted all African captives and their descendants, she hones in on the repercussions of ungendering for the captive female and her descendants. As she elaborates, ungendering marked individuals and simultaneously left a cultural and ideological mark on a nation built out of centuries of Black women's (re)productive dispossession. This cultural and ideological mark is manifest in a range of reproductive discourses, and especially in those that reflect and refract racialized idea(l)s of "motherhood" and "womanhood." For instance, the infamous Moynihan Report inflicted such a forceful blow on Black women at the time of its publication that the impact continues to be felt across generations. Indeed, as many have pointed out, this impact is evident in decades of punitive and dehumanizing US social policy targeted at Black mothers and their children.[10] In Spillers's titular formulation, she expands her point about the Moynihan Report further, pushing it into the domain of language by observing that the process of ungendering in slavery today structures the distinctly "American grammar" of her article's title. This American grammar can be thought of as a hegemonic way of thinking, talking, writing about, and ultimately materializing the racialized gender formations that organize the relations of (re)production in racial capitalism both in the past and present.

To understand the process of ungendering as cultural, ideological, material, and at once time traveling, it is helpful to recall that, although "Mama's Baby, Papa's Maybe" principally treats the Middle Passage, the slave trade, and the New World plantation, it is bookended by meditations that shift readers into Spillers's present moment in order to explore "the afterlife of reproductive slavery." [11] For instance, Spillers begins her article with a discussion of the mistaken attribution of a supposedly matriarchal function to enslaved women in social scientific work and social policy recommendations, noting the repercussions of the positing of a "black matriarchate" emergent out of slavery on Black women and their families. Because Spillers shuttles readers back and forth across time, I regard her article as an exemplary expression of what I elsewhere describe as "Black feminism's philosophy of history"—an account of the unfolding of time that refuses ideas of linear progress and simultaneously reveals the imbrication or constellation of the slave past and the racial capitalist present (Weinbaum, *Afterlife*). In depicting slavery and her present moment of writing as involved in a complex relationship of historical reciprocity, Spillers argues that the Moynihan Report endures and resonates because it is representative of an entire "class of symbolic paradigms" (66) that together ensure slavery's lasting impress on the language used to describe and materialize our world. Ultimately, Spillers argues that the American grammar of her title encapsulates the problem that is her article's focus: existence of ungendering as a medium of violence and a technology of power that was brewed up in slavery and that persists in the racial capitalist (and therefore biocapitalist) present.

Although Spillers's contributions are most often regarded as psychoanalytically orientated, I am here suggesting that her meditation on American grammar allows her to advance a decidedly historical and materialist argument. As Spillers elaborates, an American grammar ungendered the captive female and continues to shape the material conditions in which (re)producers live and labor. To intervene in this situation, it is therefore necessary to expose the violence that inheres in the process of ungendering and to consider its alternative affordances. As Spillers quips, "The problem before us is deceptively simple" (66). There is a long tradition, one that the Moynihan Report taps, that dehumanizes descendants of enslaved (re)producers through destruction of both Black motherhood and kinship. While in slavery, bonds of kinship were severed by law and custom; in its wake (Sharpe), motherhood is foreclosed through targeted deployment of representations ranging from "the black matriarch" to "the welfare queen" and a rapidly proliferating range of pathologized figures, including the pregnant Black person charged with "genocide" for seeking an abortion in a post-*Roe* nation (Dana-Ain Davis; Latimer, "Abortion"; Roberts). Our task in the face of "the deceptively simple" problem before us is to comprehend the role played by the process of ungendering in the afterlife of reproductive slavery, to reappropriate the process, and to imagine other possible outcomes.

Feminist historians of slavery have treated the non-maternal and kinless status of the enslaved (re)producer through scholarship on *partus sequitur ventrem*. As they explain, this ancient doctrine originally derived from Roman law that was reanimated in Atlantic slavery to ensure that children born to enslaved women would follow the status of those who gave them life (Morgan, "Partus"; Dorsey; Berry). Beginning in the middle of the seventeenth century, *partus sequitur ventrem* was reanimated to ensure that children born to slaves residing in English, Spanish, and Portuguese colonies were regarded as lively commodities divisible into their useful bodily parts and processes. In short, like their "mothers," enslaved "children" were treated as alienable and fungible.[12] A child's price was calculable in a marketplace that reduced each to an exchange value.

In being forced to (re)produce their own and their children's kinlessness, enslaved women were subjected to the paired violations that sociologist Orlando Patterson argues made human beings into slaves: "natal alienation" and "social death." What Spillers's meditation on the process of ungendering adds to work by feminist histories of slavery and to Patterson's account of slave making is the understanding that both natal alienation and social death are processes of ungendering. As Spillers observes, the ungendering of enslaved (re)producers enabled legal evisceration of kinship, disaggregation of gestation and parturition from "motherhood," and the related disavowal of the existence of Black "femaleness" and "womanhood." Notably, Spillers theorizes the process of ungendering as both recursive and reiterative. The body of the captive female had to be transformed into property in order to be subsequently used to accumulate more property. The accumulation process was repeated across generations to maintain slave racial capitalism. This two-pronged accumulation process resulted in the (re)production of slaves whose forced participation in the (re)production of more slaves further powered the systems of dispossession, extraction, and accumulation.[13] Put otherwise, ungendering *engendered* more ungendering and thus ongoing racialized (re)productive accumulation.

At the same time that enslaved (re)producers were legally stripped of their rightful recognition as "mothers," Spillers notes that their "ethnicity" was "concentrated" (67) through their subjection to the chattel making logic of *partus sequitur ventrem*. *Partus sequitur ventrem* recursively "ethnicized"

(Spillers's preferred term) the (re)producer and in this way signaled her exile from the dominant gender formation—the racialized gender formation that equated femaleness with whiteness and organized the division of productive and reproductive labor into realms of public and private. Expanding on the work of feminist historians before her and anticipating the direction their work would take, Spillers suggests that the maintenance of a racialized gender division of labor during slavery was predicated on stabilization of the equation of womanhood with legal recognition of inclusion in domestic arrangements that divided space and labor into public and private, and thus into the forms required by (white) patriarchy. In recursively ethnicizing the (re)productive laborer as "Black," *partus sequitur ventrem* shored up idea(l)s of white motherhood and womanhood for all those who were exempted from enclosure within the doctrine's logic. As Spillers pointedly observes, in a world divided into racialized and gendered realms of public and private, "mothering . . . is the only female gender there is" (73). Circling back to her opening gambit in order to link her insights about the hegemony of white domestic space to her insights about the hegemony of American grammar, Spillers adds, "Motherhood and female gendering/ungendering appear so intimately aligned . . . [that they] speak the same language" (78).

According to the grammatical rules about which Spillers wrote, in slavery both motherhood and womanhood are exclusively white/European. Motherhood was a privilege conferred on those residing within a racialized (as white) and gendered (as female) domestic space that was ruled over by a (white) patriarch willing to bestow a patronym on those he regarded as kin. As Spillers specifies, by contrast to white/European women, enslaved (re)producers were "not regarded as elements of the domestic" (72). Such recognition would imply their belonging within a racialized and gendered metonymic chain from which they and their progeny were necessarily excluded. This chain linking together (white) motherhood, (white) womanhood, (white) paternity, (white) kinship, (white) genealogy, and, not least, (white) futurity had to be maintained in order for the "black matriarch" of the Moynihan Report to emerge as a living atavism, a figure out of time and yet pathologically stuck within its maw—a figure descended from the captive female held responsible for instigating the supposed crisis besetting "the black family," the pathological kin group imagined by Moynihan and those who influenced and were influenced by his work (Moynihan).

Use of enslaved (re)producers as engines of capital accumulation negated the possibility that gestation and parturition could be regarded as mother-making activities that conferred on them conventionally gender-marked identities and attendant bonds of kinship. As Spillers observes, instructively employing quotation marks around words whose meaning is thrown into question by the imposition of *partus sequitur ventrem*: "If 'kinship' were possible, the property relations [set in place in slavery] would be undermined, since the offspring would then 'belong' to a mother" (75). This last observation is underscored by Spillers when she subsequently adopts an admonishing tone: "One treads on dangerous ground in suggesting an equation between female gender and mothering" (78) in slavery. From the vantage point of enslavers, enslaved (re)producers were commodities characterized by the unique capacity to (re)produce chattel and thus amass surplus value for their owners. Ultimately, Spillers brings readers to the realization that by prohibiting enslaved (re)producers from laying claim to their children (and therefore to legally recognized kinship and genealogical futurity), the laws of slavery placed the captive female "out[side] of the traditional symbolics of female gender" (80) and into "an enforced state of breach in which 'kinship' loses meaning since it can be invaded at any moment . . . by the property relation" (74).

To summarize the imbricated arguments about the process of ungendering that I seek to excavate from Spillers rich text: (1) forced participation in (re)production recursively transforms the enslaved (re)producer into an ungendered and ethnicized (or racialized) source of chattel; (2) the enslaved (re)producer is denied the legal status of mother and therefore denied inclusion within womanhood, both of which emerge as presumptively white/European; and (3) *partus sequitur ventrem* brands the children of enslaved (re)producers as property that may be forced to (re)produce property across generations. By contrast to the mid-twentieth-century French feminist Simone de Beauvoir, who argues in her existential treatise on "the second sex" that "the woman" gives birth to herself as "a mother" in the act of giving birth to a child (540–88), no falsely universal power of self-actualization was available to the enslaved (re)producer.[14]

Ungendering the "Human-as-Cargo"

Up until this point, I have discussed the process of ungendering on the New World plantation. And yet, according to Spillers, ungendering does not begin on the plantation but, rather, in a different space and time: in the hold of a slave ship packed with African captives whom Spillers labels *human-as-cargo*. As Spillers observes, ungendering of the enslaved (re)producers was preceded by an a priori intellectual and specifically geospatial and mathematical calculation that first occurred in the minds of enslavers as they contemplated how best to maximize profit by filling ships bound for the New World not with gendered bodies of varied origin, mother tongue, custom, and age but, rather, with abstracted quantities of what Spillers famously denotes as *flesh*. Though numerous scholars engage Spillers idea of flesh (seeking to come to terms with its distinction from *body*), for present purposes I treat flesh as the primary by-product of Middle Passage—a by-product that is at once material, geospatial, mathematical, abstractable, and, above all, ungendered. To transform flesh into valuable property that takes up a given amount of space in the ship's hold, an atomizing calculation must numerically reduce the gendered *body* of the captive to a precise quantity of *flesh*, and then assess the amount of space said flesh will occupy within a strategically packed hold.

Of course, the calculation that reduces flesh to a quantity of human-as-cargo not only takes place in slavery but in all economic exchanges that occur in capitalism. What is unique to commodity exchange in slavery is the calculation of human value in relation to that of all other commodities, living and inanimate. It is only in the process of exchange as it takes place in slavery, in other words, that the humanness and thus the social identities to which the inhabitant of the allotted space within the ship's hold had previously laid claim are put under erasure or into what Spillers calls a "state of breach," from which there is no exit, at least from the point of view of property holders. As Spillers elaborates, the captive female stowed aboard the slave ship alongside other captives, *she* who considered *herself* and will have been recognized by others as an "indigenous" woman or girl, is transmogrified in and through the abstracting calculation made by enslavers, and then in and through the forced experiences of Middle Passage, into a quantity of flesh—a quantity of human-as-cargo that is dispossessed of home/land, mother/tongue, kin/ship, history, age, body, and, not least, gender.[15]

At the end of a passage spanning several paragraphs that begins with a discussion of the famous Brookes Plan in which Captain Perry, an antislavery investigative reporter, illustrates in detail how the owner of the vessel known as the *Brookes* calculated the space that each captive who was forced to board his ship would be allotted in the ship's hold ("let it now be supposed that every man slave is to be allowed six feet by one foot four inches for room, every woman five feet ten by one foot four, every boy five feet by one foot two, and every girl four feet six by one foot"),[16] Spillers concludes,

> Those African persons in "Middle Passage" were literally suspended in the "oceanic," if we think of the latter in its Freudian orientation as an analogy for the undifferentiated identity: removed from the indigenous land and culture, and not-yet "American" either, these captive persons, without names that their captors would recognize, were in movement across the Atlantic, but they were also

nowhere at all. Inasmuch as, on any given day, we might imagine, the captive personality did not know where s/he was, we could say that they were the culturally "unmade," thrown in the midst of a figurative darkness that "exposed" their destinies to an unknown course. . . . We might say that the slave ship, its crew, and its human-as-cargo stand for a wild and unclaimed richness of *possibility* that is not interrupted, not "counted"/"accounted," or differentiated until its movement gains the land thousands of miles away from the point of departure. Under these conditions, one is neither female, nor male, as both subjects are taken into "account" as *quantities.* The female in "Middle Passage," as an apparently smaller physical mass, occupies "less room" in a directly translatable money economy. But she is, nevertheless, quantifiable by the same rules of accounting as her male counterpart. (72)

While most readers take up Spillers ideas about the creation of flesh (and thus the body/flesh distinction) in order to engage the ontological question of the destruction of *"the* Black" as human subject (Bey; Sexton; Snorton; Wilderson, *Red*, "Reciprocity"), in relating her ideas about the creation of flesh to the abstracting economic calculation that filled the hold of the slave ship, I maintain that Spillers not only theorizes an origin point for ontological anti-Blackness in Middle Passage. She theorizes the centrality of the process of ungendering to the workings of racial capitalism tout court. For it was while honing in on the packing of the *Brookes*'s hold that Spillers brings readers to the salient realization that Atlantic slavery was predicated on a mathematical, geospatial, economic, and abstracting process of ungendering that ultimately enabled the commodification of human beings. As she succinctly observes, "the scaled inequalities" that are recommended by the owner of the *Brookes* and observed by Captain Perry "complement the commanding terms of the dehumanizing, ungendering, and defacing project" (72) that was Atlantic slavery.

Overall, the above passage reveals the role of a meticulous *counting/ accounting* in the transformation of the captive female into a quantity of flesh and thus into an ungendered quantity of human-as-cargo. Erasure of the captive female's gender identity is part of the process of commodifying the human being, and thus part of the process on which the smooth workings of slave racial capitalism depended. Related accounts of the work of mathematical abstraction and numeracy in the slave trade have been elaborated by historians Stephanie Smallwood (chaps. 2 and 3) and Jennifer Morgan (*Reckoning*, chaps. 1 and 2) through detailed analyses based on their readings of ship's logs and captains' ledger books among other available archives. Each offers formulations that inform and thicken the present interpretation of

Spillers. Smallwood writes, "Traders reduced people to the sum of their biological parts, thereby scaling life down to an arithmetical equation and finding the lowest common denominator" (43).[17] Drawing on Spillers, I add to Smallwood that the "lowest common denominator" is in fact ungendered flesh. When aggregated, ungendered flesh constituted the "complete" cargo; it functioned as a measure of the total surplus value that would be realized in specie and notes when the ship reached its destination, its hold was unpacked, and the contents sold. For Morgan, the numeracy that animates logs and ledgers leads to an understanding of the silences that characterize the archives of slavery. As she explains, captains' inattention to the presence of women on their ships, their failure to record the gender of their cargo, cannot be dismissed but rather must be interpreted as an important symptom of the numerical logic on which the trade was predicated. Whereas Morgan reads erasure of female captives from the written record as "a crucial originary moment when . . . gendered categories of meaning became constitutive of the most profoundly inscribed racial subordination," drawing on Spillers I add that erasure of gendered categories from the archives of slavery (and from too much of the scholarship that is based on them) testifies loudly to the power of the process of ungendering. As Morgan further speculates, inattention to the presence of women on board ships may paradoxically speak to the violent and wonton sexual (ab)use to which enslaved women and girls were subjected: "For slave traders, refusing to record the sex ratios on board their ships was perhaps part of their ideological strategy for rationalizing the trade" (49). I find that Morgan's observation is anticipated by Spillers who writes, "The sexual violation of captive females and their own express rage against their oppressors did not constitute events that captains and crews rushed to record" (73).

Through discussion of the ungendering that is part and parcel of the abstracting calculation of commodification, Spillers compels readers to recognize that the logic that filled the hold of the ship was forwarded on the plantation, where it again was used to rationalize dispossession, extraction, and accumulation. More specifically still, once the process of ungendering was set in motion, it could be episodically mobilized to rationalize the consumption of enslaved (re)productive labor and its products. Indeed, the process of ungendering was structural. Its reiteration was a constitutive feature of an American grammar that ultimately enabled the materialization of both an economic system and a national culture across time. The rules of this American grammar structured and materialized the Brookes Plan, the implementation of the doctrine of *partus sequitur ventrem*, the Moynihan Report and the public policy emergent from it, and the entire class of symbolic paradigms on which the report drew, to which it contributed, and that it advances.

Because I hope that this article contributes not only to scholarship on Spillers but also to that on racial capitalism, I pause to summarize its arguments in familiar Marxist terms: "Mama's Baby, Papa's Maybe" ought to be treated as an addition to Marx's theory of so-called primitive accumulation that centers interconnected processes of racialization and ungendering. This is because it simultaneously extends, blends, and critiques Marx's story of capitalism's inception, Robinson's concept of racial capitalism, and Federici's account of enclosure of the reproductive commons. As it does so, it shows us that racial capitalism is predicated on an abstracting mathematical, geospatial, and economic calculation that negates gender in the process of packing the hold of the slave ship, forecloses the captive female's claim to "motherhood" and "womanhood" by forcing her participation in (re)productive labor governed by the doctrine of *partus sequitur ventrem*, and ultimately precludes the enslaved (re)producer's recognition as a rights-bearing human subject who might otherwise be entitled to the status and protections (albeit always partial) afforded by inclusion in the racialized and gendered relations of legally recognized kinship and domesticity. In sum, according to Spillers the (re)production of both chattel and kinlessness (or social death and natal alienation) are together tethered to the process of ungendering that was set in motion both when the captive female's body was transformed into flesh and when it was forced to participate in the reproduction of the relations of (re)production that subtend slave racial capitalism.

No Stopping at the Gender Question

Twenty years after publication of "Mama's Baby, Papa's Maybe: An American Grammar Book" Spillers joined a group of Black feminist scholars including Shelly Eversley, Farah Griffin, Saidiya Hartman, and Jennifer Morgan to collectively reflect on its stakes. One question the group took up was Spillers's relationship to the poststructuralist feminist theory that was being celebrated in the 1980s as she wrote. Spillers's response to this question is instructive in that she retrospectively understands herself not to have written with the intent of critiquing then dominant theories inattentive to race and racism (though she does this so well!). Rather, she recalls writing in order to identify and explore the problem of "black women stopping at the gender question" (Spillers et al. 304). "Stopping at the gender question," failing to push beyond gender as principal object of investigation and most valued analytical lens was a necessity for Spillers because of the "refusal of certain gender privileges to black women historically" (Spillers et al. 304). Put otherwise, Spillers recalls recognizing that because ungendering was and remains central to ongoing dehumanization of Black women, she found it necessary to push beyond gender. She did this by neither assuming gender as a given analytic priority nor as an identity available to all comers. And she therefore did not rely on the presumption of universal access to recognition as either a mother or a woman. As she elaborates further, in writing her watershed article she sought "to go *through* gender to get to something *wider*" (304, my emphasis). Spillers assumed neither gender's presence nor the relevance of the feminist frameworks proffered by those who surrounded her in the academy. Rather, she found that she was preoccupied with questions about what had been gone through to create an exclusively white claim to the status of human being, and, especially, what had been too readily assumed about the racialization of both human motherhood and womanhood. Indeed, Spillers retrospectively describes her focus as being identification of the racialized and gendered exclusions that were and continue to be enacted to solidify a raced (as white) and gendered (as male) construct of the "human" precisely because she recognized that for the captive female and her descendants gender was and remains episodically evaporated, foreclosed, refused, denied, disavowed, or entirely negated.[18]

By contrast to those who presumptively regard gender as available for the taking—albeit as always already insufficient as the only mark of a subject's identity—Spillers sought to go *through* gender to get to something *wider*. Indeed, it was in this spirit that she created her account of an American grammar structured around a racialized process of ungendering. As she explains, when writing "Mama's Baby, Papa's Maybe" she searched for "a vocabulary" that would enable her undertaking, but found that such a vocabulary was not "immediately available" (Spillers et al. 301). Identification of what was missing, moreover, led to realization that she would need to gesture toward the invention of a "new syntax" that might yet enable her work. This new syntax, or what she also describes as a new "semantic field/fold" ("Mama's Baby," 80), would ideally enable revelation of the process of ungendering to which the captive female was subjected in Middle Passage, on the New World plantation, and beyond.

Notably, the process of ungendering is not only connected to violence but also to what Spillers forecasts (in the passage that is quoted above) as "a wild and unclaimed richness of *possibility*" (72) that is unwittingly unleashed by the abstracting mathematical, geospatial, and economic calculations that first made slave racial capitalism go. On the one hand, the italicized term, *possibility*, signals the devastating reality to which the doctrine of *partus sequitur ventrem* was attached in slavery. This is the speculative economic possibility that enslavers sought to realize by laying claim to the wild and unclaimed riches extracted from flesh forced to (re)produce the system of slave racial capitalism when the slave ship "gain[ed] the land thousands of miles away from the point of departure" (72). On the other hand, the term *possibility* gestures toward so much more. Indeed, it directs attention to the captive female's potential transgression, resistance, and refusal of forced participation in racialized (re)productive accumulation and thus to an audacious insistence on the *possibility* of existence beyond the dehumanizing conditions that have been imposed. In doing so, it suggests that the process of ungendering might simultaneously constitute a profound violation and an opening. It might be an immediately violent and violating process and a process with unknown outcome—a process that is double-edged in that it heralds alternative forms of fungibility and lability, and thus alternative modes of being in and relating to the world that are irreducible to the abstracting calculations that subtended slavery. Put simply, ungendering might be a wayward process that affords rich future *possibility* even though it has historically been used to reap violence.

This is the "wild and unclaimed richness of *possibility*" that Black studies scholars such as C. Riley Snorton and Tiffany Lethabo King (among others) have located in Spillers's work. As Snorton influentially argues in *Black on Both Sides*, the process of ungendering that transpires in slavery can and should be linked to transness and, conversely, transness to Blackness. As King powerfully attests in *The Black Shoals* and elsewhere (Wilderson and King), writing in partial counterpoint to Afropessimists (Wilderson, *Red*; Sexton) who often position Spillers (in my view mistakenly) as a fellow proponent of their position, Blackness is neither an exclusively negative nor debilitating product of enslavement.[19] It is always also a fungible and therefore defiant source of oppositional ontological, social, and political formation. As King elaborates, "there is *possibility* and *futurity* when one is rendered outside of human coordinates" ("Abolishing" 79). In sum, the process of ungendering that is slavery's fount and legacy holds within it the *possibility* that those caught up in the process might yet challenge, refuse, exceed, or perhaps even transcend the confines of the forms of capitalism that are enabled by racialized (re)productive accumulation.

By way of conclusion, I track further into the realm of *possibility* to speculate about reproduction untethered from gender and to consider the import of this in the context of the contemporary movement for reproductive justice. Thoughts limned here are admittedly in process and thus are ones I hope to continue to think through alongside others committed to realization of substantive reproductive freedom in the United States and elsewhere around the world. In brief, I follow Spillers in imagining what an insurgent understanding of the "wild and unclaimed richness of *possibility*" that is afforded by the process of ungendering might ideally contribute to collective thinking about a shared future that might yet represent a radical rupture with the form of ongoing racialized (re)productive accumulation that I have argued today characterizes both racial capitalism and biocapitalism (Weinbaum, *Afterlife*; "Reproducing"; "Slave Episteme").

A Different Reproductive Future?

At the very end of her article Spillers swerves (Butler 29) off the main road she has traveled and explores in her final paragraphs the "new syntax" or "semantic field/fold" that she has argued might be afforded by our coming to terms with the imposition of the myth of the "Black matriarchate," or what she in this instance labels the myth of "Mother Right" (80) using language adopted from anthropologist Claude Meillassoux. As Spillers elaborates, for enslaved (re)producers and their descendants, "Mother Right" emerges from a perverse torquing of white reason. In the Atlantic world such a supposed *right* is a "negating feature of [Black] human community" (80) insofar as racialized (re)productive accumulation remains an ongoing process that systematically refuses motherhood to Black (re)producers and either entirely forecloses or violently devalues Black kinship in its attempt to decimate Black humanity. But Spillers observes, "Mother Right" must also be recognized as a patently false imposition, a grammatical rule that ought to be broken or entirely refused. "Mother Right" (like "Black matriarchate") disavows as it misnames the process of ungendering in slavery and beyond. Therefore, "Mother Right" ought to be deconstructed and not only displaced but also replaced, so that it becomes possible to clear space for thinking about racialized reproduction beyond gender and thus in relation to what amounts to an alternative humanist project of futurity. As Spillers announces in concluding her article, once the "play of paradox" that characterizes the process of ungendering is revealed and understood, it becomes "our task to make a place for . . . [the] different social subject" who represents the legacy of this process going forward (80).

As Spillers elaborates in the retrospective exchange about her essay discussed above, when she invoked this "different social subject," she did not intend to allude to "a thing that is somehow male *and* female" (Spillers et al. 304). Rather, she was imagining "a kind of humanity that we seem very far from" in retrospect, but that she nonetheless "used to think black culture was on the verge of creating" (304). Despite her acknowledgment of her reservations ("used to think . . . ") about the immanence of an unprecedented "kind of humanity," Spillers nonetheless acknowledges that in 1987 she optimistically ended her watershed article on a final, future-oriented note. This note chimes deeply with Afrofuturist (and Afro-optimist) sensibilities that were in the mid-1980s just beginning to take form in other quarters (Brown). Thus, Spillers is channeling the zeitgeist when, in her article's concluding paragraphs, she cosmically forecasts Black futurity in an alternative idiom, one that pushes through gender as we know it to renegotiate the fraught relationship among Blackness, reproduction, and motherhood to get at something wider. Indeed, Spillers closes by forecasting Black futurity in a subjunctive idiom that requires cessation of ongoing racialized (re)productive accumulation and the violent dispossession and extraction that have subtended it.

Drawing out her final cosmic note in order to improvise on it, Spillers surmises that "the African-American male" has been "handed" by the captive female and her descendants in ways he cannot escape and that have removed him from "the fiction of the father" ("Mama's Baby," 80), from the fiction of paternal power that has been and remains reserved for white men. To grab hold of an "aspect of his own personhood" that might yet liberate him from this fiction, it is the "heritage of the mother that . . . [he] must regain" (80). For "the African-American male," Spillers explains, *possibility* inheres in the ability to say " 'yes' to the 'female' within" (80). As others including Snorton have noted, with this remark Spillers appears to call for "the African-American male" to embrace the *possibility* that is opened up by the historical process of ungendering "handed" through time by the captive female whose gender was negated in Middle Passage, who was refused recognition as mother, and whose descendants are today identified by any number of dehumanizing names, including those monikers with which Spillers opens her article: " 'Peaches' and 'Brown Sugar,' 'Sapphire' and 'Earth Mother,' 'Aunty,' and 'Granny' " (65).

For Black women descended from the captive female forced to (re)produce her own and her children's kinlessness, Spillers suggests that the path to liberation is related but distinct. For these "different social subjects" the liberatory project entails reclamation of "the monstrosity" foisted on enslaved (re)producers and their descendants. Black women's liberation, she clarifies, will not be realized by "joining the ranks of gendered femaleness" (80). Rather, it will require "gaining the insurgent ground" occupied by those who dare to self-name, self-make, and ultimately "rewrite . . . a radically different text for female empowerment" (80). No doubt, this "radically different text" closely resembles Spillers's own. It is a text that deconstructs, displaces, and replaces a disabling American grammar that has in the past been used to abet the process of ungendering. It is a future text, as Fred Moten suggests in an allusive nod to Spillers (and to Luce Irigaray, Spillers's French feminist contemporary), that must be recognized as part of the Black radical tradition precisely because it entails "a cutting and abundant refusal of closure." As Moten explains, "This refusal of closure is not a rejection but an ongoing and reconstructive improvisation . . . this reconstruction's motive is the sexual differentiation of sexual difference" (288).[20]

In an uncanny convergence, Loretta J. Ross, one of the founders of the movement for reproductive justice, suggests that a set of parallel moves should be made in its pursuit. In a 2017 article, Ross argues that reproductive justice as both a framework and praxis ought to encompass analysis of the experiences and needs of all people, not only cis women.[21] She specifies that she is thinking about what it means for reproductive justice to encompass the human rights of trans people, gender-nonbinary people, and those who seek to push beyond gender in order to live other possibilities (291). In short, Ross suggests that reproductive justice ought to be capacious enough to risk embrace of the *possibility* that Spillers understood to inhere in the process of ungendering, in the unhinging of reproduction from gender when imagining "the new social subjects," born in slavery's wake, who seek "to go *through* gender to get to something *wider*."

Though admittedly the bulk of Ross's article is concerned with advancing women's reproductive freedom—a project that takes on renewed urgency in our post-*Roe* moment—in my preferred reading it also embraces the "wild and unclaimed richness of *possibility*" that Spillers first located in the process of ungendering. And perhaps this is unsurprising as Ross expressly invokes Spillers in a key passage in which she appears to take up insights gleaned from Spillers in her ongoing battle against reproductive injustice in the context of racial capitalism. As Ross observes, in working toward reproductive justice it is necessary to begin with the needs of Black women and from there create a praxis that redresses the wrongs done to all pregnant people and all potentially reproductive bodies (301). These wrongs began with the Black body's ungendering in slavery and its reduction to flesh. Today's wrongs include a host of related violations such as the Black body's transformation into a laboratory for social and medical experimentation (surgical procedures, drug trials, forced sterilization and cesarean section, non-consensual testing with long-term contraceptives such as Depo-Provera, etc.), disproportionate incarceration and shackling during childbirth, destruction of the social contract through so-called welfare reform, and, not least, denial of access to adequate childcare, health care, housing, food and clean water as well as all the other material resources that are not simply desired but required by every pregnant person and by all those who hope to become parents or seek access to resources that allow them to remain childless. In short, to achieve reproductive justice, Ross argues, racial capitalism must be confronted and the intersection of reproduction, womanhood, and motherhood reworked. Put otherwise, we must follow Spillers in embracing the "wild and unclaimed richness of *possibility*" that inheres in the historical ungendering of (re) production—and this is so, even though this process was used to fuel slave racial capitalism and continues to fuel the practices of racialized (re)productive accumulation on which racial capitalism's expansion depends.

In the preceding pages I have followed Spillers in suggesting that ungendering is key to racial capitalist accumulation and that it might yet open up rich possibility in the afterlife of reproductive slavery. In doing so, I have taken to heart the fact that Spillers ends her article with the bold idea that the ungendered (re)productive processes that powered slave racial capitalism in the past may yet prove to be just fungible enough to open up new ways of being in, relating to, and materially reproducing our world. At the same time that Ross's invocation of Spillers clears space for expansive conceptualization of reproductive justice, my reading of Spillers suggests that those involved in realizing substantive reproductive freedom must push beyond all-too-familiar liberal calls for an invigorated politics of inclusion. As Spillers reminds us, what is needed in slavery's wake is not a proliferation of gendered identities, but rather a new syntax that might yet allow us to not only deconstruct the past but also displace and replace long-standing relationships of historical reciprocity between the process of ungendering and racialized (re)productive accumulation. In theorizing (re)production in racial capitalism, Spillers compels us to inquire into how the processes of ungendering that she identified and examined have shaped our world and continue to shape the workings of contemporary global markets for (re)productive labor and products. To this end, we must examine how the existing movement for reproductive justice might yet involve refusal of ongoing racialized (re)productive accumulation as it functions within contemporary biocapitalism. Such refusal will necessarily entail analysis of the complex processes that currently enable the circulation of all the human biological commodities (re)produced by contemporary laborers whose bodies have been reduced to "the lowest common denominator" that Spillers labeled flesh. For it is as commodified flesh that surrogates, egg vendors, and many others enter the transnational marketplace to sell their bodies, their bodily processes, and the products of their in vivo labor. Where a thorough and strategic account of the ungendering of contemporary racialized (re)productive accumulation will take us is a heretofore unexplored question that cannot be adequately answered by scholars and/or activists who rely on anachronist pieties about distinctions between productive and reproductive labor, and the supposed feminization of labor in globalization. As Spillers makes clear, truly substantive reproductive freedom requires the dismantling of the inner solidarity of slavery, racial capitalism, biocapitalism, and racialized (re)productive accumulation and acceptance of the risk involved in refusing to stop at the gender question. ▪

Alys Eve Weinbaum is professor of English in the Department of English and adjunct professor in Gender, Women, and Sexuality Studies at the University of Washington, Seattle. She is author of *The Afterlife of Reproductive Slavery: Biocapitalism and Black Feminism's Philosophy of History* (2019), which won the Sarah A. Whaley Book Prize for groundbreaking scholarship on women and labor from the National Women's Studies Association (NWSA) and an honorable mention for the Gloria Anzaldúa Book Prize for transnational scholarship in Women's Studies also from the NWSA; and *Wayward Reproductions: Genealogies of Race and Nation in Transatlantic Modern Thought* (2004).

ACKNOWLEDGMENTS

This article has benefited from dialogue that transpired over several months among members of the Reproducing Racial Capitalism workshops that Jennifer L. Morgan and I together convened in 2022 and 2023. I thank all the participants for their insight and radical imagination. I am indebted to Stephanie Clare, Brent Edwards, Caleb Knapp, Chandan Reddy, Lynn Thomas, Sasha Turner, Julia Wurr, and SJ Zhang for offering detailed feedback on various iterations of this article. Finally, a big thanks to Alexandra Meany for research assistance.

NOTES

1   The related term, *biocapital*, is usually attributed to Kaushik Sunder Rajan. Although Rajan does not explore the (re)productive character of biocapital/ism, this is the focus of the feminist scholarship in science and technology studies alluded to here.

2   "Slave breeding" is *the* "biotechnology" that facilitated the (re)production of slave racial capitalism. For this reason I elsewhere argue that contemporary slave racial capitalism ought to be retroactively recognized as a form of biocapitalism (Weinbaum, *Afterlife*).

3   Some scholars are wary about using a term that associates slaves and animals, while others recall that the term *slave breeding* was used by slave traders, owners, plantation managers, and abolitionists, and is necessary to accurate historicization (Morgan, *Reckoning*; Berry; Paugh; Smithers). The term I use in this article *enslaved (re)production*, has the advantage of both accurately describing and simultaneously shorthanding economic processes without forwarding dehumanizing language.

4 Rosalind C. Morris suggests that Marx's German term, *Ursprüngliche Akkumulation*, ought to be but has not been routinely translated as *originary accumulation*. Morris regards mistranslation as instructive in that it emphasizes the recursive and ongoing character of processes that enable capitalism's reproduction and the simultaneous construction of these processes as natural and inevitable. This insight is useful in that it illuminates the representation of the radical transformation of the relations of (re)production as always already foreclosed. Throughout this essay, I use the dominant translation because it remains most recognizable.

5 As Federici explains, *Caliban* represents work begun in the 1970s in collaboration with Leopoldina Fortunati that first appeared in Italian in 1984. Notably Federici and Fortunati formulated their ideas around the same time as Robinson and Spillers. Brief accounts of primitive accumulation are interspersed throughout Federici's subsequent writings. In these later works (*Witches*, 2018; *Re-Enchanting*, 2019; *Beyond*, 2020) she uses the term *reproductive commons*.

6 Spillers is not the first to consider the processes of ungendering in racial capitalism. Angela Davis develops similar arguments based on her assessment of the dehumanizing labor that all slaves performed. Oyèrónké Oyewùmí argues that in Yoruba society gender functioned as a Western imposition and did not exist as a meaningful social category prior to European colonization and the slave trade. Though this argument has been roundly challenged (see, for instance, Nwokeji), it remains an important reminder that African social formations were distinct from contemporaneous European ones.

7 On occasion, Spillers also refers to the "African female subject" (68) and the "African female in captivity" (73). Notably, she never questions the gender of the Africans who gave birth to captives caught up in the slave trade.

8 Recent scholarship explores the pitfalls and liberatory possibilities of assisted reproductive technologies (ARTs) (Mamo, *Queering*; "Queering Reproduction"; Smietana, Thompson, and Twine; Thompson; Keaney; Clarke and Haraway; Vertommen in this special issue) and examines how both normative and nonnormative kin making are caught up in racial capitalist logics and biocapitalist circuits of exchange. To be clear, I do not intend to argue against consumption and use of ARTs but rather to underscore the inevitability of enmeshment of contemporary (re)production in racial capitalism.

9 Gestational surrogacy uses a "donor" egg or most often an egg purchased from a "vendor" whose phenotypic traits the consumer hopes to recreate in a prospective child. Gestational surrogacy allows for the breakup of (re)productive labor into its constituent parts and enables involvement of a maximal number of (re)producers in the (re)production of the product. Today, gestational surrogacy is so dominant that it is simply referred to as surrogacy. Indeed, so-called traditional surrogacy involving a surrogate's own egg was largely phased out in the early 1990s in an effort to avoid legal challenges to "ownership" or "custody" of the child (re)produced.

10 Spillers's argument is amplified in Dorothy Roberts's account of the myriad ways in which the child welfare system destroys Black families (*Torn*).

11 "The afterlife of slavery" was first theorized by Saidiya Hartman (*Lose*). I expand Hartman's concept to highlight its reproductive logic, what I call "the afterlife of reproductive slavery."

12   When "motherhood" is thrown into uncertainty, so too is "childhood." Habiba Ibrahim draws on Spillers to argue that "childhood" is a life stage foreclosed to those directly impacted by enslavement and its aftermath.

13   Robert Nichols ("Disaggregating"; *Theft*) observes that land dispossession is a recursive form of so-called primitive accumulation because land must first be made into property in order to be dispossessed. Here I suggest that a similar dynamic characterizes (re)productive accumulation insofar as the (re)producer must first be made into flesh.

14   According to Angela Davis ("Reflections"), ungendering of the enslaved laborer is not opposed to but rather complements the hyper-sexualization that rationalizes the rape of the enslaved, an act of terror that is further incentivized by the (re)productive logic of slavery. It is perhaps because Spillers shared with Davis this insight about the complementarity of ungendering and rape in slavery that Spillers homes in on racialized (re)productive accumulation, a process that effectively necessitates both sexual (ab)use *and* the womb's enclosure through *partus sequitur ventrem*.

15   In reminding readers that African captives were "indigenous" (72), Spillers suggests the complicity between slavery and colonialism and effectively sets the stage for consideration of the connection between Blackness and Indigeneity, and Black studies and Indigenous studies in subsequent scholarship (King, Navarro, and Smith; King, "Black"; Lowe).

16   Or, as the owner of the *Brookes* recommends, taking the mathematical reduction one step further: "five females [ought to] be reckoned as four males, and three boys or girls as equal to two grown persons" (Spillers 72).

17   Smallwood is also concerned with the process of abstraction as it pertains to the filling of the ship's hold: "Slaves became, for the purpose of transatlantic shipment, mere physical units that could be arranged and molded at will—whether folded together spoonlike in rows or flattened side by side in a plane" (68).

18   In this sense Spillers was working alongside Sylvia Wynter ("Beyond"; "Unsettling").

19   Spillers also distances herself from Afropessimism (Spillers, "Hortense Spillers").

20   In Hegelian terms "this reconstruction's motive" is the negation of the negation (Moten 288). Publication of "Mama's Baby, Papa's Maybe" coincides with heightened anglophone interest in and critique of French feminist theory, including the work of Luce Irigaray.

21   Reproductive justice is based on three interconnected principles: the right to have a child under conditions of one's choosing, the right not to have a child, and the right to parent in an environment free from individual or state violence (Ross and Solinger 9).

WORKS CITED

Almeling, Rene. *Sex Cells: The Medical Market in Eggs and Sperm.* Berkeley: University of California Press, 2011.

Arruzza, Cinzia, Tithi Bhattacharya, and Nancy Fraser. *Feminism for the 99%: A Manifesto.* London: Verso, 2019.

Baptist, Edward E. *The Half Has Never Been Told: Slavery and the Making of American Capitalism.* New York: Basic Books, 2014.

Barrett, Michele. *Women's Oppression Today: Problems in Marxist Feminist Analysis*. London: Verso, 1980.

Beauvoir, Simone de. *The Second Sex*. New York: Vintage, 1952.

Beckert, Sven. *Empire of Cotton: A Global History*. New York: Vintage Books, 2014.

Beckles, Hilary McD. *Natural Rebels: A Social History of Enslaved Black Women in Barbados*. New Brunswick, NJ: Rutgers University Press, 1997.

Berry, Daina Ramey. *The Price for Their Pound of Flesh: The Value of the Enslaved, from Womb to Grave, in the Building of a Nation*. Boston: Beacon, 2017.

Bey, Marquis. "The Trans*-ness of Blackness, and Blackness of Trans*-ness," *TSQ* 4, no. 2 (2017): 275–95. https://doi.org/10.1215/23289252-3815069.

Bhattacharya, Tithi, ed. *Social Reproduction Theory: Remapping Class, Recentering Oppression*. London: Pluto, 2017.

Boris, Eileen, and Rachel Salazar Parreñas, eds. *Intimate Labors: Cultures, Technologies, and the Politics of Care*. Stanford, CA: Stanford University Press, 2008.

Brown, Jayna. *Black Utopias: Speculative Life and the Music of Other Worlds*. Durham, NC: Duke University Press, 2021.

Bush, Barbara. *Slave Women in Caribbean Society: 1650–1838*. Bloomington: Indiana University Press, 1990.

Butler, Judith. *Gender Trouble: Feminism and the Subversion of Identity*. New York: Routledge, 1990.

Camp, Stephanie. *Closer to Freedom: Enslaved Women and Everyday Resistance in the Plantation South*. Chapel Hill: University of North Carolina Press, 2004.

Clarke, Adele E., and Donna Haraway. *Making Kin Not Population*. Chicago: Prickly Paradigm, 2018.

Cooper, Melinda. *Life as Surplus: Biotechnology and Capitalism in the Neoliberal Era*. Seattle: University of Washington Press, 2008.

Cooper, Melinda, and Catherine Waldby. *Clinical Labor: Tissue Donors and Research Subjects in the Global Bioeconomy*. Durham, NC: Duke University Press, 2014.

Davis, Angela Y. "Reflections on the Black Woman's Role in the Community of Slaves." *Black Scholar* 3, no. 4 (1971): 2–15. https://doi.org/10.1080/00064246.1981.11414214.

Davis, Dana-Ain. "Trump, Race, and Reproduction in the Afterlife of Slavery." *Cultural Anthropology* 34, no. 1 (2019): 26–33. https://doi.org/10.14506/ca34.1.05.

Day, Iyko. *Alien Capital: Asian Racialization and the Logic of Settler Colonial Capitalism*. Durham, NC: Duke University Press, 2016.

Deomampo, Daisy. *Transnational Reproduction: Race, Kinship, and Commercial Surrogacy in India*. New York: New York University Press, 2016.

Dickenson, Donna. *Body Shopping: Converting Body Parts to Profit*. Oxford: Oneworld, 2008.

Dorsey, Joseph C. "Women without History: Slavery and the International Politics of *Partus Sequitur Ventrem* in the Spanish Caribbean." In *Caribbean Slavery in the Atlantic World*, edited by Verene Shepherd and Hilary McD. Beckles, 165–207. Kingston, Jamaica: Ian Randle, 2000.

Eisenstein, Zillah R., ed. *Capitalist Patriarchy and the Case for Socialist Feminism*. New York: Monthly Review, 1979.

Federici, Silvia. *Beyond the Periphery of the Skin: Rethinking, Remaking, and Reclaiming the Body in Contemporary Capitalism*. Oakland, CA: PM, 2020.

Federici, Silvia. *Caliban and the Witch: Women, the Body, and Primitive Accumulation*. Brooklyn: Autonomedia, 2004.

Federici, Silvia. *Re-enchanting the World: Feminism and the Politics of the Commons*. Brooklyn: PM, 2019.

Federici, Silvia. *Revolution at Point Zero: Housework, Reproduction, and Feminist Struggle*. Oakland, CA: PM, 2012.

Federici, Silvia. *Witches, Witch-Hunting, and Women*. Oakland, CA: PM, 2018.

Franklin, Sarah. *Dolly Mixtures: The Remaking of Genealogy*. Durham, NC: Duke University Press, 2007.

Fuentes, Marisa J. *Dispossessed Lives: Enslaved Women, Violence, and the Archive*. Philadelphia: University of Pennsylvania Press, 2016.

Haley, Sarah. *No Mercy Here: Gender, Punishment, and the Making of Jim Crow Modernity*. Chapel Hill: University of North Carolina Press, 2016.

Hartman, Saidiya. *Lose Your Mother: A Journey along the Atlantic Slave Route*. New York: Farrar, Straus and Giroux, 2007.

Hine, Darlene Clark. "Female Slave Resistance: The Economics of Sex." *Western Journal of Black Studies* 3, no. 2 (1979): 123–27.

Hine, Darlene Clark. "Rape and the Inner Lives of Black Women in the Middle West." *Signs* 4, no. 4 (1989): 912–20.

Ibrahim, Habiba. *Black Age: Oceanic Lifespans and the Time of Black Life*. New York: New York University Press, 2021.

Jacobson, Heather. *Labor or Love: Gestational Surrogacy and the Work of Making Babies*. New Brunswick, NJ: Rutgers University Press, 2016.

James, Selma. *Sex, Race, and Class: The Perspective of Winning*. Oakland, CA: PM, 2012.

Johnson, Jessica Marie. *Wicked Flesh: Black Women, Intimacy, and Freedom in the Atlantic World*. Philadelphia: University of Pennsylvania Press, 2020.

Johnson, Walter. *River of Dark Dreams: Slavery and Empire in the Cotton Kingdom*. Cambridge, MA: Harvard University Press, 2013.

Jung, Moon Ho. *Coolies and Cane: Race, Labor, and Sugar in the Age of Emancipation*. Baltimore, MD: Johns Hopkins University Press, 2006.

Keaney, Jaya. *Making Gaybies: Queer Reproduction and Multiracial Feeling*. Durham, NC: Duke University Press, 2023.

King, Tiffany Lethabo. "Black 'Feminisms' and Pessimism: Abolishing Moynihan's Negro Family." *Theory and Event* 21, no. 1 (2018): 68–87. https://muse.jhu.edu/article/685970.

King, Tiffany Lethabo. *The Black Shoals: Offshore Formation of Black and Native Studies*. Durham, NC: Duke University Press, 2019.

King, Tiffany Lethabo, Jenell Navarro, and Andrea Smith, eds. *Otherwise Worlds: Against Settler Colonialism and Anti-Blackness*. Durham, NC: Duke University Press, 2020.

Latimer, Heather. "Abortion Regulation and the Afterlife of Reproductive Slavery; or, A Call to Make Abortion Natural Again." *Feminist Studies* 48, no. 2 (2022): 342–66. https://doi.org/10.1353/fem.2022.0030.

Latimer, Heather. *Reproductive Acts: Sexual Politics in North American Fiction and Film*. Montreal: McGill-Queens University Press, 2013.

Lowe, Lisa. *The Intimacies of Four Continents*. Durham, NC: Duke University Press, 2017.

Mamo, Laura. *Queering Reproduction: Achieving Pregnancy in the Age of Technoscience.* Durham, NC: Duke University Press, 2007.

Mamo, Laura. "Queering Reproduction in Transnational Bio-economies." *Reproductive BioMedicine and Society Online* 7 (2018): 24–32. https://www.ncbi.nlm.nih.gov/pmc/articles/PMC6287057/.

Markens, Susan. *Surrogate Motherhood and the Politics of Reproduction.* Berkeley: University of California Press, 2007.

Meillassoux, Claude. "Female Slavery." In *Women and Slavery in Africa,* edited by Claire C. Robertson and Martin A. Klein, 49–66. Madison: University of Wisconsin Press, 1983.

Mies, Maria. *Patriarchy and Accumulation on a World Scale: Women in the International Division of Labor.* London: Zed Books, 1986.

Morgan, Jennifer. *Laboring Women: Reproduction and Gender in New World Slavery.* Philadelphia: University of Pennsylvania Press, 2004.

Morgan, Jennifer. "*Partus Sequitur Ventrem*: Law, Race, and Reproduction in Colonial Slavery." *Small Axe,* no. 55 (2018): 1–17. https://doi.org/10.1215/07990537-4378888.

Morgan, Jennifer. *Reckoning with Slavery: Gender, Kinship, and Capitalism in the Early Black Atlantic.* Durham, NC: Duke University Press, 2021.

Morris, Rosalind C. "*Ursprüngliche Akkumulation*: The Secret of an Originary Mistranslation." *boundary 2* 43, no. 3 (2016): 29–77. https://doi.org/10.1215/01903659-3572418.

Moten, Fred. *In the Break: The Aesthetics of the Black Radical Tradition.* Minneapolis: University of Minnesota Press, 2003.

Moynihan, Daniel Patrick. "The Negro Family: The Case for National Action." 1965. In *The Moynihan Report and the Politics of Controversy,* edited by Lee Rainwater and William L. Yancey, 47–94. Cambridge, MA: MIT Press, 1967.

Nahman, Michal, Bronwyn Parry, and Sigrid Vertommen. "Introduction: Global Fertility Chains and the Colonial Present of Assisted Reproductive Technologies." *Catalyst: Feminism, Theory, Technoscience* 8, no. 1 (2022): 1–17. https://doi.org/10.28968/cftt.v8i1.37920.

Nichols, Robert. "Disaggregating Primitive Accumulation." *Radical Philosophy* 194 (2015): 18–28.

Nichols, Robert. *Theft Is Property! Dispossession and Critical Theory.* Durham, NC: Duke University Press, 2020.

Nwokeji, G. Ugo. "African Conceptions of Gender and the Slave Traffic." In "New Perspectives on the Transatlantic Slave Trade." Special issue, *William and Mary Quarterly* 58, no. 1 (2001): 47–68. https://doi.org/10.2307/2674418.

Oyewùmí, Oyèrónké. *The Invention of Women: Making African Sense of Western Gender Discourse.* Minneapolis: University of Minnesota Press, 1997.

Patterson, Orlando. *Slavery and Social Death: A Comparative Study.* Cambridge, MA: Harvard University Press, 1982.

Paugh, Katherine. *The Politics of Reproduction: Race, Medicine, and Fertility in the Age of Abolition.* Oxford: Oxford University Press, 2017.

Rajan, Kaushik Sunder. *Biocapital: The Constitution of Postgenomic Life.* Durham, NC: Duke University Press, 2006.

Roberts, Dorothy. *Torn Apart: How the Child Welfare System Destroys Black Families—and How Abolition Can Build a Safer World*. New York: Basic Books, 2022.

Robinson, Cedric J. *Black Marxism: The Making of the Black Radical Tradition*. Chapel Hill: University of North Carolina Press, 2000.

Ross, Loretta J. "Reproductive Justice as Intersectional Activism." *Souls* 19, no. 3 (2017): 286–314. https://doi.org/10.1080/10999949.2017.1389634.

Ross, Loretta J., and Rickie Solinger. *Reproductive Justice: An Introduction*. Berkeley: University of California Press, 2017.

Rudrappa, Sharmila. *Discounted Life: The Price of Global Surrogacy in India*. New York: New York University Press, 2015.

Sexton, Jared, "People-of-Color-Blindness: Notes on the Afterlife of Slavery." *Social Text* 28, no. 2 (2010): 31–56.

Sharpe, Christina. *In the Wake: On Blackness and Being*. Durham, NC: Duke University Press, 2016.

Smallwood, Stephanie. *Saltwater Slavery: A Middle Passage from African to American Diaspora*. Cambridge, MA: Harvard University Press, 2007.

Smietana, Marcin, Charis Thompson, and France Winddance Twine. "Introduction: Making and Breaking Families—Reading Queer Reproductions, Stratified Reproduction, and Reproductive Justice Together." *Reproductive BioMedicine and Society Online* 7 (2018): 112–30. https://doi.org/10.1016/j.rbms.2018.11.001.

Smithers, Gregory D. "American Abolitionism and Slave-Breeding Discourse: A Reevaluation." *Slavery and Abolition* 33, no. 4 (2012): 551–70. https://doi.org/10.1080/01440 39X.2011.622119.

Snorton, C. Riley. *Black on Both Sides: A Racial History of Trans Identity*. Minneapolis: University of Minnesota Press, 2017.

Spar, Debora L. *The Baby Business: How Money, Science, and Politics Drive the Commerce of Conception*. Boston: Harvard Business Review, 2006.

Spillers, Hortense. "Hortense Spillers: Afro Pessimism and Its Others." Video lecture, Institute for Critical Social Inquiry at The New School, New York, June 9, 2021. Vimeo video, 1:31:04. https://vimeo.com/551629648.

Spillers, Hortense. "Mama's Baby, Papa's Maybe: An American Grammar Book." *Diacritics* 17, no. 2 (1987): 65–81.

Spillers, Hortense, Saidiya Hartman, Farah Jasmine Griffin, Shelly Eversley, and Jennifer L. Morgan. "'Whatcha Gonna Do?': Revisiting 'Mama's Baby, Papa's Maybe: An American Grammar Book': A Conversation with Hortense Spillers, Saidiya Hartman, Farah Jasmine Griffin, Shelly Eversley, and Jennifer L. Morgan." *Women's Studies Quarterly* 35, nos. 1–2 (2007): 299–309. https://www.proquest.com/scholarly-journals /whatcha-gonna-do-revisiting-mamas-baby-papas/docview/233638049/se-2.

Sweeney, Shauna. "Gendering Racial Capitalism and the Black Heretical Tradition." In *Histories of Racial Capitalism*, edited by Destin Jenkins and Justin Leroy, 58–84. New York: Columbia University Press, 2021.

Thompson, Charis. *Making Parents: The Ontological Choreography of Reproductive Technologies*. Cambridge, MA: MIT Press, 2005.

Turner, Sasha. *Contested Bodies: Pregnancy, Childbearing, and Slavery in Jamaica*. Philadelphia: University of Pennsylvania Press, 2017.

Twine, France Winddance. *Outsourcing the Womb: Race, Class, and Gestational Surrogacy in a Global Market*. New York: Routledge, 2011.

Vergès, Françoise. *The Wombs of Women: Race, Capital, Feminism*. Durham, NC: Duke University Press, 2020.

Vogel, Lise. *Marxism and the Oppression of Women*. New Brunswick, NJ: Rutgers University Press, 1983.

Waldby, Catherine. *The Oocyte Economy: The Changing Meaning of Human Eggs*. Durham, NC: Duke University Press, 2019.

Weinbaum, Alys Eve. *The Afterlife of Reproductive Slavery: Biocapitalism and Black Feminism's Philosophy of History*. Durham, NC: Duke University Press, 2019.

Weinbaum, Alys Eve. "Marx, Irigaray, and the Politics of Reproduction." *Differences: A Journal of Feminist Cultural Studies* 6, no. 1 (1994): 98–128.

Weinbaum, Alys Eve. "Reproducing Racial Capitalism." *Boston Review Forum* 44, no. 2 (2019): 85–96.

Weinbaum, Alys Eve. "The Slave Episteme in Biocapitalism." *Catalyst: Feminism, Theory, Technoscience* 8, no. 1 (2022): 1–25.

Weinbaum, Alys Eve. *Wayward Reproductions: Genealogies of Race and Reproduction in Transatlantic Modern Thought*. Durham, NC: Duke University Press, 2004.

White, Deborah Gray. *Ar'n't I a Woman? Female Slaves in the Plantation South*. New York: Norton, 1985.

Wilderson, Frank B. III. "Reciprocity and Rape: Blackness and the Paradox of Sexual Violence." *Women and Performance: A Journal of Feminist Theory* 27, no. 1 (2017): 104–11. https://doi.org/10.1080/0740770X.2017.1282122.

Wilderson, Frank B. III. *Red, White, and Black: Cinema and the Structure of US Antagonisms*. Durham, NC: Duke University Press, 2010.

Wilderson, Frank B. III, and Tiffany Lethabo King. "Staying Ready for Black Study: A Conversation." In *Otherwise Worlds: Against Settler Colonialism and Anti-Blackness*, edited by Tiffany Lethabo King, Jenell Navarro, and Andrea Smith, 52–73. Durham, NC: Duke University Press, 2020.

Wynter, Sylvia. "Beyond Miranda's Meanings: Un/silencing the 'Demonic Ground' of Caliban's 'Woman.'" In *Out of the Kumbla: Caribbean Women and Literature*, edited by Carole Boyce Davies, 355–72. Chicago: Africa World, 1990.

Wynter, Sylvia. "Unsettling the Coloniality of Being/Power/Truth/Freedom: Towards the Human, after Man, Its Overrepresentation—an Argument." *CR: The New Centennial Review* 3, no. 3 (2003): 257–336. https://doi.org/10.1353/ncr.2004.0015.

Laura Briggs

Becoming "Welfare Island"

Reproductive Labor and Racial Capitalism
in Twentieth-Century Puerto Rico

ABSTRACT From the era of enslavement to contemporary structures of debt, governing entities and capital have denied state support to Puerto Ricans, demanding instead that payments flow from the archipelago first to Spain and then to the United States. While the US welfare state is notoriously stingy, even its limited benefits have never gone to Puerto Ricans on an equal basis to residents of the states. How, then, have Puerto Ricans been perennially accused of receiving too much welfare? This article argues that Puerto Rico marks the vanishing point of the coherence of the discourse of the "welfare queen" and reveals its underlying logic: it marks Black and impoverished people's resistance, and the refusal to birth babies and raise children who are docile participants in the kind of labor force sought by capital. The "welfare queen," generalized to the archipelago as a whole, marks rebellion and fugitivity.

KEYWORDS enslavement, racial capitalism, social reproductive labor, welfare, Puerto Rico

We all know the welfare queen. She is the figure of grievance of a transnational right wing that wants to pretend impoverished people are picking their pocket, rather than the other way around. Ronald Reagan famously relied on this trope to make his case for smaller government, loosely basing her on Chicago's Linda Taylor—making her into a Black woman with a pink Cadillac who fraudulently took millions, cashing her government checks at the liquor store (Levin). There was nothing new in Reagan's fixation on "bad" Black mothers. Subsequent (and previous) generations of politicians also used a libelous narrative about "welfare" to score political points in an attempt to end government programs for impoverished parents and their children. She was the antihero of the Johnson and Nixon administrations' accounts of civil rights progress, part of the Moynihan Report's story of the

HISTORY of the PRESENT ▪ A Journal of Critical History ▪ 14:1 ▪ April 2024
DOI 10.1215/21599785-10898352 © 2024 Duke University Press

Black family as a matriarchal "tangle of pathology"—an emasculating Black woman who cowed her sons and left them unable to compete in the job market (Kelley). She was at the heart of the "culture of poverty" explicated by social scientist Oscar Lewis in the best-selling *La Vida: A Puerto Rican Family in the Culture of Poverty—San Juan and New York*; she caused programs that gave money to impoverished people to fail because she passed down the bad financial and sexual habits that led to poverty from generation to generation. She was the villain of the "third world overpopulation" narrative that reached its zenith in the 1970s as a crisis of poverty, development programs, and global security; too many babies and too few jobs led people to rise up and demand communism (Briggs, *Reproducing*; Critchlow). In Europe she has typically been an immigrant, often Muslim now, once Jewish; she has a large family that claims too many state benefits; she carries an alien culture with "oppressive" or "traditional" values, and her children contribute nothing of importance to the future of the nation and, indeed, steal the cultural patrimony of those who consider themselves the native-born. She is posited as the epitome of wasted national spending. In some ways, this story is as old and persistent as racial capitalism itself; its primary origin in the modern era is an account of the enslaved, African-descended mother that justified some of the most sadistic actions of slavers: her children were the property of enslavers, who claimed that she didn't care what happened to her children, so slavers could separate them, sometimes from birth.

"Welfare mothers" and their kin, I argue in this essay, reference a crisis of reproductive labor—populations fugitive from the demands of racial capitalism—rather than any actual transfer payments by the state. Leaning on the insights of Alys Eve Weinbaum, Rickie Solinger, Jessica Marie Johnson Halle-Mackenzie Ashby, and others in this issue, this article reads Cedric J. Robinson and Silvia Federici together to address the problem of social reproductive labor and its racialization, attending in particular to what happened after the era of enslavement in Puerto Rico. How were the meanings attached to social reproductive labor and its relationship to racial capitalism transformed, it asks, when Black mothers' children ceased to be someone else's property, and a eugenic discourse of too many (not-white) offspring began to replace the historic demand to feed capitalism's labor needs with ever more workers? How, in other words, did states and labor markets deal with the specifically racialized contradictions of dependency? On the one hand, as generations of socialist feminists and Black feminists have pointed out, childhood and children disadvantage employers—below a certain age, infants and young people cannot work, and any adult caring for them is less available for other kinds of labor. On the other hand, capitalism ultimately needs another generation of workers, birthed, socialized, and ready to serve up fast food, clean homes, punch a time clock, or head out to the fields. The discourse of the "welfare queen" marks this space—the squawking outrage of former enslavers claiming that the state is somehow paying for the raising of these children and the demand to reduce dependency and its costs to as near zero as possible. It voices their suspicion that African-descended children are not being reared and shaped properly for what capitalism demands. The social and biological reproductive labor and resources required for their birth and rearing are always, implicitly and explicitly, something *stolen*, a fraud, a cheat.

When applied to Puerto Ricans, the "welfare mother" narrative reaches the vanishing point of its coherence. Puerto Ricans are not eligible for almost any of the entitlements under the US Social Security Act that are usually said to constitute "welfare." Federici and others tell us that capital has, since the early modern period, forced people to give birth to and raise its next generation of workers, profiting off that unpaid feminized labor as surplus value. Yet after enslavement, rather than underscore the need to reproduce the workforce, a medical, public health, and (post)colonial state apparatus has, at least since the era of eugenics, instead insisted through this discourse of "welfare" that it would have been better if fewer Black and impoverished children had been born. Putting "overpopulation" together with related discourses about juvenile delinquents in the 1950s (including claims about drug-peddling youth) and student protests and general strikes, I argue, showed that "welfare mothers" were not necessarily those who received payments from the state's coffers. They more often received nothing at all. The problem of "welfare," rather, is a discourse that complains of fugitivity (Harney and Moten), of marronage (Roberts), a charge that the archipelago was in revolt and children were not being properly socialized as workers.

In recent years Puerto Rico as a whole has rhetorically been made into "welfare island," exceeding the historical grounding of this discourse in misogyny. *The Economist* entitled an ugly piece in 2006 about Puerto Rican men's supposed bad work habits "Trouble on Welfare Island," even as the Supreme Court reaffirmed a US commitment to denying its residents benefits associated with US welfare programs. It expanded this flexible discourse such that it was not even gendered female: "Half the working-age men in Puerto Rico do not work. . . . Many things have gone wrong. Most important, however, is that the United States government assumed too big a role in the Puerto Rican economy, and its largesse enabled the commonwealth's government to do the same. . . . Two federal intrusions stand out: an oversized welfare state, and misguided rules on business investment" (*Economist*). It goes on to characterize federal disability payments as the primary problem. This complaint about an "oversized welfare state" took in not only men but also children, government, and even housing, the electrical system, and roads after Hurricane María in 2017. "I hate to tell you Puerto Rico," said then-president Trump, "you're throwing our budget a little out of whack because we've spent a lot of money on Puerto Rico" (Johnson and Parker).

The irony of the welfare trope, the claim that states give away too much of their wealth to Afro-Puerto Ricans or other impoverished people is, well, *rich*. In 2022 the US Supreme Court reaffirmed that Puerto Ricans and others resident in US possessions could be understood as legally lesser—colonized, to put a finer point on it—such that its residents were not entitled to federal welfare benefits, including, specifically, disability payments. In *United States v. Vaello Madero*, the court upheld the exclusion of Puerto Rico from the Nixon-era legal change to Social Security to expand benefits to people with disabilities, creating the Supplemental Security Income (SSI) program.[1] *Vaello Madero* affirmed as precedent the holdings from 1901 to 1922, known collectively as the Insular Cases, that constituted Puerto Rico and other US possessions as neither sovereign nor fully part of the United States but "foreign in a domestic sense." The Supreme Court disenfranchised them from the US polity based on race. At the adoption of the Constitution, the court said, "all the native white inhabitants [were] endowed with citizenship." The court drew from eugenics discourses to find—in the Thirteenth Amendment, no less—a principle that because residents of what it dubbed "Porto Rico" belonged to "alien races," they need not be subject to "the administration of government and justice according to Anglo-Saxon principles"[2] Thus residents of the archipelago, while nominally US citizens after 1917, were not entitled to the protections of the Constitution or even the laws of the United States. Congress was free to make provision for Puerto Ricans to have lesser entitlements or none at all.

This was not a new state of affairs. Puerto Rico had not seen much "welfare" under the Spanish, either. Indeed, through much of its history, the archipelago was sending wealth to Spain as part of a sugarcane-and-slavery economy, just as, in the present day, it sends its wealth to the United States under a debt scheme wrought through financialized capitalism, which withdrew services and demanded excessive contributions from Black and impoverished residents. In this it is reminiscent of Reagan and Margaret Thatcher's reforms of the International Monetary Fund and World Bank that produced structural adjustment programs, or the bankrupting of New York or Detroit— all forms of racialized extraction through debt (Chakravartty and da Silva), a form of governance in the Americas belonging to Indigenous dispossession

(Byrd et al.) and the slave episteme (Weinbaum). Yet, while the ledger books of colonialism and impoverishment in the archipelago suggest that the flow of wealth is quite the opposite of what the "welfare queen" story imagines, still, this libel belongs to a particular cultural logic. Its work in Puerto Rico (as elsewhere) is ideological and racial, centering the fear that Black mothers leave work behind to raise too-free children.

The Era of Enslavement

Black women's reproductive labor has long been a problem. Even when pregnant and nursing, enslaved and African-descended women were represented in grotesque and inhuman terms in transnational medical and travel literature—squatting in the fields to give birth, then returning to hoe the next row, with elongated breasts that made them able to nurse over their shoulders without pausing in their work (Morgan 12–49; Briggs, "Hysteria" 256–61). Slavers and managers of enslaved people worried about mothers' willingness to forsake their infants and young children in order to participate in the agricultural and artisanal labor force, fearing that enslaved mothers might actually choose to care for their pregnancies and infants instead, and raise children who refused to understand themselves as enslaved. As Angela Davis wrote, the work of reproductive labor by Black women under enslavement was marked by their disloyalty to that labor system: their "role as a caretaker of a household of resistance" included "concretely encourag[ing] those around [them] to keep their eyes on freedom" (7). The work of counterinsurgency by slavers and their descendants was to denigrate this labor of freedom, claiming first that enslaved mothers did not care about their children and then, after emancipation, assailing Black mothers as idle, hypersexual, and relying on public benefits.

Puerto Rico has a long history of Black insurgency. The Caribbean's rebellious African and diasporic people took advantage of the ocean to find freedom, slipping the bonds of one island to steal their freedom on another (Martínez-San Miguel). Puerto Rico's outlying island of Vieques became a destination for maritime maroons (Hall) from St. Croix in the Danish West Indies and across the Caribbean (Beckles), like other places in the archipelago where the currents carried small boats (*yolas*)—San Juan, Ponce, Guayama, and Humacao (Dunnavant). One of the oldest maroon communities in the Caribbean was in Puerto Rico, in Loiza (Giusti-Cordero 59–62), settled in the sixteenth century (Sued Badillo and López Cantos 25–27). Between the establishment of the first sugar plantation in 1517 and emancipation in 1873, enslaved people in Puerto Rico rebelled again and again—with twenty-two slave revolts documented in the nineteenth century alone—or fled across the harrowing Mona Passage after 1791 to liberated Hispaniola, the island encompassing contemporary Haiti and the Dominican Republic (Baralt). This spirit of fugitivity in the Puerto Rican archipelago was met with repression and harsh work regimens, particularly in the cane fields, as an ever more reactionary plantocracy came to Puerto Rico from Haiti and an imperial US South, which sought to annex Caribbean islands as slave states (Levander; García Peña). Spain used Puerto Rico to replace agricultural production lost after the Haitian revolution, successfully making it one of the most intensively cultivated "sugar islands" in the world (Giusti-Cordero 58).

Labor in the cane fields, however, was not the only thing that mattered under slavery: so too did reproductive labor. It marked the slavers' work of rendering a human who could reproduce into a unit of value, whose unborn offspring could be accounted for and financialized. Under enslavement and in its aftermath, Afro–Puerto Rican women's labor to give birth to and raise their children was brutally denigrated, and they were characterized as stupid and brutish, "reduced purely to a vegetative state" or, at worst, "monstrous mothers who murdered their children" (Findlay, *Imposing* 60). They "remained inherently and permanently degenerate," unamenable to reform, even after emancipation (Lloréns, *Making* 48).

Puerto Rico was one of the last places in the Americas to end slavery, and even when it did, freedom did not automatically follow for Afro–Puerto Ricans. The work of freedom continued after emancipation, as it did elsewhere in the Caribbean and everywhere in the world slavery made (Lightfoot). Creole and Spanish landowners in Puerto Rico issued *libretas* (passbooks) from employers to ensure that formerly enslaved people were not too free, not evading waged work, or too mobile, seeking also to enforce the ongoing participation of reproducing women in the formal labor force. Although *libretas* disappeared in the twentieth century, they were renewed during World War I for sex workers, this time showing that they had been tested for syphilis (Briggs, *Reproducing* 46–73).

Scholars and activists disagree about the extent to which enslavement was primarily racial in Puerto Rico, pointing instead to the formation of a rural proletariat in the context of the relatively large number of Black free people and the unfreedom of white, Chinese, and East Indian plantation workers and the ways even white *agregados* (free sharecroppers) worked side by side with enslaved people in the cane fields (Mintz). Others insist on the key role that racial slavery played in labor and the relatively large Black diasporic population in the archipelago, brought into being in 1521 following the request to Charles V from the Bishop of San Juan for permission to purchase twenty enslaved African workers to replace Indigenous Taino workers who had died of disease (Brau 345–46; Díaz Soler 57–58).

One thing is clear, however: US rule of the islands brought a much more explicitly binary Black and white grammar of race. Following the 1898 exchange of the Puerto Rican archipelago between empires, those in the United States often understood all of Puerto Rico in terms of relative degrees of Blackness and hence generalized the trope of the lazy Black woman and her impertinent child to the whole archipelago. For example, people who would have been classified in terms of Puerto Rico's complex and ambiguous racial nomenclature under Spanish rule or in Puerto Rican vernaculars (Duany; Godreau; Rodríguez Silva) were treated simply as "white" or "colored" in the US Army's initial census in 1899. Mocking editorial cartoons caricatured the whole island as a small Black "pickaninny" in the early years of the twentieth century (Negrón-Muntaner).

Within a few decades, Puerto Rican reproduction quickly became a subject of obsessive concern for US social scientists and policymakers. In the 1930s the archipelago became a virtual laboratory for testing birth control under a theory of "overpopulation," well before that term became a descriptor of the "Third World" in general. Overpopulation in Puerto Rico was explicitly characterized as a problem within capitalism, representing the creation of more workers than there were jobs, which suppressed wages and led to social unrest. That is, Puerto Rican reproductive excess became iconic of how such labor could go awry, resulting from the production and rearing of too many children. While I have written elsewhere about this anxiety about Puerto Rican fecundity and the scientific and social scientific efforts to ensure that there were fewer offspring through birth control and sterilization programs, here I will focus on children and youth from the 1930s to the 1970s as well. There were not just too many children; they were bad at capitalism—producing criminality and sedition, bringing drugs and communism to the archipelago.

Social Reproduction and Racial Capitalism

As Alys Weinbaum argues in this issue, socialist feminists like Silvia Federici have explored the home, housework, and raising of a next generation as a site of reproductive labor, but it requires analytical work to bring these accounts into conversation with the scholarship on (slave) racial capitalism. Birthing and caring for children, cleaning, feeding the household, educating young people, and caring for the ill are essential for the reproduction of labor, part of the work that produces surplus value. Without it, the labor force could not continue to exist. Federici's *Caliban and the Witch* theorizes a history of how reproductive labor works positively: it is a demand by the state for children, for population, for social reproduction. "Starting in the mid-sixteenth century, while Portuguese ships were returning from Africa with their first human cargoes, all the European governments began to impose the severest penalties against contraception, abortion, and infanticide" (86). Midwives and others who had knowledge of pregnancy were prosecuted for witchcraft, she argues, a catchall crime of deviancy from procreative sex. For the first time, male doctors began to control labor and delivery, and, Federici writes, "in the case of a medical emergency" they "prioritized the life of the fetus over that of the mother" (87). She continues: "While in the Middle Ages women had been able to use various forms of contraceptives, and had exercised an undisputed control over the birthing process, from now on their wombs became public territory, controlled by men and the state" (89). The Church fomented misogyny and sponsored brothels and sex work in order to divide the working class by gender, encouraging men to commit crimes of sexual violence while the state burned witches accused of fornication (47). Women and feminized people were called on to reproduce the working class through their bodies, by birthing babies to feed the maw of industrial and agricultural production, and through their social reproductive labor, by feeding, clothing, and caring for the children, the ill, and the elders—those whom capitalism could not yet use or had used up—and by keeping workers themselves ready for the next long day of labor to produce the machine of surplus value that enriched the bosses by underpaying workers.

Under conditions of enslavement and in its wake (Sharpe), the key question about economies of social reproduction was always the extent to which this labor could be squeezed to the margins—how much agricultural or other work could be demanded from mothers and others who cared for children without children dying in numbers too great to sustain the labor force, how high infant mortality could rise because of maternal ill-health or lack of rest, and whether it was financially shrewd to extract this labor from those who were already enslaved themselves or from mothers in Africa whose children could be taken from them and transported to the Americas or the Caribbean. Non-white and non-European mothers and feminized people have long fit awkwardly into the framework of social reproductive labor because racist discourses have as often been about *preventing* births and withdrawing care from infants and children as about reproducing a next generation of laborers. We need a stronger account of (post)colonial spaces and reproductive labor—the places Marx associated with "primitive accumulation." From the 1930s through the 1970s, the fear was that impoverished youth and their mothers in Puerto Rico would slip the bonds of capitalist discipline, becoming fugitive to its demands for particular kinds and numbers of children. Here, as in Sigrid Vertommen's work in this issue on Palestinians in the reproductive regimes of Israel, we see the negation of reproductive labor at work, more akin to what Achille Mbembe calls necropolitics than social reproduction.

In *Caliban* Federici is revising Marx's notion of primitive accumulation. One of the things that requires analysis for Marx is that if wealth is built through the extraction of surplus value from workers, how is it that some people *begin* with the capital that allows them to build factories, enabling them to compel others to sell their labor for less than it is worth? In the liberal tradition that Marx is criticizing, Adam Smith argues that it is because initially, in the before times when there was not yet capitalism, some workers were more industrious than others, saved their earnings, and, also being clever, were eventually able to build factories and organize manufacturing, growing ever more wealthy, while their less capable counterparts were turned into workers who had to sell their labor to survive. (Adam Smith is very much alive in contemporary politics; industriousness and cleverness, as we know, continue to play a major role in today's conservative accounts of why businessmen are virtuous and should get all the good things, from political power to freedom from taxation.)

Marx, in contrast, explained this early moment—which might be better characterized as the prehistory of accumulation given the racist connotations of *primitive*—in terms of violence and expropriation. It is here that Marx comes closest to articulating something like what Cedric Robinson called racial capitalism—the ways that surplus value is produced through differentially valuing the contributions of populations marked racially as available for extra extraction, whether unpaid Slavs or Africans in the early modern period, for example, or low-paid racially minoritized immigrant farmworkers in the present. For his notion of precapitalist accumulation, Marx looked to enslavement and colonialism: "the discovery of gold and silver in America, the extirpation, enslavement and entombment in mines of the aboriginal population, the beginning of the conquest and looting of the East Indies, the turning of Africa into a warren for the commercial hunting of black-skins" (Marx 823). For Robinson, of course, this is not precapitalism at all, but capitalism itself, as many subsequent theorists have also argued (Lowe; Coulthard; Harvey). There is also a long feminist genealogy to Federici and this line of thought—the early twentieth-century theorist of imperialism, Rosa Luxemburg, suggested that primitive or previous accumulation continues alongside and within capitalism as accumulation through naked dispossession in colonial geographies. Marx also looked to the enclosure of common lands in England and the resulting depopulation of villages as strategies for the concentration of wealth as private property and hence capital. Federici adds another kind of "enclosure": of labor marked feminine, alongside enslavement, serfdom, and other kinds of wage theft or unfree labor. The routine work of housework and reproductive labor was what went on behind the scenes that made capitalism possible, and its unpaid nature was a kind of surplus value extracted from the working class as a whole.

Intriguingly, in the introduction to *Caliban*, Federici says her book was marked, and indeed necessitated, by the work of the women's movement in Nigeria, where she was teaching in the 1980s. That decade, she argued, saw a new campaign of primitive/previous accumulation, beginning with what she called "a decisive intervention by the State (instigated by World Bank) in the reproduction of the work-force: to regulate procreation rates" (3). This provocative statement bears unpacking, although she does not do it. It appears to reference the following series of events. In 1988, at the behest of international lending authorities and a technocratic elite, Nigeria officially adopted a "population control" policy to limit excess reproduction, the first country in sub-Saharan Africa to do so in twenty years, despite deeply pronatalist beliefs among many of its people and opposition from feminist groups (Robinson, "Negotiating"). This same elite initiated a misogynist campaign, blaming the high cost of living and a so-called lack of competitiveness of Nigeria internationally on women's "vanity" and the wrong kinds of social reproduction, from polygamy to bad child-rearing to a lack of nuclear family households. While the majority of Nigerians were living off the land, through subsistence agriculture and similar strategies, the technocratic elite was trying to turn them into a modern, urban proletariat, with small nuclear families appropriate to such economic strategies and the lives and households of the laborers who could serve their industries (Federici, "Interview"). It seems that it was Federici's insight into the importance of official misogyny in breaking the solidarity of a Nigerian working class, or really peasants, that led her to intervene in how Marxists narrate the relationship of reproduction to so-called primitive accumulation.

Because of *Caliban*'s focus on the early modern period, however, Federici is better at articulating why capitalism and the state compel women to bear and raise more children—doing unpaid labor to reproduce the labor force— than why officials might mark rural people's reproduction as excessive. The twentieth and twenty-first centuries in particular have seen campaigns to halt the birth of excess children in colonial and formerly colonial spaces, even as capitalism needs them to replenish the labor force. Why? There is clearly a fight over changing forms of labor needs—as in the transformation from agriculture to industrialization, and also of the relationship of the state to its citizenry. Excess children are construed as illegitimate, always potentially dependent on the government or charity institutions, even when there is, in fact, no "welfare" provision for them at all.

We need to expand Federici's account to make sense of what is both a racial and a colonial project: the state and capital's fear of Black children and youth after slavery, the consigning of them to the category of "excess," of a workforce that on the one hand is necessary to agriculture and industry but also is always, somehow, too many. How can we think about why capitalism would produce an *anti*-reproductive labor regime? Didn't the capitalist class always want more and more workers to exploit? Why demand fewer babies through an account of overpopulation? Paying impoverished people (often but not always African or African-diasporic peoples) too little to live on, criminalizing them, consigning them to prison and vicious policing, and forcing them to have abortions (Vergès); denying mothers and feminized people the resources necessary for reproductive labor; and producing children and youth as unwanted or, indeed, enemies of the state or people—this is the necropolitical reproductive project of the modern, post-slavery era. The formation of a concept of reproductive excess belongs to the same misogynist logic that Federici identifies—in which working-class women are responsible for capitalism's crises, whose "fornication" and other crimes cry out for sadistic punishments, as in the witch-burning era (Williams 1–11). Federici seems to understand that the witch (who minimizes the number of offspring) and the "welfare queen" (who has too many) are a twinned but often opposed pair. However, her account of the church and doctors forcing women to give birth and raise offspring is only partial. Despite the Nigerian campaign against overpopulation that inspired the book, the problem of reproductive excess is not what she narrates. Here, following Federici, let us explore the episteme of overpopulation, the belief that it would have been better if certain people had never been born. We need to look to the places that Marx names as the sites of the prehistory of accumulation—not just the Europe of the Enclosure Acts but also (post)colonial and slave societies, such as those in the Americas—and pose Federici's questions to the cultural work of the trope of the wayward Black mother who does not care about her offspring—whose dependency and need for care are said to steal resources from state coffers—in the context of the ongoing work of racial capitalism and accumulation outside the system of the surplus value produced through the exploitation of waged labor.

The Puerto Rican 1930s, 1940s, and 1950s

As we have seen, the casual characterization of Puerto Rico as a "welfare island" does not even minimally comport with the reality of policy or economics. The archipelago has virtually no entitlement to US welfare programs and never has. In 1935, when Congress passed the first major piece of social welfare legislation in the United States, the Social Security Act, Puerto Rico was excluded from its provisions for old-age pensions, mother's allowances in the form of Aid to Dependent Children, and other child welfare programs, and, by extension, the later expansion of the act to include Medicaid and Medicare (Amador 105). While there were some limited expansions, these were always the result of hard-fought political struggles, and Puerto Rico's foundational exclusion has remained. In effect, these exclusions require residents of the archipelago to work for wages or (and) starve. As Hilda Lloréns notes, poor and Black folks at the margins have long been required to forage and live off the land and sea (Lloréns, "Race"). To this day, Puerto Rico barely has any social welfare programs as a result of its status as part of the United States as a non-sovereign territory.

Where one lives under US rule produces major distinctions in what Hannah Arendt famously called "the right to have rights" (177). When she wrote that phrase, Arendt was referring to imperialism and the crisis for human rights produced by the extrajudicial nature of colonial spaces (Benhabib 50–52). The US government produces inequalities in status, rights, and citizenship through a nearly incomprehensible legal heterogeneity in five major and nine (or eleven) minor territories—organized and unorganized, incorporated and unincorporated, commonwealths, atolls, and guano islands—as well as 63 state-only and 567 federally recognized Indian tribal nations (and an estimated 200 non-recognized or terminated tribes), including also Alaskan Native tribal entities and corporations, Pueblos, off-reservation trust land, and tribal jurisdictional areas, not to mention Hawaiian homelands and carceral spaces like the Guantánamo Bay Detention Center. One could also look to areas under US jurisdiction or created by the United States but sloughed off, like Iraq's Green Zone (Chandrasekaran) or South Korea's camp towns (Lee). This proliferation of types of geographies, designated by lawyers and recognized by federal or state governments, produces territorially and racially differentiated areas where the US Constitution applies fully, in part, or not at all, depending almost at the whim of official entities that nevertheless claim to be rule bound (Kim). Think, for example, of Supreme Court Justice Neil Gorsuch's writing that he rejected the racism of the insular cases and their "alien races" unfit for citizenship, even as he upheld these same cases as precedent in excluding Puerto Ricans from the Supplemental Security Program in the *Vaello Madero* case. As Ann Laura Stoler and Carole McGranahan argue, "Agents of imperial rule invested in, exploited, and demonstrated strong stakes in the proliferation of geopolitical ambiguities. . . . Those terms signaling the unclarified sovereignties of US imperial breadth—unincorporated territories, trusteeships, protectorates, possessions—are not the blurred edges of what more 'authentic,' nonvirtual visible empires look like, but variants on them" (10).

The Social Security Act was born as an effort to provide support for reproductive labor, and perhaps it is thus not surprising that the people construed as belonging to "alien races" were not included in it. Women's rights activists in the United States sought to make provision for mothers, children, and elders during the Great Depression, bringing care labor into the public sphere, and its original advocates very much sought to include all US American geographies in it (Koven and Michel 277–320; Ladd-Taylor). It was, however, most effective for whites and immigrants; not only did Congress choose to exclude Puerto Ricans and others in US possessions, but also members of tribal nations and African Americans, even as these were the very people suffering the most in the 1930s.

The economic catastrophe of the Depression arrived early and with a vengeance in Puerto Rico, brought in with the 1928 category 5 Hurricane San Felipe Segundo that devastated crops, homes, and lives, and from which the archipelago did not recover for a decade. Despite the wreckage, the Hoover administration offered next to nothing to help. Puerto Ricans responded to the absence of state support during this era with intensified labor and nationalist radicalism, including strikes, boycotts, and an uprising for independence under the leadership of Pedro Albizu Campos. The United States answered with indifference.

With the election of Franklin D. Roosevelt in 1932, liberals sought to manage Puerto Ricans and their economy, specifically by introducing export-led manufacturing and manipulating reproduction and reproductive labor. The archipelago's incorporation into this new phase of racial capitalism rested on reducing the numbers of babies and children through a liberal policy of managed decline and—through birth control and sterilization—delivering a female labor force to factories by reducing their fertility, making them available as workers. The 1930s saw the beginnings of what Michelle Murphy has called "the economization of life": the elaboration of a notion of gross national product (via John Maynard Keynes) yoked to an account of national population (18). Here was the reproduction of the working class in necropolitical form—if impoverished, immigrant, Black, and other non-white mothers did not reproduce, or could not feed and care for infants and children in a way that was adequate for the maintenance of life, it would be better for the well-being of an economy that depended on the labor of women.

Blackness and reproductive excess were cited as reasons not to extend social welfare benefits to Puerto Rico. When Katherine Lenroot, director of the federal Children's Bureau, testified in favor of Puerto Rico's inclusion in Social Security in 1939, members of Congress argued that Puerto Ricans were inferior, disproportionately Black, and different from the mainland population. Congressman Thomas Jenkins (R-OH) offered a jumble of such arguments: "Of course we recognize the population of Puerto Rico is very dense," and "they are in a warm climate" (referencing an old discourse of "tropical" racial difference), not to mention, shifting to the modern idiom, that "racially they are very different from the American people, generally speaking." Moreover, Jenkins concluded that because of this racial difference, "their requirements and needs" were "not quite the same" as those of people in the mainland United States. Because Puerto Ricans were "poorer" than those living in the continental United States, he said that supporting the welfare of those in the archipelago would entail "taking on a much bigger load toward them than we are toward our own people" because of their higher birth rates. This was essentially the template for conservative arguments against including Puerto Ricans on an equal footing in social welfare programs: too many babies who are racially different from US Americans (whom some legislators endeavored to imagine as all white) and hence not entitled to be treated on an equal footing; and they are currently poor and, apparently, deserve to continue to be (Amador 125).

While some benefits were extended to Puerto Ricans under the Social Security Administration in 1939 as a result of the activism, lobbying, and arguments of radical social workers, as historian Emma Amador notes, this discourse of "too many" Puerto Ricans only intensified in the 1940s and 1950s. Sociologists who argued for a massive program of birth control for the island explicitly pointed to declines in infant mortality (from 122 per 1000 in the 1930s to 79 per 1,000 in the period from 1945) as intensifying poverty (Briggs, *Reproducing* 114). In this context and often quite blatantly, many US policymakers and even members of the Puerto Rican political class sought to direct less health care, fewer feeding programs, and fewer financial resources to Puerto Rico, even claiming that this would be best for the well-being of its residents (Morrissey). Journalist John Gunther offered a visceral account of what counted as too many people in the archipelago, one that relied implicitly on a sense of them as less than human: "Puerto Rico has been a headache to the United States for 40 years. Its poverty is a disgrace to the Stars and

Stripes. From the economic point of view the overwhelming problem of Puerto Rico is the relation of population to the land. The orphan island teems and bristles with crowded thousands." Humans don't "teem"; insects do—and it is animals, too, or rather their fur that "bristles." This animalistic discourse belongs to an older travel literature of Africa and the Americas and its "savages." Gunther continued, "Puerto Rico's poverty is caused first and overwhelmingly by overpopulation, which is in turn caused by several factors—natural fecundity for one thing, the influence of the Roman Catholic Church, and the efficiency of the United States Health Service" (Gunther 425 and cover). Or, as the Rockefeller Foundation had it,

> There they are, the teeming millions of the little island of Puerto Rico, ready to serve as handy examples for anyone who wants to damn American policies in public health. And it is a difficult example to argue away, because there is no denying the existence of the Puerto Ricans, and because there is equally no denying that most of them continue to live under deplorable, substandard conditions, despite all of the capital, experts, and technologies that have been lavished on the island during a period of fifty years through a paternalistic American policy.[3]

As with the later welfare queen, "teeming" Puerto Rico is characterized here as a wasted investment.

For a brief period after World War II, in response to the global movement for decolonization, the United States poured money into Puerto Rico as a demonstration site of the advantages of being under the noncommunist, US sphere of influence (in contrast to Cuba). Despite the policy changes in this era that included Puerto Rico in provision of old-age pensions, public health clinic allowances, and Aid to Dependent Children (ADC), poverty and unemployment persisted at high rates. The excesses of reproductive labor—too many children—became key to addressing Puerto Rico's poverty for the archipelago's first elected governor, Luis Muñoz Marín, and for mainland commentators, as "overpopulation" became the dominant idiom of Puerto Rico's problems. This analysis drove two kinds of policies: family planning and sterilization on the one hand, and strong encouragement to emigrate to the mainland on the other (Ramírez de Arellano and Seipp). Of course, one could say—and, indeed, the island's independence movement did say—that "overpopulation" was a convenient alternative to speaking of colonialism in the context of a robust international movement for decolonization throughout Africa, Asia, and Latin America, and it obscured the economic reasons for the archipelago's poverty: first an enslavement-based sugar economy, then marginalization within an increasingly global regime of free trade that centered the economic winners from an earlier era of enslavement, colonization, and its forms of globalization. It also began to reverse the logic through which the economy was understood—rather than building an economy for people, Puerto Ricans' existence became a problem for the economy. Focusing on emigration and the wish that some people should not be born represented a foundational betrayal by the archipelago's first locally elected governor.

This demand for the disappearance of the unnecessary babies of Puerto Rico in the 1930s, 1940s, and 1950s underscored the necropolitical imagination, the wish for fewer Puerto Ricans, in particular their maternal reproductive labor. Far from the forced reproduction of Federici's early modern Europe, we find a growing injunction against reproduction of the children of Black and other Puerto Rican communities. They had become disposable, unnecessary, the babies that the world (and, particularly, the United States) would be better off without. The Social Security Act's welfare—ADC, old-age pensions—was being consciously withheld and reduced by Congress. More than a demand that Puerto Ricans reproduce themselves at the bare edges of what is survivable; more than a broader tolerance for hunger, illness, and premature death among children; it is a fantasy of fewer of them "teeming" the island. Capitalism and its utterly minimalist welfare state would benefit from fewer of these lives.

The Puerto Rican 1960s and 1970s: Children and Babies Become Problematic Youth

Maternal labor and children also became key figures in the later decades of the twentieth century, and particularly crucial to explaining Puerto Rico's debt crisis during the recession of the 1970s, when male unemployment first reached 40 percent—roughly what it is at present—even as foreign factory owners sought a cheaper, more exploitable female labor force (Rios). The rising number of women in the new export-oriented, foreign- or mainland-owned factories accomplished what all the exhortations about "overpopulation" never could in an agricultural economy: sharp declines in the numbers of children per household and rising rates of the use of both birth control and sterilization. Women had to have fewer pregnancies and children to keep punching a time clock. Even so, children and rebellious youth became an emblem of what was wrong and how to fix Puerto Rico by reducing the number of Puerto Ricans.

The "bad" mother producing these unruly youth in Puerto Rico was not the Black "matriarch" of the Moynihan Report—that was a figure who belonged to a genealogy of enslavement in the US South and the civil rights movement. Rather, Puerto Rico's reproductive excess was produced by a slightly different figure, invented in relationship to a "culture of poverty," living in (post)colonial geographies and migrating to the so-called First World. In 1966, the year after Daniel Patrick Moynihan wrote his famous report, anthropologist Oscar Lewis wrote a best-selling book, *La Vida*. Novelistic in form and pornographic in content, *La Vida* is about a family living in a San Juan shantytown and eventually divided between there and New York City. According to Lewis, the family matriarch, Fernanda, is "a good-looking, dark Negro woman of about forty with a stocky, youthful figure. She had dull black eyes, heavy eyebrows and full lips" (Lewis 4–5). She does sex work, as do two of her three daughters. One reviewer described the content of *La Vida* as "sex in a thousand forms, minutely described, until the world seems a gigantic, monotonous brothel" (Bendiner 22–23). The spouses and lovers of Fernanda and her daughters enter the narrative only for the briefest of interludes, as numbers rather than people. The book offers a theory of reproduction that it terms the "culture of poverty," in which the habits of (implicitly Black) impoverished people, most notably the inability to save money or delay gratification, are passed from mothers to children. Oversexed, abusing drugs, and leading lives characterized by random violence and the pursuit of pleasure, Black women raise children who are too free to submit themselves to Protestant self-discipline. Although Lewis claimed the political mantle of the Left for his work, the book became a key text of the neoconservative Right of the 1970s and eighties that characterized Third World development programs that gave money to impoverished people of color as a waste.

By the 1960s and 1970s, even as the discourse of too many babies became an ever more prominent grammar with which to characterize the Puerto Rican archipelago, people also began disparaging the islands' young people, elaborating yet a further discourse of failed reproductive labor. There were multiple versions of how Puerto Rican youth had gone wrong, reflecting political divisions that deepened in these decades. *Independentistas*, the Puerto Rican left, complained of the Americanization of youth. Liberals worried about radicalization, arguing that young people were increasingly drawn to socialist solutions to the archipelago's problems. Conservatives complained about general strikes, the fight for minimum wages, the drugs and criminality that they insisted Puerto Rico was awash in, while Lewis's *La Vida* was narrating this version of the archipelago for a broad US audience.

Independentistas had a point; by the 1960s and 1970s, Puerto Rico was becoming rapidly Americanized, perhaps especially its youth. As the commonwealth's government pushed a population marked as "excess" to migrate beginning in the 1940s, more and more working-class families were split between the archipelago and places like New York City; Chicago; Hartford, Connecticut; Holyoke, Massachusetts; and even rural Michigan (Ayala; Findlay, "Dangerous"). At the same time, in counterpoint, the nationalist movement was undergoing a historic resurgence. A leading light of Puerto Rican letters, the *independentista* intellectual Luis Rafael Sánchez, captured this sentiment parodically but bitterly in *La guaracha del Macho Camacho*. The novel is full of the American invasion of pop culture, with US products and advertising everywhere; men who came back from the US war in Korea "scrambled" (48); politicians who dreamed of creating a hall to honor "Washington, Lincoln, Jefferson, and other founding titans of the Puerto Rican motherland" (24); and the identical Puerto Rican triplets, Hughie, Louie, and Dewey, named by their father after a Donald Duck cartoon (115). Written at a time when Ariel Dorfman's and Armand Mattelart's fierce monograph opposing American cultural imperialism, *Para leer al Pato Donald* (*How to Read Donald Duck*), was being burned in bonfires in Chile by the right-wing dictatorship of Augusto Pinochet after the US-involved 1973 military coup against Salvador Allende, *La guaracha del Macho Camacho* echoed Dorfman's critique of the Disneyfication of Latin America even as it sexualized the legacy of enslavement.

Meanwhile, liberals worried about the radicalization of youth. Socialism was in the air, confirming young people's belief that their upbringing had failed to fit them into the industrial workforce. News from Cuba—including the ongoing revelations about the involvement of the Central Intelligence Agency in the Bay of Pigs/Playa Girón invasion—continued to make headlines, while Puerto Ricans joined a global movement against imperialism and colonialism (Rivera Lugo). The feminist movement was everywhere, as young women took self-defense classes to be able to walk the streets confidently at night (*Mundo*). A new feminist organization, Mujer Intégrate Ahora, was formed in the archipelago, raising issues from sexual harassment to abortion to lesbian rights, founding the journal *El tacón de la chancleta* under the remarkable inspiration of queer Afro–Puerto Rican attorney and poet Ana Irma Rivera Lassén (Ayala and Bernabé 235). The other cataclysms of the era also resonated on the island, as decolonization and its suppression gained steam: the military coups in Bolivia, Chile, Uruguay, and Argentina; the US invasion of the Dominican Republic in 1965; the Shah of Iran, imposed by a US-backed military coup, overthrown by a revolution in 1978–79; and the ongoing decolonization struggles in Namibia, Zimbabwe, and South Africa (Rivera Lugo). Above all, there was the US war in Vietnam, Cambodia, and Laos, in which thousands of Puerto Rican youth served—in exceptional disproportion to their numbers—and that thousands of others, particularly students, opposed.

Students at the University of Puerto Rico (UPR) were engaged in their own war against Americanization, in a campaign to "puertorriqueñizar la Universidad," as Marisol LeBrón reminds us (*Policing* 144–75). Students insisted that the UPR would be a place where students could address the real problems of the archipelago, not just another locus producing managers for the ongoing Americanization of Puerto Rico. In protest of the war in Indochina, they successfully demanded that Reserve Officers' Training Corps (ROTC) be removed from campus and that students have voting power in faculty meetings and the Academic Senate. In Puerto Rico in 1971, riot police and ROTC cadets faced off against student activists, and students, police officers, and ROTC members were killed and injured at the Río Piedras and Mayagüez campuses. In the most dramatic and longest-remembered incident of the agitation, two pro-independence students were ambushed, carried off in a car, and killed by the police on a remote mountain, in what became known as the Cerro Maravilla massacre (Rosa 111–15).

Conservatives, meanwhile, worried about the working-class youth participating in the labor movement. As brutal as the war on university campuses became, it was still conspicuously less violent than the other youth struggle in the streets—that of organized labor and its objections to the ways inflation was raising the cost of everything, to the enrichment of some, even as unemployment rose to staggering levels. Strikes roiled nearly every sector, from transportation to tourism to industry and agriculture; on January 3, 1975, the boilermakers' union headquarters was destroyed by a bomb many thought was planted by the police or other state forces (Epica Task Force 78). Even as the persecution of labor grew, unions linked their power, supporting each other's strikes through the founding of the Movimiento Obrero Unido (United Labor Movement) in 1971. Unions had a voice and power they were not afraid to use (Ayala and Bernabé 232–35).

Puerto Rico's government doubled down on making labor—and youth in particular—the enemy. At a 1966 hearing the commonwealth government opposed raising the minimum wage, citing declining employment rates, particularly in agriculture. Amadeo Francis, the economic advisor to the economic development administration, argued that young people were becoming disastrously accustomed to being idle, a circumstance he was certain that a rise in the minimum wage would only exacerbate. While the reproductive labor of producing these young workers was as necessary under this regime of paid sugarcane work as it ever had been, the state sought to maintain wages below minimum wage, below what labor in the archipelago and in the continental United States believed was necessary to sustain life. In the long aftermath of enslavement, Francis dreamed of pushing these dangerous youth back into the cane fields. They were bad at being a working class, and their continued well-being and vitality was a Cold War threat. Their lives were disposable; they were part of the "teeming" excess population that official policy sought to push off the archipelago through migration or to minimize through birth control. These young people did not need living wages or education. "The chronic shortage of jobs in Puerto Rico," Francis argued, "has been contributing to the development of an institutional group of young men who have voluntarily withdrawn from, or never entered, the labor force. These young people show signs of developing a most undesirable attitude both toward work per se" and, he added, in a nod toward the dangers of decolonization struggles, "toward a community that is unable to afford them either decent jobs appropriate to their limited levels of skill and education or, alternatively, professional and vocational preparation adequate to enable them to participate productively in the community's common endeavor."[4] Given the excessive reproduction throughout the archipelago, he insisted, there was not going to be an improvement any time soon in education, which basically left working the cane at low wages as a form of social incorporation that would keep dangerous young men from entering the struggle for decolonization.

While largely white university students from the wealthier classes were increasingly criminalized as "terrorists" in the 1970s (women and men alike), the militancy of working-class youth was likewise turning them into public enemies and potentially violent guerillas in the image of Che Guevara. The parallel move for the largely Black young people of the *caseríos*, the public housing projects that increasingly dotted the island, particularly in larger cities, was to call them juvenile delinquents and drug addicts—an opening move in what would become mass incarceration of these "extraneous" people (LeBrón, *Policing*). This, too, was a way of marking a failure to become an industrial working class, with drugs, sex, and communism marking their mothers' reproductive labor gone awry. "Drug abuse, particularly among youthful Puerto Ricans, tears at the social fabric and contributes to crime and delinquency in all of Puerto Rico's major cities," opined US Representative Lester Wolff from New York, in 1979, as the House Select Committee on Narcotics Abuse and Control opened its special three-day hearings on the island, blaming drugs on an inter–Latin American traffic, even as locals repeated the common sense of Puerto Ricans: drugs, and drug abuse, came to Puerto Rico from Cuba, New York, and Chicago.[5] Juvenile delinquency was said to be on the rise, as was drug addiction. Although Puerto Ricans themselves were not at all persuaded that they had a drug problem, it was the opening move in imagining Latinx youth as criminals and drug traffickers, even when they had nothing to do with the movement of narcotics—the beginning of marking them as a class for mass incarceration, another instantiation of seeing these young, disproportionately Black youth as excess and in need of removal.

As Puerto Rico underwent unprecedented cultural and economic change in this era, the response to it focused on youth, with critics expressing revulsion at young people themselves. The archipelago was indeed rapidly becoming culturally and economically transformed, with jobs and wealth moving away from agriculture, and, as unemployment and a rising cost of living took hold in the archipelago even more profoundly than in the continental United States, with increasingly militant labor and students struggling for a more hopeful future. Yet their optimism and vision were met with disdain as they were nudged toward migration, and vigorous campaigns of repression and birth control expressed the hope that in the future, fewer of them would be born.

In this context of growing radicalism, unrest, and independence, activists won another extension of "welfare" to the archipelago: in 1974 food stamps (*cupones*) were introduced to Puerto Rico. They became the key welfare provision—together with public housing—that enabled the increasingly displaced working class and their children to continue eating and living with a roof over their heads. In 1982, however, food stamps were judged to be too generous for Puerto Ricans, a population marked for death and diminishment, and under Reagan, the island was instead given a block grant that dramatically reduced benefits to individuals. Similarly, Puerto Rico was treated unequally—often dramatically so—under Medicaid, Medicare, and Supplemental Security Income. In the decades after the 1970s, these inequalities continued and were repeated for other anti-poverty programs, including those that largely replaced Aid to Families with Dependent Children: the Earned Income Tax Credit and the Child Tax Credit (Greszler). For the wealthy and middle class, there was a jobs program: the rapid expansion of the commonwealth's government, which provided good jobs for those with an education, even as they grumbled about far less expensive welfare measures for feeding poor children, complaining that *cupones* would destroy agriculture and industry (Banítez de Rodríguez; Silvestri).[6] Meanwhile, unsurprisingly, the best welfare handouts were reserved for mainland-based corporations, which, from 1976 to 2005 were invited under section 936 of the tax code to relocate subsidiaries to the island and pay no taxes. When this tax loophole was closed under Bill Clinton, Puerto Rico's economy began the long, slow slide that brought it to its current disasters.

The Welfare Trope as Political Hurricane

At mid-twentieth century, at the height of the Cold War and its relentless pressure to show that Puerto Ricans, like African Americans and impoverished people in the United States generally, would not do better under communism, the US response to the low standard of living among Puerto Ricans was to blame it on "too many children"—on excessive reproduction—even as incomes began their considerable, albeit unsustained, rise. Mainland social science and newspapers were, if anything, less sympathetic to Puerto Rico's children and youth, turning them into a "relief problem," with no real children anywhere visible, only "the absence of childhood as a specially prolonged and protected stage in the life cycle, [and an] early initiation into sex," in the words of Oscar Lewis. By the 1970s Puerto Rican youth on the island were thoroughly a problem, whether "idle" young men who might become revolutionaries, juvenile delinquents, drug addicts, labor radicals, or restive students. These much more explicitly harsh characterizations of Puerto Rican children and youth produced more of the same, perhaps more so—subminimum wages, an incipient war on drugs, the continued unequal insertion into the US social safety net, and, occasionally, the killing of students. As objects of pity or fascination, or imagined as dangerous and disposable, the children and youth—as well as the working class that could reproduce the same—brought fear and loathing, but never largesse or justice.

Mid-twentieth-century development programs led to long-term debt across the Caribbean and the wider Third World—and for Haiti, that debt began in the early nineteenth century, with former French slavers, then the United States, looting its treasury (Gamio et al.). This financialized capitalism is a slightly different context from Marx's surplus value derived from underpaying factory laborers; it is capital transformed into perpetual (re) payment without the workers or factories. Puerto Rico has suffered through a debt crisis of more recent provenance—dating from the 1990s—but it, too, has been locked into a status of virtually perpetual repayment through an austerity program directed by a fiscal control board that sought to do away with minimum wages and reliable old-age pensions. One member of the board promoted the view that minimum wages and pensions reduced the number of jobs. These doctrines were produced at least in part through an account of the 1970s, an era of explosive labor militancy, general strikes, and rising costs for the wealthy. This work is not just done through an account that demonizes unions (and the costs of rising minimum wages and other benefits), but one that points to children as the demons, socially, of this era.

The legacies of the welfare queen have, if anything, intensified in the twenty-first century. Relief from the disasters of Hurricanes María and Irma (which inflicted serious damage to the eastern edge of Puerto Rico and the Virgin Islands only a week before María) was one of many arenas in which conservatives with decision-making authority over millions of people in the archipelago engaged in ugly caricatures of Puerto Rico with roots in narratives of the welfare queen. A few weeks after the hurricanes, Andrew Biggs, a scholar associated with the neoconservative American Enterprise Institute (AEI) think tank and an appointed member of the Fiscal Oversight and Management Board for Puerto Rico (FOMB), said that the archipelago was like "the alcoholic who hits rock bottom and says, 'OK, we're bankrupt now, and we have really got to change the way we're doing things." The FOMB is an independent entity within the Puerto Rican government established by US Congress through the Puerto Rico Oversight, Management, and Economic Stability Act (PROMESA) of 2016, with the mandate to help Puerto Rico achieve fiscal responsibility with pro-growth fiscal reforms and renew access to capital markets. Puerto Ricans call it "la junta," a term for an illegitimate governing group, usually established after a coup, underscoring its unelected nature and the power of those who control the finances to govern, in effect, and the ways it has operated to harm working- and middle-class Puerto Ricans by allowing corporations and hedge funds to set the terms of repayment. All seven members of FOMB are appointed by the president of the United States. The governor of Puerto Rico, or the governor's designee, is an ex officio member of the oversight board without voting rights.

At a panel presentation sponsored by AEI, Biggs laid out a neoconservative vision for the archipelago ended the following: the minimum wage that Puerto Ricans had won in the 1970s, labor rules requiring just-cause termination, paid sick days for employees, paternity leave, and overtime pay. Despite the contempt of the political class in the archipelago for impoverished and Black Puerto Ricans, Biggs saw Puerto Ricans as an undifferentiated mass who, like all welfare queens, lacked willpower and self-discipline. They had to be forced to do hard work and difficult things. "The reality is, the government doesn't want to do these things," Biggs said of eliminating pensions and minimum wage. "If you let them not do them, they won't do them." He continued, "A problem with labor supply on the island is the phase out of welfare benefits," because miserable wages and benefits would make even the exceedingly minimal "welfare" more attractive to (always implicitly Black) women with children (Fang).

Puerto Rico has, in recent years, experienced crises natural and unnatural— hurricanes and earthquake swarms, corrupt politicians, and debt. In 2022, almost exactly five years to the day after María, Hurricane Fiona wiped out the electrical grid all over again. Austerity budgets in response to the debt have left schools closed and neglected (Alhindawi and Katz), even as crypto tycoons from the states have bought up prime real estate (Morales; Bonilla). Even with the highest vaccination rate in the United States, half a million people got COVID-19—one-sixth of the population. As the award-winning artist ADÁL had it, the people of the archipelago were a population marked for death and elimination—"Muerto [dead] Rico" (Catlin; LeBrón, *Against*). Indeed, they always had been.

The trope of the welfare mother did devastating political work as a discourse of the welfare cheat was applied to the entire archipelago. Ten days after Hurricane María, when many of the sick and injured still awaited rescue that often never came (Bonilla and LeBrón), Trump tweeted out a characterization of the whole archipelago that leaned heavily on the welfare mother: "[They] want everything to be done for them and it should be a community effort. 10,000 Federal workers now on island doing a fantastic job." In subsequent weeks, as people sought emergency grants from FEMA or even tarps to cover their roofs to protect themselves and what remained of their belongings from the elements, only 30 percent received FEMA grants (compared to 60 percent in Texas in a storm a month earlier), despite the ongoing characterization of all Puerto Ricans as welfare "cheats" (Panditharatne). Puerto Rican homes and land have long had a preponderance of informal property title, with only 70 percent of properties even registered with governments. Not only did FEMA fail to adapt to the local situation, but when they did finally show up to assess the damage, many did not even speak Spanish and hence could not explain to residents who they were and what they were doing there (Panfil). When Congress allocated hurricane relief funds, the Department of Housing and Urban Development (HUD) refused to release them, sitting on $18 billion in rebuilding aid for years, because, it said, "Given the Puerto Rican government's history of financial mismanagement, corruption, and other abuses, we must ensure that any HUD assistance provided helps those on the island who need it the most. This process must be handled in a prudent manner with strong financial controls to mitigate the risk to Federal taxpayers" (Touchberry).

Revolt

Yet for all their pain and troubles, Puerto Ricans fought back as they always have. This land of slave rebellions and uncounted general strikes in the years that followed enslaved people's freedom organized what became known as the Verano Boricua (Puerto Rican Summer) protests in 2019, and they overthrew the governor. A leaked and published transcript of a derisive chat on the messaging app Telegram among Governor Ricky Rosselló and his circle of appointed officials proved a bridge too far. People's anger boiled up against the political class's contempt for people's suffering after the hurricane (including jokes about covering up the story of the bodies piled up in local morgues that gave lie to the official death toll in only double digits) and the racism, homophobia, transphobia, and misogyny that met calls for a state of emergency about femicide. Hundreds of thousands of people from across the political spectrum poured into the streets (Hostetler-Díaz; Zambrana). This situation is an echo of the 1970s, when wave after wave of general strikes signaled a refusal of the effort to break unions or, especially but not exclusively for people of African descent, to return to sugarcane fields with machetes under a burning sun.

In the face of all this struggle and heartbreak in Puerto Rico, it is perhaps still true that one of the most serious blows the archipelago has sustained is neither natural disaster nor the imposition of a colonial finance apparatus through the law called PROMESA. What has made all of them worse is the return of the old libel: the suggestion that what ails the commonwealth is "welfare," and the related insistence that fewer Puerto Ricans—a kind of negative reproductive labor—is what the archipelago needs. It is the resurgence of the welfare queen as the key trope that tells us we are in the presence of a crisis of reproductive labor. The welfare mother, that enduring sign of the refusal of Black women to work for wages while simultaneously raising children—children who might not ultimately grow into workers who are "productive" (exploitable) members of the labor force—was and continues to be mobilized by the political right to describe the conundrum and the contempt of the capitalist class for reproductive labor and the reproduction of Afro-Puerto Rican youth.

From the fights of the 1930s through the 1970s over the incorporation of Puerto Rico into the Social Security program to complaints about drug addicts and communists, the labor of reproduction has been, since slavery ended, explicitly disparaged by Puerto Rico's ruling class and its colonizers from the states. The issue of how racial capitalism was to find a cheap, docile workforce is perennially in crisis, and excessive young people—or "overpopulation"—provided an economic language by which to mark their lives as disposable. Puerto Ricans' excessive reproduction has long provided a vivid figure for the archipelago. Early in the twentieth century, US newspapers and popular discourse about policy imagined Puerto Rico as a geography of excessive reproduction of the less than human, the animalistic Black and Brown children who were too much. This is an image that persisted through the Depression, New Deal, development, and financial capitalist crisis eras. It never served Puerto Ricans; rather, it became part of the broader US political imaginary that enabled their exclusion from much of the social safety net, which, even when added later, always at a lower rate, disadvantaged Puerto Ricans by design.

Yet from the era of enslavement to the Verano Boricua, Puerto Ricans have revolted again and again against their emplacement in a global economy as exploited agricultural, industrial, and service workers, as well as reproducers, whose job is to produce surplus value and a next generation—but not too many. The welfare queen is a discourse of counterinsurgency, an effort to contain rebellions large and small. Its claim that the (colonial) state is supporting working-class and impoverished people, and especially their children, is almost comic, especially in Puerto Rico, where by statute and design there is somewhere between very little and zero state support for young people. Yet across centuries, from slave revolts, uprisings for independence, general strikes, student movements, protests against unjust debt, the feeding of neighbors and rebuilding of communities after hurricanes, and a people taking to the streets to bring down a governor, Puerto Ricans have fought for and celebrated living in each generation against a demand for their death and diminishment. ▨

Laura Briggs is professor of women, gender, sexuality studies and adjunct professor of history at the University of Massachusetts, Amherst. She is author of a number of books and numerous articles on reproduction, race, and the United States in Latin America, including the award-winning *Somebody's Children: The Politics of Transracial and Transnational Adoption* (2012) and *Reproducing Empire: Race, Sex, Science, and U.S. Imperialism in Puerto Rico* (2002).

ACKNOWLEDGMENTS

I am grateful to the editors of this special issue, Alys Eve Weinbaum and Jennifer L. Morgan, and to the other members of the Reproducing Racial Capitalism workshop that they convened, including Rickie Solinger, Caleb Knapp, Sasha Turner, Jessica Marie Johnson, SJ Zhang, Sigrid Vertommen, Halle-Mackenzie Ashby, Vanessa Agard-Jones, and Diana Paton, who offered invaluable help and engagement with this essay. Thanks to Christen Smith for help in thinking through the long history of the feminist movement in Nigeria, and Pam Butler for their thoughtful suggestions. Tiarra Cooper provided fantastic editorial assistance.

NOTES

1   United States v. Vaello Madero, 596 U.S. ___ (2022).
2   Downes v. Bidwell, 182 U.S. 244 (1901).

3   Unsigned internal policy document. January 1952. Rockefeller Archive Center, Rock-
    efeller Foundation Files, Record Group 3.2, Series 900; Sub-Series, Pop-1, box 57,
    folder 312.

4   Statement of Amadeo I. D. Francis, Economic Adviser to the Administrator, Eco-
    nomic Development Administration of the Commonwealth of Puerto Rico. United
    States. Congress. Senate Committee on Labor and Public Welfare. *Amendments to the
    Fair Labor Standards Act (Puerto Rico):* Hearing before the Subcommittee on Labor.
    Part 3—San Juan, Puerto Rico (January 3, 4, and 5, 1966). Washington: U.S. G.P.O.,
    1977, pp. 1461–62.

5   Lester Wolff, Chairman, presiding. United States. Congress. House Select Commit-
    tee on Narcotics Abuse and Control. *The Scope of Drug Abuse in Puerto Rico: Supply and
    Demand Reduction. Hearing.* (April 19, 20, and 21, 1979). Washington: U.S. G.P.O., 1979,
    p. 2; Testimony of Ronald Seibert, Special Agent in Charge, DEA San Juan, pp. 8, 14;
    15; testimony of Capt. Nelson Segarra, Narcotics Division, Puerto Rico Police De-
    partment, pp. 11, 19.

6   For example, the Ferré administration increased the number of public employees
    from 100,000 in 1968 to 150,000 in 1973.

WORKS CITED

Alhindawi, Diana Zeyneb, and Jonathan Katz. "The Disappearing Schools of Puerto
    Rico." *New York Times Magazine,* September 12, 2019. https://www.nytimes.com
    /interactive/2019/09/12/magazine/puerto-rico-schools-hurricane-maria.html.

Amador, Emma. "'Women Ask Relief for Puerto Ricans': Territorial Citizenship, the Social
    Security Act, and Puerto Rican Communities, 1933-1939." *Labor* 13, nos. 3-4 (2016):
    105-29.

Arendt, Hannah. *The Origins of Totalitarianism.* New York: Harcourt Brace Jovanovich,
    1973.

Ayala, César J. "The Decline of the Plantation Economy and the Puerto Rican Migration
    of the 1950s." *Latino Studies* 7, no. 1 (1996): 61-90.

Ayala, César J., and Rafael Bernabé. *Puerto Rico in the American Century: A History Since
    1898.* Chapel Hill: University of North Carolina Press, 2009.

Banítez de Rodríguez, Celeste. "Rafael Hernández Colón: Los dos primeros años."
    El mundo, January 1, 1975.

Baralt, Guillermo A. *Slave Revolts in Puerto Rico: Conspiracies and Uprisings, 1795-1873.* Trans-
    lated by Christine Ayorinde. Princeton, NJ: Markus Wiener, 2007.

Beckles, Hilary. "From Land to Sea: Runaway Barbados Slaves and Servants, 1630-1700."
    Slavery and Abolition 6, no. 3 (1985): 79-94.

Bendiner, Elmer. "Outside the Kingdom of the Middle Class." *Nation,* January 2, 1967, 22-23.

Benhabib, Seyla. *The Rights of Others: Aliens, Residents, and Citizens.* New York: Cambridge
    University Press, 2004.

Bonilla, Yarimar. "For Investors, Puerto Rico Is a Fantasy Blank Slate." *Nation,* February
    28, 2018. https://www.thenation.com/article/archive/for-investors-puerto-rico-is-a
    -fantasy-blank-slate/.

Bonilla, Yarimar, and Marisol LeBrón. *Aftershocks of Disaster: Puerto Rico before and after
    the Storm.* New York: Haymarket Books, 2019.

Brau, Salvador. *Puerto Rico y su historia*. Valencia: Imprenta de Francisco Vives Mora, 1894.

Briggs, Laura. "The Race of Hysteria: 'Overcivilization' and the 'Savage' Woman in Late Nineteenth-Century Obstetrics and Gynecology." *American Quarterly* 52, no. 2 (2000): 246–73.

Briggs, Laura. *Reproducing Empire: Race, Sex, Science, and U.S. Imperialism in Puerto Rico*. Oakland: University of California Press, 2002.

Byrd, Jodi A., Alyosha Goldstein, Jodi Melamed, and Chandan Reddy. "Predatory Value: Economies of Dispossession and Disturbed Relationalities." *Social Text* 36, no. 2 (2018): 1–18.

Catlin, Roger. "The Award-Winning Artist ADÁL Has Died. Read One of His Final Interviews." *Smithsonian Magazine*, January 4, 2021. https://www.smithsonianmag.com /smithsonian-institution/behind-devastating-prize-winning-image-adals-muerto -rico-180975010/.

Chakravartty, Paula, and Denise Ferreira da Silva. "Accumulation, Dispossession, and Debt: The Racial Logic of Global Capitalism—an Introduction." *American Quarterly* 64, no. 3 (2012): 361–85.

Chandrasekaran, Rajiv. *Imperial Life in the Emerald City: Inside Iraq's Green Zone*. New York: Alfred A. Knopf, 2006.

Coulthard, Glenn. *Red Skin, White Masks: Rejecting the Colonial Politics of Recognition*. Minneapolis: University of Minnesota Press, 2014.

Critchlow, Donald T. *Intended Consequences: Birth Control, Abortion, and the Federal Government in Modern America*. Oxford: Oxford University Press, 2001.

Davis, Angela. "The Black Woman's Role in the Community of Slaves." *Black Scholar* 3, no. 4 (1971): 2–15.

Díaz Soler, Luis Manuel. "Historia de la Esclavitud Negra en Puerto Rico 1493–1890." PhD diss., Louisiana State University, 1950.

Dorfman, Ariel, and Armand Mattelart. *Para leer al Pato Donald: Comunicación de masa y colonialism*, rev. ed. 1972; repr., México: Siglo Veintiuno Editores, 2010.

Duany, Jorge. *The Puerto Rican Nation on the Move*. Chapel Hill: University of North Carolina Press, 2002.

Dunnavant, Justin P. "Have Confidence in the Sea: Maritime Maroons and Fugitive Geographies." *Antipode* 53, no. 3 (2021): 884–905.

The Economist. "Trouble on Welfare Island." May 25, 2006. https://www.economist.com /united-states/2006/05/25/trouble-on-welfare-island.

Epica Task Force. *Puerto Rico: A People Challenging Colonialism*. Illus. by Luis Cancel. Ecumenical Program on Central America and the Caribbean, 1976.

Fang, Lee. "After Hurricane Maria, Key Republican Compares Puerto Rico to 'the Alcoholic Who Hits Rock Bottom.'" *Intercept*, November 14, 2017. https://theintercept .com/2017/11/14/puerto-rico-hurricane-maria-promesa-andrew-biggs/.

Federici, Silvia. *Caliban and the Witch: Women, the Body, and Primitive Accumulation*. Brooklyn: Autonomedia, 2004.

Federici, Silvia. "Interview with Silvia Federici: Wages for Housework." Interview by Louise Toupin. *Pluto Press* (blog), November 2018. https://www.plutobooks.com /blog/silvia-federici-wages-for-housework-interview-louise-toupin/.

Findlay, Eileen Súarez. "Dangerous Dependence or Productive Masculinity? Gendered Representations of Puerto Ricans in the US Press, 1940–50." *Radical History Review*, no. 128 (2017): 173–98.

Findlay, Eileen Súarez. *Imposing Decency: The Politics of Sexuality and Race in Puerto Rico*. Durham, NC: Duke University Press, 1999.

Gamio, Lazaro, Constant Méheut, Catherine Porter, Selam Gebrekidan, Allison McCann, and Matt Appuzo. "Haiti's Lost Billions." *New York Times*, May 20, 2022. https://www .nytimes.com/interactive/2022/05/20/world/americas/enslaved-haiti-debt-timeline .html.

García Peña, Lorgia. *Translating Blackness: Latinx Colonialities in Global Perspective*. Durham, NC: Duke University Press, 2022.

Giusti-Cordero, Juan A. "Labour, Ecology, and History in a Puerto Rican Plantation Region: 'Classic' Rural Proletarians Revisited." *International Review of Social History* 41, no. S4 (1996): 53–82.

Godreau, Isar P. *Scripts of Blackness: Race, Cultural Nationalism, and U.S. Colonialism in Puerto Rico*. Champaign: University of Illinois Press, 2000.

Greszler, Rachel. *Congress Should Not Give Puerto Rico Federal Tax Subsidies*. Washington, DC: Heritage Foundation, March 22, 2016. https://www.heritage.org/taxes/report /congress-should-not-give-puerto-rico-federal-tax-subsidies.

Gunther, John. *Inside Latin America*. New York: Harper and Brothers, 1941.

Hall, Neville A. T. "Maritime Maroons: 'Grand Marronage' from the Danish West Indies." *William and Mary Quarterly* 42, no. 4 (1985): 476–98.

Harney, Stefano, and Fred Moten. *The Undercommons: Fugitive Planning and Black Study*. New York: Autonomedia, 2013.

Harvey, David. "The 'New' Imperialism: Accumulation by Dispossession." In *Karl Marx*, edited by Kevin B. Anderson and Bertell Ollman, 213–41. New York: Routledge, 2012.

Hostetler-Díaz, Jean. "Photo Essay: The Power of Popular Protest: El Verano Boricua." Photography by Vanessa Díaz and Federico Cintrón-Moscoso. *Latin American Perspectives* 47, no. 3 (2020): 13–17.

Johnson, Jenna, and Ashley Parker. "Trump Hails 'Incredible' Response in 'Lovely' Trip to Storm-Torn Puerto Rico." *Washington Post*, October 3, 2017.

Kelley, Robin D. G. *Yo' Mama's Disfunktional!: Fighting the Culture Wars in Urban America*. Boston: Beacon, 1997.

Kim, Jodi. *Settler Garrison: Debt Imperialism, Militarism, and Transpacific Imaginaries*. Durham, NC: Duke University Press, 2022.

Koven, Seth, and Sonya Michel. *Mothers of a New World: Maternalist Politics and the Origins of Welfare States*. New York: Routledge, 1993.

Ladd-Taylor, Molly. *Mother-Work: Women, Child Welfare, and the State, 1890–1930*. Urbana: University of Illinois Press, 1995.

LeBrón, Marisol. *Against Muerto Rico: Lessons from the Verano Boricua*. Cabo Rojo, PR: Editora Educación Emergente, 2021.

LeBrón, Marisol. *Policing Life and Death: Race, Violence, and Resistance in Puerto Rico*. Oakland: University of California Press, 2019.

Lee, Na Young. "The Construction of United States Camptown Prostitution in South Korea: Transformation and Resistance." PhD diss., University of Maryland, 2006.

Levander, Caroline. "Confederate Cuba." *American Literature* 78, no. 4 (2006): 821–45.

Levin, Josh. *The Queen: The Forgotten Life behind an American Myth*. New York: Little, Brown, 2019.

Lewis, Oscar. *La Vida: A Puerto Rican Family in the Culture of Poverty—San Juan and New York*. New York: Random House, 1996.

Lightfoot, Natasha. *Troubling Freedom: Antigua and the Aftermath of British Emancipation*. Durham, NC: Duke University Press, 2015.

Lloréns, Hilda. *Making Livable Worlds: Afro-Puerto Rican Women Building Environmental Justice*. Seattle: University of Washington Press, 2021.

Lloréns, Hilda. "The Race of Disaster: Black Communities and the Crisis in Puerto Rico." *Black Perspectives* (blog), April 17, 2019. African American Intellectual History Society. https://www.aaihs.org/the-race-of-disaster-black-communities-and-the-crisis -in-puerto-rico/.

Lowe, Lisa. *The Intimacies of Four Continents*. Durham, NC: Duke University Press, 2015.

Martínez-San Miguel, Yolanda. *Coloniality of Diasporas: Rethinking Intra-colonial Migrations in a Pan-Caribbean Context*. New York: Palgrave Macmillan, 2014.

Marx, Karl. *The Process of Capitalist Production*. Book 1 of *Capital: A Critique of Political Economy*. Vol. 1. 1867; repr., New York: Cosimo Classics, 2007.

Mbembe, Achille. *Necropolitics*. Durham, NC: Duke University Press, 2019.

Mintz, Sidney W. "The Culture History of a Puerto Rican Sugar Cane Plantation: 1876– 1949." *Hispanic American Historical Review* 33, no. 2 (1953): 224–51.

Morales, Ed. *Fantasy Island: Colonialism, Exploitation, and the Betrayal of Puerto Rico*. New York: Bold Type Books, 2019.

Morgan, Jennifer L. *Laboring Women: Reproduction and Gender in the New World Slavery*. Philadelphia: University of Pennsylvania Press, 2004.

Morrissey, Marietta. "The Making of a Colonial Welfare State: U.S. Social Insurance and Public Assistance in Puerto Rico." *Latin American Perspectives* 33, no. 1 (2006): 23–41.

El Mundo. "Elogian Puertorriqueña en diario sesiones de Congreso E.U." January 1, 1975.

Murphy, Michelle. *The Economization of Life*. Durham, NC: Duke University Press, 2017.

Negrón-Muntaner, Frances. "The Crisis in Puerto Rico Is a Racial Issue. Here's Why." *Root*, October 12, 2017. https://www.theroot.com/the-crisis-in-puerto-rico-is-a-racial -issue-here-s-why-1819380372.

Panditharatne, Mekela. "FEMA Has Rejected Sixty Percent of Assistance Requests in Puerto Rico. Why?" *Slate*, June 15, 2018. https://slate.com/technology/2018/06 /hurricane-maria-aftermath-fema-rejects-60-percent-of-assistance-requests.html.

Panfil, Yuliya. "How the Biden Administration Can Fix This Part of the Disaster Housing Crisis." *Slate*, December 16, 2020. https://slate.com/technology/2020/12/fema-climate -disaster-aid-proof-home-occupancy.html.

Ramírez de Arellano, Annette B., and Conrad Seipp. *Colonialism, Catholicism, and Contraception: A History of Birth Control in Puerto Rico*. Chapel Hill: University of North Carolina Press, 1983.

Rios, Palmira N. "Export-Oriented Industrialization and the Demand for Female Labor: Puerto Rican Women in the Manufacturing Sector, 1952–1980." *Gender and Society* 4, no. 3 (1990): 321–37.

Rivera Lugo, Carlos. "La lucha por los derechos humanos." *Claridad*, special section, December 15–21, 1978: 10–11.

Roberts, Neil. *Freedom as Marronage*. Chicago, IL: University of Chicago Press, 2015.

Robinson, Cedric J. *Black Marxism, Revised and Updated Third Edition: The Making of the Black Radical Tradition*. Chapel Hill: University of North Carolina Press, 2021.

Robinson, Rachel Sullivan. "Negotiating Development Prescriptions: The Case of Population Policy in Nigeria." *Population Research and Policy Review* 31, no. 2 (2012): 267–96.

Rodríguez-Silva, Ileana. *Silencing Race: Disentangling Blackness, Colonialism, and National Identities in Puerto Rico*. New York: Palgrave Macmillan, 2012.

Rosa, Alessandra M. "Resistance Performances: (Re)constructing Spaces of Resistance and Contention in the 2010–2011 University of Puerto Rico Student Movement." PhD diss., Florida International University, 2015.

Sánchez, Luis Rafael. *Macho Camacho's Beat (La guaracha del Macho Camacho)*. Translated by Gregory Rabassa. McLean, IL: Dalkey Archive, 1980.

Sharpe, Christina. *In the Wake: On Blackness and Being*. Durham, NC: Duke University Press, 2016.

Silvestri, Reinaldo. "Ferré dice cupones evitar revolución." *El mundo*, September 2, 1977.

Stoler, Ann Laura, and Carole McGranahan. "Introduction: Refiguring Imperial Terrains." In *Imperial Formations*, edited by Ann Laura Stoler, Carole McGranahan, and Peter C. Perdue, 173–210. Santa Fe, NM: School for Advanced Research, 2007.

Sued Badillo, Jalil, and Angel López Cantos. *Puerto Rico Negro*. Río Piedras: Editorial Cultural, 1986.

Touchberry, Ramsey. "HUD Is Violating the Law by Withholding Billions in Disaster Aid from Puerto Rico, Democrats Say." *Newsweek*, September 2019. https://www.newsweek.com/hud-violating-law-withholding-puerto-rico-disaster-relief-democrats-say-1458109.

Trump, Donald (@realdonaldtrump). " . . . want everything to be done for them when it should be a community effort. 10,000 Federal workers now on Island doing a fantastic job." Twitter, September 30, 2017, 7:29 a.m. https://twitter.com/realDonaldTrump/status/914089888596754434?s=20.

Vergès, Françoise. *The Wombs of Women: Race, Capital, Feminism*. Translated by Kaiama L. Glover. Durham, NC: Duke University Press, 2020.

Weinbaum, Alys Eve. *The Afterlife of Reproductive Slavery: Biocapitalism and Black Feminism's Philosophy of History*. Durham, NC: Duke University Press, 2019.

Williams, Patricia. *The Alchemy of Race and Rights: Diary of a Law Professor*. Cambridge, MA: Harvard University Press, 1992.

Zambrana, Rocío. *Colonial Debts: The Case of Puerto Rico*. Durham, NC: Duke University Press, 2021.

Caleb Knapp

"Much-Abused Luke"
Slavery, Sexual Terror, and Protest

ABSTRACT This essay revisits a familiar but seldom discussed anecdote of same-sex sexual abuse in the archive of Atlantic slavery: the story of Luke in Harriet Jacobs's *Incidents in the Life of a Slave Girl* (1861). Through a close reading of Luke's story, the article advances three claims: (1) the history of slavery is also a history of same-sex sexual terror, (2) the sexual terror of slavery included reproductive sexual violence but was not limited to it, and (3) *Incidents* is ultimately a story about sexual terror and protest against it in the form of fugitivity. In making these arguments, the article intervenes into current conversations in the feminist historiography of slavery, capitalism, and reproduction and contributes to emerging work on same-sex sexual relations in the context of enslavement. It closes with a short reflection on the stakes of Luke's story for historiography on sexuality.

KEYWORDS slavery, sexual violence, history of sexuality, reproduction, protest

Late in the narrative of her life, *Incidents in the Life of a Slave Girl* (1861), Harriet Jacobs recounts a chance meeting between two enslaved fugitives—herself and Luke, an acquaintance of hers from North Carolina.[1] Luke had just reached New York, where he, like Jacobs, stuck to side streets to elude slave catchers and citizens turned bounty hunters by the passage of the 1850 Fugitive Slave Act. Commencing what Jacobs calls a "reign of terror" (245) on Black people in the United States, the bill mandated national recognition of slaveholders' property claims and ordered all citizens, under threat of penalty, to assist in fugitive apprehension and rendition.[2] When they cross paths, Luke is on his way to Canada, having successfully escaped a trader. Introducing him to readers, Jacobs offers his backstory, one of the few accounts of same-sex sexual violence in the archives of North American slavery. It begins with the death of Luke's master and Luke's transfer as property to the master's profligate son, who required constant bedside attendance, having lost the facility of his limbs owing to what the text suggests is deviant

HISTORY of the PRESENT ▪ A Journal of Critical History ▪ 14:1 ▪ April 2024
DOI 10.1215/21599785-10898363 © 2024 Duke University Press

sexual behavior (Wallace 89–90; Abdur-Rahman, "'Strangest Freaks'" 232). The task of waiting on the debilitated bachelor fell to Luke and proved thankless, for impairment made the young man irascible. At whim and over trivial matters, he lashed Luke until he could no longer lift the whip. If Luke resisted, the slaveholder called for the constable, whose services became increasingly necessary as the arm of the libertine grew weaker. Condemning this master for acts of perversion against "much-abused Luke" (248), Jacobs relates that some days the "cruel and disgusting wretch" (247) ordered Luke to wear nothing but a shirt that could be easily stripped off for a flogging. In language that bespeaks the sexual nature of Luke's subjection, Jacobs writes that the master "lay there on his bed, a mere degraded wreck of manhood" and "took into his head the strangest freaks of despotism," some of which were "too filthy to be repeated" (247). Throughout the antebellum period sex acts between men were typically named through reference to the unspeakable and coded in terms like the ones Jacobs uses, including *disgusting, filthy,* and *degraded* (Downs). The anecdote, in other words, indicates that Luke suffered sexual harm at the hands of his master (and the police).

The existing historiography on slavery has examined the sexual violence of bondage but situations like Luke's remain underexplored—a robust theoretical accounting of same-sex sexual harm under slavery is still needed. Leading historians in the first half of the twentieth century rarely acknowledged the sexual abuse of enslaved women by masters, typically dismissing it as the outcome of enslaved women's promiscuity and opportunism or as evidence of mutual affection between masters and slaves (Stampp 359–60; Genovese 413–31). A wave of Black feminist historiography in the 1970s, 1980s, and 1990s critically revised this narrative, highlighting enslaved women's routine exposure to sexual assault, overturning pervasive myths of Black female hypersexuality, critiquing racialized constructions of feminine chastity, and exposing the paradoxes of consent under slavery. This scholarship makes previously obscured forms of sexual violence legible and details how enslaved women navigated the sexual conditions of their enslavement, yet it remains largely focused on sexual harms between enslaved women and masters (Davis, "Reflections," *Women*; Hine, "Female," "Rape"; hooks; White; Carby; Spillers; Hartman; Davis, "'Don't Let Nobody'"; Painter). Building on this body of work, recent feminist studies of slavery have focused on the centrality of enslaved women's reproduction to chattel bondage in the Americas. This scholarship offers an implicit account of sexual subjection in which rape and other forms of sexual abuse constitute means of achieving biological procreation and social reproduction. The inclination of this research has been to frame sexual encounter under slavery within a reproductive teleology in which sexual violation figures predominantly in an instrumental sense as a tool for the management and exploitation of enslaved women's reproductive capacities, on which slavery depended (Roberts; Morgan, *Laboring, Reckoning*; Weinbaum, *Wayward, Afterlife*; Schwartz; Turner; Berry). This literature has made invaluable contributions to the fields of women's history, labor history, and the historiography of slavery and capitalism, but its tendency to collapse sexual violence into reproductive violence leaves Luke's sexual abuse—which cannot neatly be elucidated as reproductive labor exploitation—in need of further explanation.

The literature on sexuality cannot fully illuminate Luke's situation either. The impulse in the historiography on sexuality, especially sexuality prior to the invention of the homosexual, has been to focus on instances of nonnormative desire and its regulation as opposed to instances of same-sex sexual violence. Since at least the gay liberation movements of the 1970s and the contemporaneous rise of social history, scholars of sexuality have scoured the historical record in search of subjects who might constitute the antecedents of today's queer populations and movements. This endeavor—looking for ourselves in the past to give ourselves a history—has produced a persistent evidentiary turn to the archive in the historiography on sexuality and has generated a documentary trove of aberrant practices of sex and gender as well as an eclectic genealogy of individuals who by their records of social deviance might be recuperated into a queer history of the present (Katz, *Gay American History, Gay/Lesbian Almanac, Love Stories*; Faderman; Benemann; Rupp; Bronski).[3] This research has made tremendous inroads toward upending the dominant narratives of perversion that have long consigned sexually transgressive subjects to moral censure, criminalization, and historical obscurity. Yet it is limited by its tendency to frame sexuality in terms of desire, pleasure, and agency—it has largely presumed that sexuality is a feature of the interiority of an individuated liberal subject and that such subjects come into historical view by willfully engaging in forms of romantic love, affective intimacy, and erotic pleasure that buck existing norms (LaFleur, *Natural History*, "Whither Rape"). Accordingly, the scholarship has not yet fully accounted for forms of same-sex sexual encounter—like Luke's—that cannot be understood as expressions of mutual desire between willing subjects or recovered as admirable acts of self-liberation that challenge sexually oppressive orders. Put simply, the two fields to which one would turn to make sense of Luke's story—the historiography of slavery and the historiography of sexuality—stop short of untangling it. The anecdote thus offers an opportunity (one I take up here) to consider how Luke's story might rework and expand existing research on slavery and sexuality.

In this essay I revisit the anecdote on Luke in an effort to advance three related claims, all of which emerge out of close readings of Luke's story and its relation to the arguments Jacobs develops throughout *Incidents*. The first is that histories of slavery are also histories of same-sex sexual terror. The historiography on Atlantic slavery has not yet fully appreciated this point. I begin by arguing that Black feminist thinkers, including Angela Davis and Dorothy Roberts, have laid the groundwork for theorizing slavery as a formation of systemic sexual terror and that Jacobs anticipates this conceptualization of slavery through the narration of her own story and Luke's. Inviting readers to consider sexual violence under slavery as a form of terror grounded in the organization of property rights, Jacobs emphasizes the fact that same-sex sexual violence is an intrinsic feature of chattel bondage. What her account of Luke calls to the fore is that slavery was a structure of racial domination that entailed sexual terror not just against enslaved women but all enslaved people and that same-sex sexual terror constituted an essential element of slavery. In making this argument, I position this essay as a contribution to the emerging subfield of slavery studies that focuses on unpacking same-sex sexual relations under slavery.[4]

The second argument I advance here is that sexual terror under slavery includes reproductive sexual exploitation but is not reducible to it. Feminist scholars have extensively demonstrated that *Incidents* tells the story of enslaved women's uniquely gendered experiences of sexual violence. As Jennifer L. Morgan, Alys Eve Weinbaum, Sasha Turner, and others have argued, slavery perpetuated itself through the exploitation of enslaved women's biologically and socially reproductive labor. The law of maternal descent dictated that legal unfreedom and racial Blackness would descend through the enslaved mother's line. For this reason, sexual violence against enslaved women could be—and often was—used as an instrument whereby enslaved laboring populations were reproduced. Sexual terror under bondage thus held distinctly gendered meaning in relation to enslaved women. As I see it, Luke's story does not contravene this point. In what follows, I suggest that *Incidents* proposes the truth of what might at first seem like a paradox— sexual terror under slavery was gendered and sexual terror under slavery had no gender. Telling Luke's story, Jacobs advances an account of sexual terror capacious enough to capture its instrumental use for the gendered reproductive exploitation of enslaved women as well as for the racial domination of all enslaved people. Through the anecdote, *Incidents* moreover engages in a discursive struggle over the meaning of sexual violence—that is, it makes an argument about what should count as sexual abuse, how it should be understood in relation to reproductive exploitation, and who should be considered targets of sexual terror. Taking cues from Jacobs, I approach sexual violence not only as a fact of enslaved people's lived experience but also as an idea that is taking shape, in flux, and highly contested during the time of Jacobs's writing. In this sense, I read *Incidents* as an argument about the very way in which sexual violence should be conceptualized as a category of knowledge.

My third and final argument is that *Incidents* is a book about protest against sexual terror in the form of fugitivity. What is notable about the anecdote on Luke is not simply the sexual nature of his punishment but the fact that it appears in "The Fugitive Slave Law," a chapter dedicated to Jacobs's account of the 1850 mandate on enslaved runaways. For Jacobs the Fugitive Slave Act shatters any pretension of the North as a geography of freedom. Though she finds temporary refuge in New York, Jacobs explains that, under the order, she is "as subject to slave laws as I had been in a Slave State" (249). This narrative context makes Luke's story a mirror of Jacobs's own: Luke and Jacobs both experience sexual terror and pursue fugitivity. Luke's story represents only one of many anecdotes—most of which involve Jacobs—dealing with sexual violence in the text. Early in the narrative Jacobs explains that, as she entered her fifteenth year, her master, Dr. Flint (James Norcom), began to "whisper foul words in my ear" (33), pressing her to submit to sexual demands. His pursuit proving relentless, Jacobs bears children to a different white man, Mr. Sands (Samuel Tredwell Sawyer), garnering a modicum of protection from Flint by virtue of Sands's interposition. Yet Flint continues hounding Jacobs, jeopardizing her children's safety so long as she refuses him. Intuiting that the danger to her children (Joseph and Louisa Jacobs) will diminish if she places herself beyond Flint's reach, Jacobs hides first among friends, next in a swamp, and then for seven years in the attic of the house belonging to her grandmother (Molly Horniblow) before fleeing north. Through these acts of provisional self-defense and familial protection, Jacobs enters a condition of fugitivity. In the final section of the essay, I suggest that the shared condition of fugitivity between Luke and Jacobs matters as much for the present analysis as the differences between their experiences of sexual terror. Ultimately, through Luke's story and her own, *Incidents* frames fugitivity as a form of protest against the sexual terror of slavery. Finally, the essay closes with a brief reflection on the stakes of the foregoing arguments for the historiography on sexuality.

Sexual Terror and the Fugitive Slave Act

In the context of US slavery, sexual violence was an instrument of terror. Black feminist scholars have emphasized that slavery inherently entailed the systemic exercise of sexual subjection. In her 1971 pioneering essay on rape, gendered labor, and slavery, "Reflections on the Black Woman's Role in the Community of Slaves," Angela Davis argues that enslaved women were burdened with the task of not only laboring in the fields but also maintaining the domestic conditions required to sustain the lives of enslaved laborers. This gendered arrangement made the enslaved woman a key agent of social reproduction for the enslaved community.[5] Davis points out that the enslaved woman found herself in a unique position: she was specially situated to promote and participate in resistance to slavery. Her gendered role allowed her to curate an insurgent consciousness among the inhabitants of the slave quarters and foment insurrection in a range of forms. Davis notes that the historiography on enslaved resistance, though rich, had up to the time of her writing focused on organized revolts led by enslaved men and had ignored contributions to collective struggle made by enslaved women.[6] Davis emphasizes that the exceptional position of the enslaved woman enabled her to contribute in distinctly gendered ways to enslaved resistance but also made her vulnerable to gendered practices of counterinsurgency—including rape. The sexual subjection of the enslaved woman, for Davis, constituted an attack on both the individual woman and the enslaved community at large. Slaveholders leveraged sexual violence against enslaved women as a way of quelling collective insurgency.[7] Davis frames sexual violence as an instrument of terror, arguing that "the American slaveholder's sexual domination never lost its openly terroristic character" ("Reflections" 13). In *Killing the Black Body*, her 1997 foundational study of Black women's reproduction, Dorothy Roberts echoes this point: "The fact that white men could profit from raping their female slaves does not mean that their motive was economic. The rape of slave women by their masters was primarily a weapon of terror that reinforced whites' domination over their human property" (29–30). Both Davis and Roberts frame sexual violence as an instrument of terror deployed to suppress insurgency and secure domination.[8]

In keeping with these observations, I prefer the term *sexual terror* throughout this essay to describe sexual violence visited on enslaved people. In using this term, I emphasize two things—first, that sexual subjection was systemic under slavery and, second, that sexual violence was inherent to racial enslavement. To insist on the systemic nature of sexual terror under slavery is to refuse the fiction that sexual violence is best understood as an expression of unrestrained desires, sadomasochistic impulses, or desperate bids for domination on the part of a few bad slaveholders. It is to call attention to the institution of slavery itself as a structure of sexual domination in which the nation as a whole participated, regardless of individual people's records of abuse, while also acknowledging harms perpetrated by slaveholding individuals. I also use the term *sexual terror* to indicate that sexual violence was intrinsic—not secondary or supplementary—to racial slavery. One of the most crucial interventions advanced by Davis, Roberts, and others is that sexual violation is part and parcel of enslavement—it is not some kind of gendered "add-on" to bondage that must only be taken into account when studying the lives of enslaved women, or a concern that can be dropped when considering the essential features of the institution, or a side effect of the racial domination that slavery requires. Instead, as Davis and Roberts show, sexual terror constitutes a core feature of racial slavery's social organization and material history.

Thinking about sexual violence as terror is useful for making sense of Luke's sexual abuse. It would be a mistake to assert that Luke's social position in bondage directly correlated to that of the enslaved woman Davis describes. There is little evidence that Luke was subjected to domestic labor apart from caregiving for his master. Luke does not appear to have been situated in the same way as enslaved women to foment collective insurgency through the social reproduction of the enslaved community. So, while his sexual abuse might not constitute evidence of counterinsurgency tailored to the suppression of collective resistance, it might nonetheless represent, in Roberts's words, a "weapon of terror that reinforced whites' domination over their human property" (29). The same-sex overtones of Luke's assault have been well established, but what begs further attention is the explicit language of terror—those "strangest freaks of *despotism*" (247; my emphasis)—through which Jacobs names the tyrannical character of Luke's subjection made all the more terrible by the declining physical vitality of the slaveholder and the extension of his "freaks" through the literal arm of the constable. As the text suggests, it is precisely because his master occupies a position of dependency on Luke, a situation that troubles the dynamic of power between them, that his master resorts to acts of "despotism," involving officers of the law in the process of asserting his dominion over Luke as property. Luke encounters what might be described as a kind of sexual terror—sexual subjection through which the slaveholder reestablishes the relation of property between owner and chattel—even if that sexual terror did not signify in the same way as the sexual terror deployed against enslaved women.[9]

Reading Luke's story as one about sexual terror shifts critical attention away from questions of individual desire toward the systemic nature of sexual harm under enslavement. Part of what confounds attempts to explain Luke's experience within modern frameworks for thinking sexuality is the tendency to conceptualize sexuality as an indication and expression of an individual's interior desire, pleasure, and will. Despite work to the contrary, the idea that sexuality inheres in the body and desires of the individuated subject has remained stubbornly persistent over time (LaFleur, *Natural* 189–206; "Whither Rape"). Yet such accounts of sexuality offer little to clarify what happens to Luke. To raise questions about the individual pleasures and desires of Luke or his master is ultimately to back oneself into ethical quandaries and interpretive dead ends. Asking whether the young slaveholder sexually desired Luke or found his subjection gratifying leads to speculative claims about the master that are historically impossible to substantiate and miss the point of the story in that they neglect the issue of Luke's harm. Questions about Luke's sexual desire or experience of the erotic are not only equally impossible to prove but also exceptionally fraught—for they lead us to query whether, to use a colloquial phrase, Luke "wanted it."[10] Prioritizing questions of desire or pleasure when approaching the story of Luke risks deploying a victim-blaming logic to make sense of the anecdote—it opens the possibility of disregarding the systemic nature of the harm he faced by making him responsible for the terror visited on him. If Luke "wanted it," then he becomes an agent of his own victimization by desiring some part of his subjection. In this framing, the systemic nature of sexual terror under slavery disappears. Foregrounding sexual terror in Luke's story directs our critical focus away from the questions of individual desire and pleasure toward the issue of the systemic character of the sexual violence that defined the institution of slavery.

This shift from the individual to the systemic makes it possible to account for sexual violence against Luke in ways that exceed the narrow legal framing of rape around individual consent. As has been widely demonstrated, the British common law definition of rape—the forcible carnal knowledge of a female against her will and without her consent—formed the basis of the legal codification of sexual violence in the antebellum United States (Block; Freedman). This definition of rape establishes the presence or absence of consent as the dividing line between legally permissible sexual encounter and sexual violence. Yet proving consent before the law has shown itself to be an obstinately difficult task. Attempts to identify the presence or absence of consent have typically turned on the identification of surrogate legal forms such as the presence or absence of force, resistance, or desire, and the presence of desire in the context of a sexual encounter has often served as an index of consent (Block; Owens, "Consent"; LaFleur, "Whither Rape"). When analysis of the relation between Luke and his master is rooted in the question of desire, the conversation feeds back into the consent/nonconsent binary. The alternative to the suggestion that Luke "wanted it," in other words, is to propose that he did not desire the sexual encounters he experienced and thus was raped. Yet the claim of rape raises interpretive challenges as well, the foremost of which is that it sidesteps the question of sexual terror as a systemic phenomenon by fixing our attention again on the agency and desires or non-desires of an individual. To be clear, I am neither disputing the fact that Luke was sexually assaulted nor suggesting that any objection he expressed to his assault does not matter. Rather, the point is this: the law's narrow conceptual framing of rape around the question of individual consent cannot apprehend the structural nature of sexual violence under slavery. Accounting for the sexual abuse that Luke and other enslaved people experienced requires grappling not just with individual instances of sexual harm but also with the systemic operation of sexual terror as a technology of enslavement.

Arguing that Luke was raped proves difficult for at least three additional reasons: the gendered framing of rape law, the invisibility of consent in sodomy law, and the legal priority given to slaveholders' property rights. Legal acknowledgment of rape has long been contingent on the formal recognition of a liberal subject who can refuse consent. Historians of sexual violence have demonstrated that early US law tethered the possibility of sexual nonconsent to legal personhood—only someone who possessed legal personhood before the law could advance rape claims (Block; Freedman). Yet, as Saidiya Hartman has shown, enslaved people only acquired legal personhood in the process of being held culpable for crime. Hartman's foundational *Scenes of Subjection* (1997) demonstrates that the rape of the enslaved woman thus constituted a legal oxymoron. Because the enslaved woman could neither give nor refuse consent as a nonperson before the law, the rape of an enslaved woman was legally impossible (Hartman 79–112). As a legal nonperson himself, Luke was equally unable to give and refuse legally recognized consent, but the impossibility of his rape has a slightly different legal genealogy on account of his gender. Rape law throughout the antebellum period presumed the heterosexual nature of the violation it codified as well as the genders of perpetrators and victims: rape named a form of violence visited on a woman by a man. Accusations of rape thus required proof of a nonconsenting legal person gendered as a woman. The legal gendering of rape as "female" injury left male rape out of the question. It was impossible to conceptualize Luke's subjection as sexual assault through the rubric of rape law, for rape law required a female victim.

Luke's rape was legally impossible, owing not only to the gendering of rape law but also to the invisibility of consent in the framing of sodomy law. The idea that men could be subject to sexual violence by other men was legally unthinkable. In North Carolina, where Luke was enslaved, no legal distinction existed between same-sex sexual encounter characterized by consent versus violence. In 1837 the state adopted a statute from British law criminalizing sodomy, buggery, and other forms of sex between men under the rubric of "crimes against nature" (Spence).[11] The law reads: "Any person who shall commit the abominable and detestable crime against nature, not to be named among christians [sic], with either man or beast, shall be adjudged guilty of felony, and shall suffer death without benefit of clergy" (*Revised Statutes* 192). What the phrasing of the legal code makes clear is that sex acts between men constituted legally criminal behaviors, regardless of the forced or voluntary nature of those acts. The notion of a difference between mutually willing same-sex intimacy and same-sex rape was legally inconceivable because all sexual encounters between men were deemed acts of violence and perversion. Lack of consent, in other words, was not legally required to make sex between men a felony. Under the law, there was no such thing as male-male rape—the fact that it involved two men, assault or not, made it a "crime against nature."[12]

Luke's story suggests that the right of the slaveholder to use his property as he saw fit took priority over the legal criminalization of sodomy, thus further contributing to the legal impossibility of Luke's rape. One might think that sodomy's illegality would have led to the prosecution of Luke or his master for "crimes against nature." But Jacobs demonstrates the opposite. Law enforcement got involved but not in the way one might expect: the constable shows up to facilitate, rather than prohibit, Luke's sexual violation. The local officer occupies a puzzling and consistently overlooked presence in the story. According to the anecdote, law enforcement supported the young slaveholder in his persecution of Luke so routinely and openly that everyone around—including Jacobs—seems to have known about it. The same-sex nature of Luke's sexual abuse and the constable's participation in it appear to have been something of an open secret. If most histories of same-sex sexual encounter materialize in the furtive glance, the coded missive, the clandestine rendezvous, and the like, this one proceeds in full view of the neighborhood—there is little surreptitious about it. For as much as the passage on Luke indicates that sex acts between men represented socially reprehensible behavior, it also suggests that the sexualized despotism of slaveholders was so fully normalized that the young master could call the cops to assist him in Luke's abuse and that, when summoned, law enforcement would show up and contribute to rituals of same-sex sexual violence without batting an eye—or, perhaps more accurately, in the name of upholding the law. The story invites readers to consider the possibility that, from the vantage point of the law, the right of the slaveholder to use his property as he saw fit held priority over legal concerns about "crimes against nature" to the extent that the constable could be called on to assist the master in the perpetuation of those "crimes" if it meant safeguarding the master's property rights.

The way the constable gets involved in Luke's situation clues readers in to the fact that the law—through the logic of property rights—justified sexual terror under slavery, including same-sex sexual terror. Jacobs explains early in the narrative that Dr. Flint sanctioned his sexual encroachments against her through recourse to his property claim on her: "He told me I was his property; that I must be subject to his will in all things" (34). Hartman puts it thus: the enslaved woman "existed only as an extension or embodiment of the owner's rights of property" (82). That the sexual violation of Jacobs would be, in Hartman's phrasing, "cloaked as the legitimate use of property" (80) is a fact Flint knew well. And it seems Luke's young master understood this fact too. He knew he could call the constable again and again to aid him in what might have in different contexts been legally incriminating sexual behavior. The arrival of the constable in the young slaveholder's bedroom announces the cloaking of group same-sex sexual assault as the legitimate use of property and as the legal enforcement of the right of the slaveholder to exercise his will over his property. The constable in this sense figures as a metonym for the law—he is an embodiment of antebellum Southern law actively involved in the erasure of Luke's sexual harm under the auspices of defending the slaveholder's legal property rights.

The Fugitive Slave Act implemented at the national level the legal protection of property rights that the constable put into practice at the local level. The seemingly incongruous appearance of a story about same-sex sexual violence in a chapter on the Fugitive Slave Act casts the congressional legislation in an unconventional light, suggesting that the law is an act—that is, both an instantiation and a legal authorization—of sexual terror. The bill extends legal recognition of enslavers' property rights to the borders of the nation and in so doing expands the domain within which slave owners can legally wield sexual terror against those they call their property. Jacobs's narration of Luke's sexual abuse within the context of a larger meditation on the "reign of terror" (245) enacted by the Fugitive Slave Act suggests that the law quite literally widens the territory within which slaveholders can claim the right to use their property as they see fit and turns all Americans into guarantors of that right. Put differently, one might say that, in the wake of the Fugitive Slave Act, all citizens become the constable. Even if they do not participate in the sexual abuse of Luke, they are required by the law to protect his master's right to property by assisting in the capture and return of Luke as a fugitive. Luke's master likely died prior to the passage of the law (when Luke meets Jacobs, he has escaped the trader to whom he was sold after his master's death). Yet, speaking metaphorically, after the passage of the fugitive bill, the reach of the slaveholder extends no longer just through the arm of the constable but through the arm of every citizen in the nation. The Fugitive Slave Act meant that the right of the slaveholder to exercise sexual violence against Luke suddenly held legal protection in the North. And not just that—the law made everyone everywhere custodians of that right.

This legal arrangement of power is sexual terror visible in its systemic form. Sexual terror under slavery was not limited to the "reign of terror" put into effect by the Fugitive Slave Act, but, as *Incidents* suggests, the Fugitive Slave Act did protect slavery as a system of sexual terror. Others have talked about sexual violence in connection to the fugitive slave law, but mostly with respect to enslaved women (Weinbaum, *Afterlife* 61–87; Owens, *Consent* 56–83). Luke's story demonstrates that the sexual terror of slavery extended to all enslaved people. Jacobs's inclusion of the anecdote in the chapter on the Fugitive Slave Act is necessary—otherwise it is too easy to think that the sexual violence Luke experienced is a kind of harm that can be boiled down to something that happened in the South between a master and slave whose individual sexual desires existed at cross purposes. One of the most salient points Jacobs makes through the narration of Luke's subjection is that the sexual violence of slavery must be recognized as sexual terror—a "despotism" of sorts—that was fundamental to the institution of slavery, legally protected by law, and pervasive in its reach regardless of the actions of individual enslavers. *Incidents* proposes that slavery was, structurally, a form of sexual terror. In making this point, Jacobs must be understood as contributing to a long Black feminist genealogy of thought that includes the arguments of theorists like Davis and Roberts.[13] The attention given to sexual terror in this genealogy invites us to shift our historiographical concern away from questions about individual desire and pleasure, consent versus nonconsent, and the legal definition of rape, toward consideration of the systemic formations of sexual terror that cannot be apprehended within these frameworks.

Sexual Terror and the Question of Reproduction

Luke's story compels contemporary readers to confront questions about the relation between sexual and reproductive violence anew. The inclination within recent feminist scholarship on slavery has been to frame sexual violence as an instrument of enslaved women's forced reproduction in both biological and social senses. In a profound reorientation of the dominant historiography, which has long neglected gender as a framework for historical analysis, the work of scholars, including Morgan, Weinbaum, Turner, and others, demonstrates that the history of chattel bondage is a history of enslaved women's reproductive exploitation. Explicating how slavery reproduced itself through the expropriation of the labor of Black women's wombs, this work has tended to examine sexual violence predominantly through the lens of reproduction. New research has begun to take this scholarship in a different direction, focusing away from procreative sexual violence against enslaved women to theorize other sexual practices under slavery, including concubinage, the so-called "fancy" trade, and informal marital arrangements between masters and slaves. Yet this work, too, figures sexual violence largely in relation to its reproductive expediency, zeroing in on the socially rather than biologically reproductive instrumentality of enslaved women's sexual subjection (Finley). One of the central questions the existing scholarship raises is whether all forms of sexual subjection under slavery can be understood through reproductive paradigms. What I wish to propose through a further reading of Luke's story is this: *Incidents* suggests that the sexual terror of slavery entails forms of violence that both contribute to and exceed slavery's reproductive imperative.

It should not be missed that sexual terror against Luke occurs in the context of his caregiving labor. According to the narrative, Luke's sexual abuse begins at the point he is appointed as caretaker for his master. Describing the slaveholder, Jacobs writes: "The fact that he was entirely dependent on Luke's care, and was obliged to be tended like an infant, . . . seemed only to increase his irritability and cruelty. As he lay there on his bed, . . . he took into his head the strangest freaks of despotism" (247). The "strangest freaks" mentioned here constitute one of the strongest indications of Luke's sexual abuse (Abdur-Rahman, "'Strangest Freaks'"). The passage suggests that these "freaks" arise in consequence of the slaveholder's slackening grip on dominance. Jacobs writes that sickness lowers the slaveholder to being "tended like an infant"—a comparison that strikingly evokes the waning of his physical capacity and appearance of authority. The essence of the analogy likening the master to an infant inheres in their shared condition of total dependence on another, a state from which the master increasingly reasserts his power over Luke through sexualized acts of subjection.

Luke's labor—a form of caretaking—is socially reproductive. The infant reference calls to mind the labor of the wet nurse and the nanny, roles frequently performed by enslaved women caregivers in white households throughout the antebellum period.[14] One of the most enduring interventions of the literature on social reproduction has been the insistence on wages for such labor (at least when it is performed by married white women), including housework, care work, and other unremunerated forms of socially reproductive labor (Dalla Costa and Jones; Federici 15–22). The streetside conversation Jacobs shares with Luke on encountering him in New York suggests that they each understood his caregiving as a form of unpaid labor and in a sense anticipates the feminist wages-for-housework argument. During the conversation, Luke explains that he has taken money that belonged to his master in order to carry himself to Canada. Defending his actions, Luke proposes that he holds a "right" to the money as payment for "workin all my days" (248). Reflecting on Luke's rationale, Jacobs concurs: "I agree with poor, ignorant, much-abused Luke, in thinking he had a *right* to that money, as a portion of his unpaid wages" (248). The text in this way frames Luke's subjection as uncompensated care labor. Accordingly, it makes sense to read the sexual abuse of Luke as an instrument of his reproductive labor exploitation—to a point. In his bedside appointment, Luke engages in a type of work social reproduction theorists have long identified as unwaged domestic labor that contributes to the reproduction of the social organization of power under capitalism (Dalla Costa and Jones; Fortunati; Mies; Dalla Costa; Glenn; Weeks; Federici; Bhattacharya; Fraser). One might read sexual terror against Luke therefore as a means of extracting socially reproductive labor from him and of reinforcing his role as a reproductive laborer.

Yet, in my reading of *Incidents*, this argument misses the point of Luke's story. The anecdote, as I see it, is not ultimately about slavery's reproduction but about slavery's sexual terror. As Luke's case suggests, the sexual violence of slavery contributed to the perpetuation of the institution and functioned as a powerful tool for compelling enslaved people to work—but it cannot be exhaustively explained by the need for slavery to reproduce itself.[15] Jacobs's use of *despotism* to describe the young master's relationship to power is instructive here. The term combines implications of both absolute control and rule through the exercise of arbitrary cruelty, tyranny, and force. The term evokes meanings similar to *reign of terror*—the phrase Jacobs uses to characterize the implementation of the Fugitive Slave Act. The story of Luke, in other words, challenges readers to conceptualize slavery as a structure of domination that orders the social through the deployment of acts of terror that include reproductive sexual assault as well as sexual predations that possess no immediately discernible procreative or socially reproductive outcome. The sexual terror of slavery is, in Jacobs's account, an instrument of domination, not just an instrument of reproduction. If nothing else, Luke's story offers sexual terror as a rubric expansive enough to grapple with sexual harms that both fall within and exceed the scope of the reproductive.[16]

Part of what makes *Incidents* so challenging as an account of sexual violence under slavery is that it appears to be saying two contradictory things: sexual terror is gendered and sexual terror has no gender. On the one hand, Luke's story disrupts the conventional framing of sexual violence in rape law as a form of female-gendered harm. The portrait of violence Jacobs offers through the passage on Luke suggests that sexual terror cannot be understood in singly gendered terms as female; rather, it is visited on all enslaved people regardless of gender. Yet, on the other, the bulk of *Incidents* represents a pointed critique of the gendered nature of sexual harm under slavery. One of the text's most frequently cited lines, which Jacobs expresses on giving birth to a daughter, gestures to the unique forms of sexual violence enslaved women and girls faced: "Slavery is terrible for men; but it is far more terrible for women" (100). The truth of this line is borne out by the narrative, as Jacobs details from its earliest chapters to the last ones the relentless sexual threat she endures from Dr. Flint. The lesson of the text in this respect is that sexual violence under slavery possessed specifically gendered dimensions and that enslaved women encountered sexual terrors that enslaved men did not.

The apparent contradiction between these two propositions—that sexual terror is gendered and that sexual terror has no gender—is a false paradox. What Jacobs shows readers through the inclusion of Luke's story in her own is that both are true simultaneously. *Incidents* makes it clear that slaveholders wielded sexual terror against all enslaved people and that doing so buttressed their domination of those in bondage. At the same time, it also shows that the law of maternal descent gave sexual violence against enslaved women distinctly gendered meanings.[17] As slavery took hold in the British colonies, the logic of maternal descent solidified into law, suturing the procreative capacities of the enslaved woman to the reproduction of legal unfreedom and racial Blackness. By the time of Jacobs's enslavement in North Carolina, this rule of heritability, the legal doctrine of *partus sequitur ventrem* (Latin for "offspring follows the belly"), had become ubiquitous in the North American context (Morgan, "*Partus*"). Jacobs reminds readers of this often. When as a young woman she falls in love with a free Black carpenter, her dream of happy marriage is overshadowed by the reality that their children, through her maternity, would be enslaved (52). When Flint threatens to sell her children, Jacobs laments that the law indeed protected his right to do so, for they inherited her unfree legal status: "slaveholders have been cunning enough to enact that 'the child shall follow the condition of the *mother*,' not the father; thus taking care that licentiousness shall not interfere with avarice" (99). Sexual violence against Jacobs carried the potential to reproduce enslavement through her maternity.

The same cannot be said of sexual violence against Luke. Legal unfreedom would not be inherited through his paternity. The sexual abuse visited
on him by his master carried no potential to transfer his unfree legal status
onto offspring. Most important for the point at hand is not that his same-sex
sexual subjection could not lead to the birth of children but rather that his
sexual abuse could not pass on his status as a slave to future generations,
since his procreative labor power was neither socially nor legally endowed
with the capacity to do so.[18] Rather than trying to determine how Luke's
same-sex sexual abuse differed from the sexual violation of enslaved women,
then, *Incidents* suggests that perhaps it makes most sense to flip this formulation around and consider how the procreative sexual subjection of enslaved
women differed from all other forms of sexual terror under bondage. Enslaved
women's procreative labor served as the keystone of the entire social logic of
capitalist property relations under slavery. What mattered was the fact that
the enslaved woman necessarily passed racial Blackness and chattel status
on to her progeny—that she would, in Hazel V. Carby's words, give "birth
to property and, directly, to capital itself in the form of slaves" (25). One
could argue that slavery therefore did not, from a purely theoretical stand-
point, require the sexual exploitation of enslaved men—at least not in the
same way as it required the sexual exploitation of enslaved women—to reproduce slavery's relations of property, kinship, and unfreedom.[19] That the
wombs of enslaved women held the legal capacity to transmit unfreedom dis-
tinguished the procreative sexual subjection of enslaved women from other
instances of sexual terror under slavery, including the abuse of enslaved men
like Luke. The distinction inhered in the specificity of the gendered social
meanings attributed to enslaved women's reproductive labor power.

By the time of Jacobs's writing, antislavery writers had started to define
the sexual violence of bondage in relation to the reproductive exploitation of
enslaved women. In his 1853 treatise on the laws of antebellum slavery, legal
theorist and abolitionist William Goodell bluntly articulates an objection to
bondage that antislavery activists had by that point rehearsed for decades:
"Another prominent use of slave property, in the case of females capable of
being mothers, is that of *breeders* of slaves" (82). The observation was meant
to incriminate slavery on the grounds that it deployed sexual violence for the
generation of profit through forced reproduction, for the birth of enslaved
children not only expanded the real property of slaveholders but also afforded them the opportunity to sell enslaved offspring for cash. Countless
objections to the profitability of enslaved women's sexual subjugation appear
in the antislavery record. The abolitionist contention might be summarized thus: slavery incentivizes masters' sexual relations with enslaved

women because such relations lead to the expansion of slaveholders' capital; therefore, slavery must be ended. For abolitionists, the sexual incentive baked into the structure of slavery constituted an offensive moral problem that they denounced loudly and continuously. In doing so they discursively solidified the idea that the sexual violence of slavery was equivalent to reproductive sexual exploitation.

In telling Luke's story, Jacobs challenges readers to conceptualize sexual violence more capaciously. The anecdote encourages us to see sexual violence under slavery as an instrument of domination rather than just as a means to a reproductive end. It shows that all enslaved people faced sexual terror even as sexual terror against enslaved women was uniquely freighted with the implications of maternal descent law. Ultimately, in folding the story of Luke into her own, Jacobs participates in an antebellum discursive struggle over how sexual violence should be defined: she advances an unconventional account of what should count as sexual violation, how we should understand its relation to reproductive exploitation, and who should be considered subject to sexual terror under slavery.

Fugitivity as Protest

Fugitivity in *Incidents* constitutes a protest against slavery's order of property rights and the sexual terror that those property rights authorized. It would not be quite right to say that fugitivity in the text represents a simple objection to ownership on the part of Luke and Jacobs, although it is true that in taking flight from bondage both Jacobs and Luke refused to be owned. By "protest" I mean embodied and discursive articulations of alternatives to dominant formations of property and ownership, alternatives that constitute the basis of what Cedric J. Robinson characterizes as the "Black radical tradition." Put another way, I understand protest as the expression of radical ways of being, knowing, and relating to others that are distinct from and beyond the sphere of what is possible within social and economic orders defined by liberal arrangements of property and the logics of European colonial modernity.[20] Protest, as I use it, takes a range of forms.[21] Robinson argues in *Black Marxism* that, from the sixteenth to the nineteenth centuries, a radical tradition of insurgency against bondage cohered through enslaved people's disparate practices of fugitivity, marronage, and revolt. These practices, according to Robinson, reveal a collective insistence on the preservation of alternatives, rooted in African traditions of thought, to racial capitalism, European liberalism, and the logic of property rights that subtends both. For Robinson it is precisely the pervasiveness of instances of fugitivity like Luke's and Jacobs's that gives the historian a window onto the fact of the

Black radical tradition's existence. Elaborating Robinson's notion of fugitivity, Fred Moten characterizes it as the enactment of "a fundamental dispossession of ownership as such so that owning is, itself, disowned" (343). Running away is thus not merely backlash on the part of Luke or Jacobs to being owned or sexually terrorized. It represents a form of protest: at once a deliberate unraveling of the property right as the ordering principle of social relations and an improvisation that calls into historical possibility different ways of imagining and living how to be in the world.

What *Incidents* suggests is that fugitivity represents protest not just against slavery but also against the sexual terror that constituted it. Robinson largely neglects questions of gender and sexuality in his analysis of Black radicalism, yet the point that enslaved women contributed uniquely and foundationally to the shape of the Black radical tradition has been well substantiated. According to Moten, when enslaved women took charge of their procreative capacities, their actions represented "engagement in forms of reappropriative challenge to the extraction of surplus from their bodies" (334)—forms of reappropriative challenge that unsettled the subjugation of their reproductive capacities under slavery. In her study of slavery and its legacies of reproductive extraction, Weinbaum takes this argument further:

> In resisting sexual assault, committing infanticide, attacking and sometimes murdering their abusers, becoming fugitives, aborting or preventing unwanted pregnancies, or electing to mother their children . . . , enslaved women . . . refused to participate in the reproduction of the slave system, in the smooth reproduction of the relations of production, and in the (re)production of the human commodities that sustained it. (*Afterlife* 79)

What I wish to draw into additional and explicit focus is that fugitivity entailed protest not only against reproductive sexual violence but also against the wide range of sexual abuses—reproductive and otherwise—that Jacobs elevates for consideration through the rubric of sexual terror. The enactment of Black radical alternatives to slavery through fugitivity on Jacobs's part and Luke's is the enactment of alternatives to a regime of terror that turned on the relentless reproductive and nonprocreative sexual domination of enslaved people.

For Jacobs the sexual terror of slavery is rooted in the liberal organization of property—which she rejects unequivocally. As has been widely discussed in criticism on *Incidents*, Jacobs disdains the purchase of her freedom at the end of the narrative. Though her grandmother had offered to part with "all she had" (193) to buy her freedom, Jacobs swears never to accept her grandmother's money in exchange for liberty: "I resolved that not another cent of her hard earnings should be spent to pay rapacious slaveholders for what they call their property" (193). On reaching the North, Jacobs again confronts the chance to gain freedom through purchase. Jacobs receives a letter from Flint's daughter containing an ultimatum demanding that she return or pay for her freedom. Jacobs withholds a reply but shares her reaction to the letter with readers: "It seemed not only hard, but unjust, to pay for myself. I could not possibly regard myself as a piece of property" (240). In the final pages of the text, Mrs. Bruce, her employer, offers to pay for Jacobs and Jacobs refuses, stating her intent instead to set off for California like her brother (256–57). Jacobs feels shock and indignation on learning that Mrs. Bruce has purchased her freedom against her wishes: "So I was *sold* at last! A human being *sold* in the free city of New York! The bill of sale is on record, and future generations will learn from it that women were articles of traffic in New York, late in the nineteenth century of the Christian religion. . . . I well know the value of that bit of paper; but much as I love freedom, I do not like to look upon it" (257). The emphasis Jacobs twice places on the word *sold* suggests her extreme displeasure with her reduction to the status of property in the process of being freed through a market transaction. Pursuit of freedom through fugitivity was likely preferable to Jacobs over freedom through purchase if for no other reason than the fact that it skirted the capitalist process of commodification and the system of liberal property rights—the same system of property rights that Flint used to justify her sexual subjugation.

Perhaps Luke chose fugitivity for the same reason. The property rights of his master authorized sexual terror against him through the arm of both his master and the constable. Based on his story, Luke certainly appears to have favored fugitivity over freedom through purchase. He may have been able to buy his way out of slavery, for, when he runs into Jacobs, he has amassed enough money to carry himself to Canada. Jacobs asks whether he needs funds for his trip, and he responds in the negative, explaining that when his master died, he placed "some of his bills" (248) in a pair of trousers. After his master's burial, Luke asks for the pants and receives them, the money still pocketed away. Luke attests to a "mighty hard time" (248) keeping this money from the trader but asserts that he accomplished the feat. Yet, despite being in possession of money, Luke opts for flight. It is ultimately a matter of conjecture whether Luke harbored the same antipathy as Jacobs toward buying freedom, and it is unclear whether he possessed enough cash or even the opportunity to buy himself. But the fact that he ran suggests that he saw fugitivity as his best shot at liberation. Addressing Jacobs's concern that he might be recaptured under the Fugitive Slave Act, Luke explains that the danger of seizure is less immediate for him than it is for Jacobs, since traders were unlikely to track fugitives if they could not expect to apprehend them straightaway (248). Escaping the trader gave Luke a chance to minimize the probability of his recapture, and he took it. Yet, whatever the expediency of flight for Luke, one might also read into his fugitivity a statement of protest against the property rights that served as the basis of sexual terror against him. In this sense, as divergent as their stories are, Luke and Jacobs share one thing in common: they protested their subjection to the sexual terror of slavery through fugitivity.

Conclusion

Rather than presenting an account of sexual violence that frames it as a stable, transhistorical object of analysis, *Incidents* presents sexual violence as both a material fact of enslavement and as a contested category of knowledge in flux throughout the antebellum period. The text's representation of sexual violence indexes it as a site of urgent social, legal, and political struggle over who should be considered subject to sexual terror, how its relation to reproduction should be understood, and how sexual abuse should be defined. Readers of the text might thus understand the project of *Incidents* to be in large part one of revising and stretching the day's accounts of sexual harm so as to call into view the ways in which enslaved people—Luke and Jacobs included—suffered sexual terror and protested it. The text remains today one of the most salient accounts of sexual violence under slavery. It has stakes for contemporary historiography in that it pushes theorizing of sexual violence beyond its current boundaries in the existing scholarship on slavery, inviting us to understand how the deployment of sexual abuse under slavery exceeded its reproductive instrumentality and operated as a structure of sexual terror against all enslaved people.

For the bulk of this essay, I have focused on the stakes of Luke's story for the feminist historiography on slavery, but in closing I want to briefly consider the stakes of the anecdote for scholarship on the history of sexuality. Though they cannot be exhaustively answered here, Luke's story raises a set of lingering questions: What might the history of sexuality look like if it started with the account of Luke's abuse rather than instances of mutual desire and romantic intimacy? How might Luke's story rewrite what we think we know about the history of sexuality? How might existing histories of sexuality expand and change when routed through archives of racial enslavement? Much of what makes the story of Luke so profound is that it holds the potential to rework foundational and long-standing premises in the historiography on sexuality. Despite Michel Foucault's famous rejection of the repressive hypothesis in the *History of Sexuality, Vol. 1* (1976), the idea that the history of same-sex sexuality is characterized by archival loss, destruction, erasure, and paucity remains dominant (Marshall and Tortorici; Arondekar, *Abundance*). In the opening line of the introduction to his field-defining documentary history of lesbians and gay men in the United States, Jonathan Ned Katz writes: "We have been the silent minority, the silenced minority—invisible women, invisible men" (*Gay American History* 1). Though penned almost fifty years ago, the sentiment of this line lingers in the study of sexuality's history. Put simply, the existing historiography still tends to presume that cases of same-sex sexuality are few and far between in the archive, hard to find because they have been silenced, speak in code, or are utterly lost to history. The enduring documentary impulse in the field betrays this assumption—the aim is often to recover those stories of same-sex sexuality that can be retrieved from the violence of history and to grieve those that cannot.

Yet the anecdote on Luke suggests that perhaps past instances of same-sex sexual encounter are not so hard to find. Indeed, if Luke's story is to be believed, same-sex sexual terror was a constitutive feature of racial bondage. Scholars of slavery have in recent years begun to document the overwhelming presence of same-sex sexual violence (and protest against it) in the archives of racial enslavement. What they have shown is that such abuse was pervasive, out in the open, and quotidian: mistresses wielded sexual power over enslaved women, and masters asserted sexual dominance over enslaved men (Tinsley, "Black Atlantic"; Glymph; Scott; Foster, "Sexual Abuse," *Rethinking Rufus*; Abdur-Rahman, "'Strangest Freaks,'" *Against the Closet*; Woodard; Fuentes; Martínez, "Sex"; Downs; Aidoo; Berry and Harris; Jones-Rogers; Johnson). Perhaps the challenge for the historiography of sexuality, then, is not to track down whatever rare examples of same-sex romance exist in the conventional archives of sexuality but to start looking in a different place: the archives of slavery. Doing so will require reckoning with the widespread presumption that the central agenda of the historian of sexuality is to unearth stories of liberal empowerment that reveal how some people expressed nonnormative love, mutual desire, erotic pleasure, and affective intimacy despite disciplinary regulation, criminalization, and moral censure. The abuse of Luke raises the possibility that perhaps same-sex sexual encounters in the past are not so hidden and not so celebratory. Everyone in the neighborhood—including Jacobs—seems to have known what happened to Luke. The constable participated in it. By reading archives of slavery as archives of sexuality, we might get a different account of sexuality's history as one of sexual terror and racial violence.[22] In this way, the anecdote on Luke suggests the need to revisit—and rethink—the stories we tell about the history of sexuality. ▪

Caleb Knapp is a Cassius Marcellus Clay Postdoctoral Associate in the Department of History at Yale University and is affiliated with the Yale Research Initiative on the History of Sexualities. He is currently working on a book manuscript that examines how antislavery discourse contributed to the development of modern sexual knowledges.

ACKNOWLEDGMENTS

I am indebted to Alys Eve Weinbaum for generous, consistent, and close engagement with my work and for help articulating the arguments of this essay at key moments in its production. Thanks also to Jennifer L. Morgan and Alys Eve Weinbaum for feedback on countless versions of this article as well as to Sasha Turner, who offered me comments at an early stage of writing. I am grateful to Greta LaFleur, Michael Raka, Chandan Reddy, Jey Saung, Stephanie Smallwood, the members of the Reproducing Racial Capitalism workshop, and the editors of *History of the Present* for engaged feedback and support.

NOTES

1   *Incidents* identifies people using pseudonyms. Jacobs refers to herself as Linda Brent throughout the text. Literary scholarship on *Incidents*, however, tends to identify Jacobs by her real name while maintaining the usage of pseudonyms for everyone else. I stick to this convention and, for clarity, provide historical names (when available) on introducing pseudonyms.

2   Punishment for noncompliance included the possibility of fines totaling $1,000 and up to six months of jail time (Quarles 197–222; Sinha 500–542).

3   This evidentiary turn has become a focal point of inquiry in the fields of queer history and the history of sexuality. For work that considers the origins and stakes of this turn, see Arondekar, *For the Record* and *Abundance*; Martínez, "Archives," "Sex"; Arondekar et al., "Queering"; Marshall and Tortorici.

4   Throughout this essay I employ the term *same-sex* with a caveat, using it to name sexual relations between men or between women while acknowledging that sex is not a biological marker of gender, that sex and gender are fluid and not fixed in the body, and that same-sex relations would not have been described as such by people living during the antebellum period. Nonetheless, taking it with a grain of salt, I prefer *same-sex* over terms less apt and perhaps more obfuscating (such as *queer* or *homosexual*) to distinguish, for example, sexual terror visited on enslaved men by masters (something Luke experiences) from sexual terror visited on enslaved women by masters (something Jacobs experiences).

5   My usage of *enslaved community* is an adaptation of historian John W. Blassingame's well-known phrase "slave community" (Blassingame).

6   On this point, I have found the essay by SJ Zhang in this volume particularly instructive.

7   My reading of Davis is indebted to Alys Eve Weinbaum's reading of Davis in "Gendering the General Strike" and *The Afterlife of Reproductive Slavery* (especially 61–87).

8   My thinking on sexual violence as an instrument of terror has been additionally shaped by Sarah Haley's notion of gendered racial terror in *No Mercy Here*.

9   My account of Luke's situation is in conversation with Emily A. Owens's reading of *Incidents* as a text about sexual terror under slavery. Owens focuses on the sexual terror to which Jacobs is subject. Here I draw into focus the sexual terrorism Luke experiences (*Consent in the Presence of Force*, 56–83).

10 I pick this phrasing up from Owens (*Consent in the Presence of Force*, 56–83). For different takes on the possibility of erotic pleasure in the context of enslavement, see Scott; Tinsley, *Thiefing*; Johnson; Lindsey and Johnson.

11 In practice the law did not pertain to women, as women were not considered capable of committing sodomy (Spence 316).

12 For a detailed history of North Carolina's "crime against nature" law (a version of which remains in effect today), see Spence; Eskridge.

13 I thank Jessica Marie Johnson for help on this point.

14 The essay by Halle-Mackenzie Ashby and Jessica Marie Johnson in this volume has been especially helpful for my thinking on Black women's caregiving in the context of slavery and freedom.

15 In troubling social reproduction as a generalizable explanatory theoretical framework, I have found the article by Laura Briggs in this special issue particularly helpful.

16 In thinking through this point, I have found the essay by Rickie Solinger in this volume particularly instructive. Part of what I read Solinger to be illustrating is the fact that the sexual is not reducible to the reproductive, even as the reproductive is a pivotal feature of the sexual within formations of white supremacy.

17 Alys Eve Weinbaum's essay on "ungendering" as the fulcrum of primitive accumulation in this special issue and Hortense Spillers's essay on "ungendering" ("Mama's Baby") have been enormously instructive for my thinking on this point. I consider the work of gender in the context of sexual terror to be different from, but complementary to, the processes of "ungendering" that Spillers and Weinbaum describe. I favor the language of "gendered and having no gender" when describing sexual terror to highlight the ways that sexual violence operates both as a tool for the reproductive subjugation of enslaved women in particular and as a tool for the domination of enslaved people in general, regardless of gender. What I wish to emphasize with my formulation is that these deployments of sexual violence exist simultaneously and without contradiction in North American formations of enslavement.

18 I have found Sigrid Vertommen's essay in this volume especially helpful for thinking through differences in the political stakes of nonprocreative sex in different historical contexts.

19 I thank Sasha Turner for helping me appreciate and put words around this point.

20 I thank Alys Eve Weinbaum for suggesting "protest" as the rubric through which to name the insurgency against sexual terror that *Incidents* articulates.

21 Here I join the other essays in this volume in the effort to proliferate the categories through which rebellion against slavery and its legacies can be identified and analyzed.

22 My thinking on this point is inspired by and in dialogue with LaFleur's argument in "Whither Rape."

WORKS CITED

Abdur-Rahman, Aliyyah I. *Against the Closet: Black Political Longing and the Erotics of Race.* Durham, NC: Duke University Press, 2012.

Abdur-Rahman, Aliyyah I. "'The Strangest Freaks of Despotism': Queer Sexuality in Antebellum African American Slave Narratives." *African American Review* 40, no. 2 (2006): 223–37.

Aidoo, Lamonte. *Slavery Unseen: Sex, Power, and Violence in Brazilian History.* Durham, NC: Duke University Press, 2018.

Arondekar, Anjali. *Abundance: Sexuality's History.* Durham, NC: Duke University Press, 2023.

Arondekar, Anjali. *For the Record: On Sexuality and the Colonial Archive in India.* Durham, NC: Duke University Press, 2009.

Arondekar, Anjali, Ann Cvetkovich, Christina B. Hanhardt, Regina Kunzel, Tavia Nyong'o, Juana María Rodríguez, and Susan Stryker. "Queering Archives: A Roundtable Discussion." Compiled by Daniel Marshall, Kevin P. Murphy, and Zeb Tortorici. *Radical History Review*, no. 122 (2015): 211–31.

Benemann, William E. *Male-Male Intimacy in Early America: Beyond Romantic Friendships.* New York: Routledge, 2006.

Berry, Daina Ramey. *The Price for Their Pound of Flesh: The Value of the Enslaved, from Womb to Grave, in the Building of a Nation.* Boston: Beacon, 2017.

Berry, Daina Ramey, and Leslie M. Harris, eds. *Sexuality and Slavery: Reclaiming Intimate Histories in the Americas.* Athens: University of Georgia Press, 2018.

Bhattacharya, Tithi. "Introduction: Mapping Social Reproduction Theory." In *Social Reproduction Theory: Remapping Class, Recentering Oppression,* edited by Tithi Battacharya, 1–20. London: Pluto, 2017.

Blassingame, John W. *The Slave Community: Plantation Life in the Antebellum South.* 1972; rev. and enlarged ed., New York: Oxford University Press, 1979.

Block, Sharon. *Rape and Sexual Power in Early America.* Chapel Hill: University of North Carolina Press, 2006.

Bronski, Michael. *A Queer History of the United States.* Boston: Beacon, 2011.

Carby, Hazel V. *Reconstructing Womanhood: The Emergence of the Afro-American Woman Novelist.* New York: Oxford University Press, 1987.

Dalla Costa, Mariarosa. "Capitalism and Reproduction." *Capitalism, Nature, Socialism* 7, no. 4 (1996): 111–20.

Dalla Costa, Mariarosa, and Selma Jones. *Women and the Subversion of Community.* Bristol, UK: Falling Wall, 1973.

Davis, Adrienne. "'Don't Let Nobody Bother Yo' Principle': The Sexual Economy of Slavery." In *Sister Circle: Black Women and Work,* edited by Sharon Harley and the Black Women and Work Collective, 103–27. New Brunswick, NJ: Rutgers University Press, 2002.

Davis, Angela. "Reflections on the Black Woman's Role in the Community of Slaves." *Black Scholar* 3, no. 4 (1971): 2–15.

Davis, Angela Y. *Women, Race, and Class.* New York: Vintage, 1983.

Downs, Jim. "With Only a Trace: Same-Sex Sexual Desire and Violence on Slave Plantations, 1607–1865." In *Connexions: Histories of Race and Sex in North America*, edited by
Jennifer Brier, Jim Downs, and Jennifer L. Morgan, 15–31. Urbana: University of Illinois Press, 2016.

Eskridge, William N. Jr. *Gaylaw: Challenging the Apartheid of the Closet*. Cambridge, MA:
Harvard University Press, 1999.

Faderman, Lillian. *Surpassing the Love of Men: Romantic Love and Friendship between Women
from the Renaissance to the Present*. New York: William Morrow, 1981.

Federici, Silvia. *Revolution at Point Zero: Housework, Reproduction, and Feminist Struggle*.
Oakland, CA: PM, 2012.

Finley, Alexandra J. *An Intimate Economy: Enslaved Women, Work, and America's Domestic
Slave Trade*. Chapel Hill: University of North Carolina Press, 2020.

Fortunati, Leopoldina. *The Arcane of Reproduction: Housework, Prostitution, Labor, and Capital*. Translated by Hilary Creek, edited by Jim Fleming. Brooklyn: Autonomedia,
1995.

Foster, Thomas A. *Rethinking Rufus: Sexual Violations of Enslaved Men*. Athens: University of
Georgia Press, 2019.

Foster, Thomas A. "The Sexual Abuse of Black Men under Slavery." *Journal of the History
of Sexuality* 20, no. 3 (2011): 445–64.

Foucault, Michel. *An Introduction*. Vol. 1 of *The History of Sexuality*. Translated by Robert
Hurley. 4 vols. New York: Vintage, 1990.

Fraser, Nancy. "Crisis of Care: On the Social-Reproductive Contradictions of Contemporary Capitalism." In *Social Reproduction Theory: Remapping Class, Recentering Oppression*, edited by Tithi Bhattacharya, 21–36. London: Pluto, 2017.

Freedman, Estelle B. *Redefining Rape: Sexual Violence in the Era of Suffrage and Segregation*.
Cambridge, MA: Harvard University Press, 2013.

Fuentes, Marisa J. *Dispossessed Lives: Enslaved Women, Violence, and the Archive*. Philadelphia: University of Pennsylvania Press, 2016.

Genovese, Eugene D. *Roll, Jordan, Roll: The World the Slaves Made*. New York: Vintage, 1976.

Glenn, Evelyn Nakano. *Forced to Care: Coercion and Caregiving in America*. Cambridge, MA:
Harvard University Press, 2010.

Glymph, Thavolia. *Out of the House of Bondage: The Transformation of the Plantation Household*. New York: Cambridge University Press, 2008.

Goodell, William. *The American Slave Code in Theory and Practice: Its Distinctive Features
Shown by Its Statutes, Judicial Decisions, and Illustrative Facts*. New York: American and
Foreign Anti-Slavery Society, 1853.

Haley, Sarah. *No Mercy Here: Gender, Punishment, and the Making of Jim Crow Modernity*.
Chapel Hill: University of North Carolina Press, 2016.

Hartman, Saidiya. *Scenes of Subjection: Terror, Slavery, and Self-Making in Nineteenth-
Century America*. New York: Oxford University Press, 1997.

Hine, Darlene C. "Female Slave Resistance: The Economics of Sex." *Western Journal of
Black Studies* 3, no. 2 (1979): 123–27.

Hine, Darlene Clark. "Rape and the Inner Lives of Black Women in the Middle West."
Signs 4, no. 4 (1989): 912–20.

hooks, bell. *Ain't I a Woman: Black Women and Feminism*. New York: Routledge, 2015.

Jacobs, Harriet A. *Incidents in the Life of a Slave Girl, Written by Herself*. 1861; enlarged ed., edited by Jean Fagan Yellin. Cambridge, MA: Belknap Press of Harvard University Press, 2009.

Johnson, Jessica Marie. *Wicked Flesh: Black Women, Intimacy, and Freedom in the Atlantic World*. Philadelphia: University of Pennsylvania Press, 2020.

Jones-Rogers, Stephanie. *They Were Her Property: White Women as Slave Owners in the American South*. New Haven, CT: Yale University Press, 2019.

Katz, Jonathan Ned. *Gay American History: Lesbians and Gay Men in the U.S.A.* New York: Harper Colophon, 1976.

Katz, Jonathan Ned. *Gay/Lesbian Almanac: A New Documentary*. New York: Harper & Row, 1983.

Katz, Jonathan Ned. *Love Stories: Sex between Men before Homosexuality*. Chicago: University of Chicago Press, 2001.

LaFleur, Greta. *The Natural History of Sexuality in Early America*. Baltimore, MD: Johns Hopkins University Press, 2018.

LaFleur, Greta. "Whither Rape in the History of Sexuality? Thinking Sex Alongside Slavery's Normative Violence." *Journal of the History of Sexuality*, 33, no. 2 (forthcoming 2024).

Lindsey, Treva B., and Jessica Marie Johnson. "Searching for Climax: Black Erotic Lives in Slavery and Freedom." *Meridians* 12, no. 2 (2014): 169–95.

Marshall, Daniel, and Zeb Tortorici. "(Re)Turning to the Queer Archives." Introduction to *Turning Archival: The Life of the Historical in Queer Studies*, edited by Daniel Marshall and Zeb Tortorici, 1–31. Durham, NC: Duke University Press, 2022.

Martínez, María Elena. "Archives, Bodies, and Imagination: The Case of Juana Aguilar and Queer Approaches to History, Sexuality, and Politics." *Radical History Review*, no. 120 (2014): 159–82.

Martínez, María Elena. "Sex and the Colonial Archive: The Case of 'Mariano' Aguilera." *Hispanic American Historical Review* 96, no. 3 (2016): 421–43.

Mies, Maria. *Patriarchy and Accumulation on a World Scale: Women in the International Division of Labour*. Atlantic Highlands, NJ: Zed Books, 1986.

Morgan, Jennifer L. *Laboring Women: Reproduction and Gender in New World Slavery*. Philadelphia: University of Pennsylvania Press, 2004.

Morgan, Jennifer L. "*Partus Sequitur Ventrem*: Law, Race, and Reproduction." *Small Axe*, no. 55 (2018): 1–17.

Morgan, Jennifer L. *Reckoning with Slavery: Gender, Kinship, and Capitalism in the Early Black Atlantic*. Durham, NC: Duke University Press, 2021.

Moten, Fred. "Uplift and Criminality." In *Next to the Color Line: Gender, Sexuality, and W. E. B. Du Bois*, edited by Susan Gillman and Alys Eve Weinbaum, 317–49. Minneapolis: University of Minnesota Press, 2007.

Owens, Emily A. "Consent." *differences* 30, no. 1 (2019): 148–56.

Owens, Emily A. *Consent in the Presence of Force: Sexual Violence and Black Women's Survival in Antebellum New Orleans*. Chapel Hill: University of North Carolina Press, 2023.

Painter, Nell Irvin. *Southern History across the Color Line*. Chapel Hill: University of North Carolina Press, 2002.

Quarles, Benjamin. *Black Abolitionists*. New York: Da Capo, 1969.

The Revised Statutes of the State of North Carolina. Vol. 1. Raleigh: Turner & Hughes, 1837.

Roberts, Dorothy. *Killing the Black Body: Race, Reproduction, and the Meaning of Liberty.* New York: Vintage, 1999.

Robinson, Cedric J. *Black Marxism: The Making of the Black Radical Tradition.* Chapel Hill: University of North Carolina Press, 1983.

Rupp, Leila J. *Sapphistries: A Global History of Love between Women.* New York: New York University Press, 2009.

Schwartz, Marie Jenkins. *Birthing a Slave: Motherhood and Medicine in the Antebellum South.* Cambridge, MA: Harvard University Press, 2006.

Scott, Darieck. *Extravagant Abjection: Blackness, Power, and Sexuality in the African American Imagination.* New York: New York University Press, 2010.

Sinha, Manisha. *The Slave's Cause: A History of Abolition.* New Haven, CT: Yale University Press, 2016.

Spence, James R. "The Law of Crime against Nature." *North Carolina Law Review* 32, no. 3 (1954): 312–24.

Spillers, Hortense J. "Mama's Baby, Papa's Maybe: An American Grammar Book." *Diacritics* 17, no. 2 (1987): 64–81.

Stampp, Kenneth M. *The Peculiar Institution: Slavery in the Ante-Bellum South.* New York: Vintage, 1989.

Tinsley, Omise'eke Natasha. "Black Atlantic, Queer Atlantic: Queer Imaginings of the Middle Passage." *GLQ* 14, nos. 2–3 (2008): 191–215.

Tinsley, Omise'eke Natasha. *Thiefing Sugar: Eroticism between Women in Caribbean Literature.* Durham, NC: Duke University Press, 2010.

Turner, Sasha. *Contested Bodies: Pregnancy, Childrearing, and Slavery in Jamaica.* Philadelphia: University of Pennsylvania Press, 2017.

Wallace, Maurice O. *Constructing the Black Masculine: Identity and Ideality in African American Men's Literature and Culture, 1775–1995.* Durham, NC: Duke University Press, 2002.

Weeks, Kathi. *The Problem with Work: Feminism, Marxism, Antiwork Politics, and Postwork Imaginaries.* Durham, NC: Duke University Press, 2011.

Weinbaum, Alys Eve. *The Afterlife of Reproductive Slavery: Biocapitalism and Black Feminism's Philosophy of History.* Durham, NC: Duke University Press, 2019.

Weinbaum, Alys Eve. "Gendering the General Strike: W. E. B. Du Bois's *Black Reconstruction* and Black Feminism's 'Propaganda of History.'" *South Atlantic Quarterly* 112, no. 3 (2013): 437–63.

Weinbaum, Alys Eve. *Wayward Reproductions: Genealogies of Race and Nation in Transatlantic Modern Thought.* Durham, NC: Duke University Press, 2004.

White, Deborah Gray. *Ar'n't I a Woman? Female Slaves in the Plantation South.* 1985; rev. ed., New York: W. W. Norton, 1999.

Woodard, Vincent. *The Delectable Negro: Human Consumption and Homoeroticism within U.S. Slave Culture,* edited by Justin A. Joyce and Dwight A. McBride. New York: New York University Press, 2014.

Sigrid Vertommen

Surrogacy at the Fertility Frontier

Rethinking Surrogacy in Israel/Palestine
as an (Anti)Colonial Episteme

ABSTRACT Surrogacy is a popular assisted reproductive practice in Israel, and it has been legal since 1996, albeit, until recently, only for married heterosexual couples. Same-sex couples who aspired to genetic parenthood were therefore "forced" to look for available surrogates abroad, in countries such as the United States, India, Nepal, Mexico, and Russia. This resulted in the emergence of a lucrative transnational surrogacy industry in Israel that relies on the reproductive labor power of racialized egg cell providers and surrogates in the global South, East, and North. While much of the existing research on surrogacy in Israel explains its ubiquity by centering cultural accounts of Jewishness, this article rethinks contemporary policies, practices, and markets of assisted reproduction from the vantage point of the "colonial episteme," by unpacking the complex "intimacies" and reproductive afterlives of settler colonialism and racial capitalism in Israel/Palestine. The article argues that surrogacy operates both as a demographic frontier in the consolidation of a Jewish state in Israel/Palestine and as a commodity frontier for the accumulation of capital in a booming surrogacy industry. Surrogacy and other reproductive technologies also emerge as sites of reproductive resistance through practices of surrogacy strikes and sperm smuggling.

KEYWORDS surrogacy, Israel/Palestine, frontier, settler colonialism, biocapitalism.

There is something revolutionary about being at the frontier of something new. Someone has to be the first one, someone has to be the pioneer.
—Gay surrogacy advocate about Tammuz, Israel's first gay surrogacy agency

In 1996 Israel became one of the first countries in the world to legalize commercial surrogacy. While surrogacy will soon be allowed for all Israelis, regardless of sexual preference, initially the Embryo Carrying Agreement Law permitted surrogacy only for married heterosexual couples, explicitly excluding same-sex couples and singles from accessing this reproductive

HISTORY of the PRESENT • A Journal of Critical History • 14:1 • April 2024
DOI 10.1215/21599785-10898374 © 2024 Duke University Press

service.[1] This fostered the emergence of a transnational surrogacy sector in the early 2000s, consisting of Israeli surrogacy agencies, fertility clinics, and law firms that specialize in family and migration law and recruit and contract offshore surrogates and egg cell providers in countries where these practices are either allowed or not regulated at all. Israel's transnational surrogacy industry caters not only to same-sex commissioning parents who wish to have a biologically related child, but also to heterosexual couples who prefer to look for cheaper and more readily available surrogacy arrangements abroad.

This article uses commercial surrogacy as a lens to analyze the broader political economy of (assisted) reproduction in Israel/Palestine, at the crossroads of ongoing histories of settler colonialism and racial capitalism. Contrary to much of the existing research that explains the ubiquity of surrogacy in Israel from a cultural and religious perspective, this article rethinks contemporary policies, practices, and markets of assisted reproduction from the vantage point of the "colonial episteme"; and it unpacks the reproductive "intimacies" of racial capitalism, empire, and settler colonialism in Israel's surrogacy regime (Lowe). I will do so by introducing the frontier as an analytical trope to conceptualize and grasp the variegated (anti)colonial-capitalist relations of Israel's surrogacy regime.

The idiom of the "frontier" has been sparking Zionist imaginaries since the late nineteenth century when Jewish *halutzim* or pioneers from all over the world were encouraged to redeem the "Land of Israel" and "make its deserts bloom" through productive work, farming, and homesteading (Efron). In Zionist historiography, this is considered the constitutive period, with the pioneer as "the quintessential moral and economic subject for national conquest and development in Historic Palestine" (Neumann 3). Through their continuous conquest of the supposedly empty land on the frontiers of historic Palestine, the pioneers instilled the Jewish people's "perennial rebirth," to use Frederick Jackson Turner's frontier terminology, after centuries of diasporic persecution and presumed degeneration (Weiss; Massad). Until now, "frontier" was used as a catchy metaphor to foreground Israel's advanced and innovative position or "chutzpah" in the field of science, technology, health, and medicine. However, as critical science and technology studies scholars demonstrate, frontier imaginaries of scientific progress, modernity, and civilization often materialized only through violent and necropolitical practices of displacement and dispossession of Indigenous and enslaved populations (Harding; Franklin).

In Israel/Palestine, I will argue, gestational surrogacy materializes first and foremost as a demographic frontier in the consolidation of a Jewish state, at the expense of Palestinian life. In dialectical relation to that, surrogacy also operates as a commodity frontier in which an outsourced reproductive labor force of "Caucasian" (and other racialized) surrogates and egg cell vendors are providing the "cheap inputs" for Israel's fertility industry (Moore). Drawing on extensive ethnographic fieldwork research conducted along the surrogacy frontier in Israel/Palestine (2012–19) and the Republic of Georgia (2018), consisting of participatory observations in surrogacy agencies and fertility clinics in Tel Aviv, Haifa, Nablus, Tbilisi, and Batumi, and semi-structured interviews with Israeli, Palestinian, and Georgian fertility doctors, surrogacy brokers, government officials, commissioning parents, (gay) surrogacy advocates, and critics from civil society organizations, I will unpack the intricate ways in which gestational surrogacy is put to work and contested in Israel/Palestine in relation to its triangular population economy of settlers, Natives, and racialized reproductive workers.

In doing so, I make three contributions to the existing scholarship on reproduction, conquest, and empire. First, I bring Israel/Palestine and Zionism's settler colonial present into the debates on the grammars, logics, and modalities of reproduction under racial capitalism (Spillers). Second, this article looks at the myriad genealogies of conquest in contemporary assisted reproductive technology (ART) regimes with their distinct yet mutually constitutive reproductive logics of removal, accumulation, and exploitation. Building on the astute insights from Black feminist scholarship on the crucial role of reproduction in plantation and slave economies, my research on Israel/Palestine suggests that the epistemic condition of possibility of surrogacy is grounded not only in slavery and four hundred years of "slave breeding" but also in genocide and the centuries-old ongoing removal of Indigenous peoples. Third, I explore how these stratified reproductive logics also impact the articulation of reproductive resistance by looking at the diverging ways that surrogacy strikes and sperm-smuggling practices have been imagined and materialized in Israel/Palestine.

Hagar and the Genesis of Surrogacy in the Holy Land

To start unpacking some of the epistemic intimacies of racial capitalism, slavery, and settler colonialism in Israel/Palestine, I offer the Old Testament figure of Hagar as a fertile point of departure. This story from Genesis is often discursively framed as the first case of surrogacy, and during my interviews with Israeli fertility treatment providers, they often used it to provide cultural and religious legitimations for the popularity of ARTs and surrogacy in Israel. The story goes that the matriarch Sarah, when realizing she was infertile and unable to provide Abraham with a son, asked her Egyptian slave Hagar to be inseminated with her husband's sperm, so that their son could be Abraham's successor and father of a great nation. Yet, intimidated by the pregnant Hagar, who began to feel confident in her new role as surrogate for the patriarch's future child, Sarah banished Hagar to the desert. According to Jewish and Islamic tradition, Ishmael, the son of Hagar and Abraham, went on to become the father of the Arab-Islamic nation, while Isaac, the "real" son of Sarah and Abraham, went on to become the father of the Jewish nation. Some scholars used this badly managed surrogacy arrangement as a metaphor for the so-called conflict between the State of Israel and Palestinians (De Sutter and Delrue). According to *New World Encyclopedia*, the expulsion of Hagar is "a key text in interfaith relations between Judaism and Islam," symbolizing for Palestinians their expulsion from their homeland in 1948, while Jewish tradition believes that "Sarah was justified to use forceful measures to defend the life of her son Isaac and the Jewish nation from perceived Palestinian encroachments."[2]

Despite Hagar's biblical role as a surrogate for Abraham and Sarah, in present-day surrogacy arrangements in Israel it is highly unlikely that Hagar would be of Egyptian descent, and she would surely not be a Muslim Palestinian woman. On the contrary, the State of Israel actively avoids using the wombs or egg cells of Palestinian women for third-party reproductive services for Jewish Israelis. There are even laws in Israel prohibiting "interreligious" egg donation or surrogacy agreements between Jews, Christians, and Muslims (Vertommen, "Towards"). Instead, Israeli intended parents and their fertility brokers are increasingly contracting transnational surrogates in countries like Thailand, Nepal, Georgia, or Mexico and using egg cells from Ukrainian, Czech, or Romanian women in their reproductive quest for a biologically related child.

Remarkably, there is another group of racialized women who have come to identify with Hagar and her role as slave, handmaiden, and housewife. Black scholars in gender and theology studies have related the surrogacy story of Hagar to that of the millions of Black enslaved women whose wombs were violently appropriated and controlled by their masters and plantation owners for over four hundred years in the reproduction of property, power, and capital. Angela Davis, for instance, noted that enslaved Black women "possessed no legal rights as mothers of any kind. Considering the commodification of their children—and indeed, of their own persons—their status was similar to that of the contemporary surrogate mother" ("Surrogates" 212).

Alys Eve Weinbaum refers to these analogies as the slavery-surrogacy nexus, arguing that the persistence of what she calls the slave episteme continues to frame the racialization of reproductive and gestational labor in the biocapitalist present. She writes that "surrogacy must be linked to slavery and thus recognized as a racialized capitalist formation because it is in and through slavery that surrogacy becomes intelligible" ("Gendering" 457). Weinbaum's 2019 book includes a discussion of *Sisters in the Wilderness*, the 1993 treatise by womanist theologian Dolores Williams, who suggested that through Hagar "Black women's history . . . [becomes visible] as reproduction history . . . as history that uses labor as a hermeneutic to interpret Black women's biological and social experience of reproducing and nurturing the species and as an interpretive tool for analyzing and assessing Black women's creative productions as well as their relation to power" (*Afterlife* 135). The figure of Hagar speaks to generations of Black women who relate not only to the reproductive exploitation and expulsion she faced but also to her willpower to resist and overcome these imposed hardships.

I am sharing this biblical anecdote not only to illustrate the contested religious genealogies of surrogacy in the Holy Land but also to make an analytical point about how the messiness of historical and contemporary practices of reproduction becomes visible in and through surrogacy, with its gendered and racialized stratifications and divisions of labor that are shaped by epistemic legacies of slavery and settler colonialism. Hagar's story epitomizes many of the surrogacy narratives that will animate this article: the pronatalist imperatives to reproduce the nation, the exploitation of racialized women's reproductive labor power that this pronatalism requires, the expulsion of Natives who are viewed as a reproductive threat, and the fertile modes of resistance that are enabled in and through the reproductive sphere. Yet, despite the many resemblances between Black and Indigenous conditions of womanhood, I will argue in this article that, unlike Black women, Palestinian women are not so much racialized through the hermeneutic of reproductive labor and exploitation as through the hermeneutic of demographic replacement, genocide, and dispossession, considering the hesitance or outright "refusal," as Patrick Wolfe termed it, of the Israeli settler polity to depend on Indigenous reproductive labor power (*Traces of History*).

The article treats the stratified ways in which gestational surrogacy in Israel/Palestine materializes as both a demographic frontier and a commodity frontier in relation to its triadic population economy, based on several (international) surrogacy stories and case studies that emerged during my fieldwork between 2012 and 2019. Complicating the dyadic model of settler versus Native, Black scholars introduced a triadic population model of "European-Negro-Indian" or "White-Black-Red" to understand the complex relations of colonial conquest, slavery, and genocide (Wynter; Wilderson;

King). Congruently, Lorenzo Veracini, in his work on settler colonialism, argued that Israel/Palestine, similar to other settler colonial formations such as Australia, Canada, and the United States, is historically shaped as a triangular population economy, consisting of Jewish Israeli settlers, Indigenous Palestinians, and "imported" workers, who are all governed and racialized through different re/productive logics (*Settler Colonialism*). Put differently, reproducing racial capitalism in Israel/Palestine requires the plentiful reproduction of (Ashkenazi) Jewish Israelis, problematizes Palestinian procreation as a "demographic threat," and exploits the reproductive labor power of racialized (migrant) workers, including elderly care workers, sex workers, and egg cell providers and surrogates. The final part of the article examines how surrogacy operates not only as a frontier of demographic replacement and capital accumulation but also as a frontier of resistance, by discussing the surrogacy strike and sperm smuggling as two diverging types of reproductive sabotage.

Surrogacy as a Demographic Frontier: From Interreligious Zygotes to Racialized Wombs

Gestational surrogacy has become one of the newer and more popular reproductive technologies through which Israelis are exerting their right to parenthood, a right that is deemed so fundamental that it is recognized by political leaders and the judiciary alike. In the well-known Israeli court case of *New Family v. Approvals Committee for Surrogate Motherhood Agreements*, Justice Mishael Cheshin famously stated: "The right to parenthood is at the foundation of all foundations, at the infrastructure of all infrastructures, the existence of the human race, the ambition of man and the basis of that right as the profound need to have a child which burns in the soul . . . man's instinct of survival [is] . . . the necessity for continuity" (Schuz 199).

With an average of 3.1 children per woman, Israel is the most fertile of the OECD (Organisation for Economic Co-operation and Development) countries, where the average hovers around 1.7 children.[3] This "reproductive imperative," as Meira Weiss termed it, is deeply entrenched not only among heterosexual couples but also in Israel's gay community. In 2014 the main theme of the Tel Aviv Gay Parade was rainbow family life and equality, and the famous Israeli song "Children Are Joy, Children Are Blessing" was chosen as the event's theme track.[4] In one of my interviews with Dan, a gay father of two surrogacy babies with an American surrogate, he explained:

> I grew up in Israel, and these are the values that the society I grew up in has given me. When I go to Europe and I speak to gay people about the opportunity

of becoming parents, people raise an eyebrow and tell me: "Why should we become parents?" When I meet with people in Europe who go through the surrogacy process they usually have one child. Here in Israel we all want twins and that's only the beginning. (Tel Aviv, July 13, 2017)

Uri, the head of the Association of Gay Fathers said, "I think it's part of the Israeli and maybe even Jewish ethos that you become part of the tribe when you produce your own offspring" (Tel Aviv, July 9, 2017).

Since its establishment in 1948, the State of Israel has been known for its pronatalist policies, aimed at high birth rates and large families. Israeli scholars documented how this pronatalist stance has been institutionalized through various funds, councils, and committees, including the Heroine Award for mothers with at least ten children (1949), the Committee for Natality Problems (1962), the Demographic Center's Fund for Encouraging Birth (1968), and the Israel Council on Demography (2002). These initiatives offered financial support for reproducing large families, social and welfare benefits for (working) mothers, and high child allowances (Hashash; Birenbaum-Carmeli and Carmeli). The same pronatalism can be discerned concerning the usage, regulation, and subsidizing of assisted reproductive technologies, including in vitro fertilization (IVF) and intracytoplasmic sperm injection, gamete donation, surrogacy, and pre-implantation genetic diagnosis and screening. Israel has more fertility clinics per capita than any other country in the world. Measured by the number of IVF treatment cycles per capita, Israelis are by far the biggest consumers of IVF in the world.[5]

Many of these reproductive technologies are generously sponsored by the state. For instance, the government funds for every Israeli citizen up to age forty-five—regardless of ethnic, religious, or marital background—an unlimited number of IVF cycles for the birth of a first and second child. Israel's pronatalist stance is often explained and legitimized through cultural narratives of Jewishness that emphasize the importance of reproduction in Jewish culture, history, and tradition. Some authors refer to the first religious commandment that prescribes Jews "to be fruitful and multiply and replenish the earth." Others refer to the violent histories of anti-Semitism to which Jewish communities in Europe and Russia have been subjected for centuries, culminating in the Holocaust and the extermination of six million Jewish lives, in this way transforming individual procreation into a matter of collective survival (see, for instance, Kahn; Ivry; Teman). However, a recent bulletin on fertility trends by the Taub Center for Social Policy Studies in Israel suggested that these cultural arguments do not hold up when comparing Israeli Jews to Jews elsewhere in the world. The report states that, "although they often share the same history, fertility among Jews in other developed countries is significantly lower—including among Jews living in Europe, where welfare policies are more generous than in Israel" (Taub Center). While cultural narratives of Jewishness are important, albeit insufficient, to explain Israel's pronatalist drive, the report's conclusion, that the reasons behind Israel's "exceptional" fertility trends "remain a mystery," is less convincing.

Drawing on the inspirational body of work by Indigenous scholars and/or scholars on settler colonialism on the gendered, embodied, and reproductive grammars of settler colonial formations, I have been arguing in my work that there is nothing mysterious or exceptional about Israel's pronatalism, when taking into account Zionism's ongoing histories of conquest and demographic replacement in Israel/Palestine (see, for instance, Shalhoub-Kevorkian, *Birthing, Security*; Smith; Abdo; Yuval-Davis and Stasiulis; Wolfe, "Settler," *Traces*; Jacobs; Morgenson; TallBear). Settler colonialism is an old scholarly paradigm that has recently been picked up again by researchers from all over the world who want to understand the political, economic, social, and cultural past and present of settler societies, including the United States, Canada, Australia, Zimbabwe, South Africa, and Algeria (see, for instance, Jabary-Salamanca et al.; Lentin; Shalhoub-Kevorkian; Wolfe, "Settler," *Traces*). According to Patrick Wolfe's structuralist approach, settler polities have two defining features: (1) territorial expansion and the maximum accumulation of Indigenous land, and (2) the demographic transfer of the settler population to the newly acquired lands. He argues that this double movement of territorial accumulation and demographic settlement is undergirded by a societal logic of elimination of the Native population and their claims to their land, culture, and history. This is also a highly gendered and reproductive process (Wolfe, "Palestine").

Similar to other settler colonial formations, including Australia or the United States, the Zionist demographic zero-sum project in Israel/Palestine follows a bio/necropolitical grammar of reproduction, in which the fruitful reproduction of the settler population presupposes the non-reproductivity of Indigenous populations (Ghanim). Analyzing historical and contemporary fertility policies in Israel/Palestine, Jacqueline Portuguese and Rhoda Kanaaneh each argue that these were primarily designed by the State of Israel to benefit its Jewish citizenry, and not Palestinians whose supposedly high fertility rates have been framed by Israeli media and policymakers alike as a "ticking demographic time bomb" for the survival of the Jewish state. One famous example was the Heroine Mother Award, a prize initiated by Prime Minister David Ben Gurion in 1949 to grant all mothers a financial compensation and a personally signed letter on the birth of their tenth child. The award was dropped after ten years when it turned out that it was mostly Palestinian mothers in Israel who claimed it. Portuguese concluded that Israel, in its attempt to create and consolidate a Jewish demographic majority in a Jewish state, has been as concerned with lowering the Palestinian birth rate as it has with raising the Jewish one. She also stressed that this never resulted in a straightforward anti-natalism toward Palestinians. Unlike other settler colonial societies such as Australia or the United States, Israel has no history of forced sterilizations or abortions of Indigenous women. Moreover, Palestinian citizens in Israel (unlike those in the West Bank and the Gaza Strip) are legally entitled to the same fertility treatments as their Jewish compatriots. My research suggests nonetheless that Palestinians in Israel are often restrained from exercising their reproductive rights equally. This is because of not only Islamic and Christian restrictions to third-party reproduction but also, as I will show, because of settler colonial realities on the ground.

In 1996, when the Embryo Carrying Agreement was put in place, a state committee was appointed to approve and authorize the surrogacy contracts between the Israeli surrogate and the intended parents. The law included a religious clause, requiring the surrogate carrier and the intended mother to share the same religion. The same religious logic was repeated in 2010 with the introduction of the Egg Donation Law, requiring the egg provider and egg recipient to both have the same religion. The introduction of these strict religious requirements was justified as a way to harmonize both surrogacy and egg donation practices according to halakhic principles, since Judaism follows matrilineal standards by which the religion of a newborn is determined by the mother's religion.

Halakhic standards generally define the mother as the one who carries the baby, favoring gestational motherhood over genetic motherhood. However, with the arrival of assisted reproductive technologies, there has been a fragmentation of different maternal roles—genetic, mitochondrial, gestational—creating strong disagreements among the rabbinical authorities about who or what defines motherhood, and thus Jewish kinship (Kahn; Ivry). In an interview with a prominent rabbi, who was then president of Israel's National Bioethics Committee and expert in medical halakhic ethics, the stakes of the rabbinical debates on motherhood were clarified:

> There are at least four opinions among Jewish rabbis. One says that the genetic material is the important one, so the egg donor is the mother. Another one says that the egg is just a chip made in China, and what is important is the pregnancy, carrying the baby, and delivering, it doesn't matter where the genetic material

comes from. A third opinion says that neither is the mother, because to be a mother you have to fulfil both functions, and once you divide there is no half mother, and since it's half and half, then there is no mother at all. A fourth position is that both are mothers, who says that we can only have one mother, we have two mothers, one is the genetic mother and one is the nurturing mother. (West Jerusalem, July 16, 2013)

Since the rabbis failed to reach a uniform opinion on what constitutes "pure" Jewish motherhood, it was decided that both the genetic and the gestational mother must have the same religion, "so that," the rabbi continued, "we know for sure what a child is, either Jewish or non-Jewish" (Jerusalem, July 16, 2013). In practice, this means that a Jewish Israeli woman cannot donate oocytes or gestate a baby for a Muslim, Druze, or Christian (who are often Palestinian) woman, or vice versa, without the approval of an Exceptions Committee. As Palestinian women rarely serve as surrogates or egg cell providers in Israel, this also means that Palestinian women are not benefiting from these reproductive services. Apart from one, none of the dozens of Israeli surrogacy agents whom I interviewed mentioned having Palestinian clients for either domestic or international surrogacy arrangements. They predominantly cater to Jewish Israeli couples, which is in line with Elly Teman's findings in her foundational study of surrogacy in Israel.

The legal advisor of the Ministry of Health explained the inclusion of the religious amendment in the Law on Egg Donation as a way to "not make more problems than we already have, and we have a lot in this country. If, for example, there would be a Jewish egg donor and a Muslim recipient, then this would cause problems because the baby would be both Muslim and Jewish (interview, West Jerusalem, February 20, 2012). Another renowned bioethicist and former member of the Bioethics Committee clarified: "We don't know what will eventually emerge as the religious attitude towards interreligious zygotes, so we decided to stay on the safe side" (interview, Tel Aviv, July 26, 2013).

Ironically, most Israelis in need of egg donation or surrogacy continued to make use of transnational egg vending and surrogacy programs with countries such as Ukraine, Georgia, Romania, and the Czech Republic, where oocyte vendors or surrogates are rarely Jewish.[6] In these cases of transnational fertility services, the State of Israel, in agreement with the chief rabbinate, solved the alleged kinship problem by encouraging the intended parents to convert the children born from this procedure to Judaism in order for them to be recognized as full-fledged Jews.[7] In the latter case, the genetic possibility of an "interreligious zygote" did not motivate Israeli policymakers to outlaw the reproductive practice. This suggests that religious legitimations hide more than they actually reveal (Ben Porat; Nahman, *Extractions*). Indeed, religious categorizations of Jews, Muslims, and Christians often tend to obscure underlying racial and ethnic classifications of Arabs/Palestinians versus Jews. As Patrick Wolfe phrased it, "In Israel, religion operates as a racial amnesty" (*Traces* 260). When asked about his opinion on the inclusion of the religious clause in the Egg Donation Law, one fertility specialist stated: "The consensus was that we didn't want to mingle between populations and to put, let's say, a Jewish egg in an Arab woman" (interview, Hadera, August 21, 2012).

Moreover, Michal Nahman's research on racializing practices of ova extraction demonstrated how Jewish Israeli women considered rejecting ova from Palestinian women in Israel. She quoted a Mizrahi Jewish couple: "Regarding the religion of the donor, we didn't talk about it, so I guess it's not relevant. Of course, it's important that she shouldn't be an Arab, ya'ni" ("Materializing" 205). Similarly, when asking a Jewish Israeli surrogate, who pointed out during our interview that she would happily gestate the babies of all Israeli couples, "from ultraorthodox couples to homosexual ones," whether she would do the same for a Muslim or Christian couple, she answered: "Of course not, they don't have the same values as us. These mothers send their children to explode themselves as suicide bombers, how can I share a surrogacy with them?" (interview, Kiryat Atta, July 21, 2017).

In her research on surrogacy and racial practices, Jaya Keaney suggested that contemporary transnational surrogacy markets flourish by presenting the womb as an empty rental space that does not shape the fetal identity. In this biogenetic business model of kinship, gestation is seen as peripheral to racial transmission. She argues that "in sharp contrast to the racialization of gametes, surrogates' wombs are deracialized." While my research on Israel/Palestine concurs that for transnational surrogacy arrangements, the "foreign" womb is indeed constructed as largely irrelevant to the racial makeup of the surrogacy baby, this "nonracializing" logic does not uphold for domestic surrogacy. Within the frontiers of the settler colony, the womb's religious and racial boundaries are closely monitored. Similar to cross-religious restrictions for marriage, adoption, and egg donation, the State of Israel demonstrates a structural reluctance to mix with the Indigenous Palestinian population, as Dafna Hirsch's research indicated. This is contrary to reproductive logics in other settler colonial formations, where Indigenous peoples have often been bioculturally assimilated into the settler body. As Wolfe summarized: "In the case of Palestinians, . . . Zionism's racialization strategy can be expressed with maximal simplicity: it is one of outright exclusion" (*Traces* 272).

Another example of surrogacy's reproductive-demographic arithmetic in Israel/Palestine can be found in gay couples' access to surrogacy services. As Adi Moreno's research on gay surrogacy in Israel indicated, at first sight, gay couples seem excluded from the state's pronatalist stance to be fruitful and multiply, by not permitting them to start a surrogacy procedure in Israel and "forcing" them to go abroad to countries such as Thailand, India, or Nepal, where—until recently—surrogacy was either legal or not regulated at all. At times, these cross-border arrangements resulted in highly mediatized surrogacy scandals in which Israeli surrogacy babies and their intended fathers got stuck abroad without the necessary papers to "return" to Israel.

In 2013, for instance, sixty-five Israeli surrogacy babies were stranded in Thailand after the Thai government refused to let the babies cross the border. Thai law awards full parental rights to the gestational mother and not to the intended parents. This is why the Israeli Ministry of the Interior initially refused to issue Israeli passports for the babies, as the Thai government would consider this child abduction. Outraged by the lack of support from the government, sections of Israel's gay community began organizing a public campaign to "bring the children home," particularly targeted at Gideon Sa'ar, then Minister of the Interior, who at that time just had a baby himself. In a well-coordinated social media action, famous Israeli celebrities posted selfies with the slogan "Gideon, your baby is home, ours isn't" on their Facebook pages. The campaign received massive media attention, and after nine days of action the Israeli authorities agreed to temporarily authorize passports for the Israeli babies in Thailand under the express condition that the Thai surrogate would sign a document relinquishing all her rights and commitments toward the newborn child. Similar events unfolded in Nepal in April 2015. After a huge earthquake hit the country, killing almost ten thousand people, it became clear that Nepal had transformed into a popular surrogacy destination for Israeli gay couples, with dozens of surrogacy babies who were unable to leave Nepal. Israel was the first country to send a humanitarian mission to Nepal, with the repatriation of the Israeli surrogacy babies and their dads as the top priority, while the Indian surrogacy mothers were left in Nepal. On the arrival of the first three young babies in Israel, the spokesperson for the Israel Defense Forces (IDF) sent out the following statement made by Lieutenant Colonel Ron, accompanied by a picture of an IDF soldier holding a tiny baby in his hands: "We have the knowledge and experience and especially the commitment to bring the residents of the State of Israel back home" (IDF, April 27, 2015).

The script in each of these surrogacy "scandals" follows a similar story-line. The Israeli intended parents publicly reported feeling abandoned by their government in their quest for parenthood. The Israeli media then followed suit by framing them as reproductive exiles who were refrained from "returning" to Israel, a highly emotive leitmotif in Jewish history. However, as Moreno argued, the State of Israel was not absent at all in facilitating these international surrogacy journeys. On the contrary, the Israeli authorities actively contributed to the regulation of the surrogacy babies by promulgating overseas surrogacy regulations for intended parents, acknowledging genetic parenthood of the parents in Israeli family courts, registering the child, issuing citizenship, arranging passports for the surrogacy babies, and even sending the army or private planes to pick up the surrogacy babies and their parents.

When one Israeli surrogacy lawyer was asked about the scandal with the Thai surrogacy babies, and whether the babies were blocked from entering Israel, she replied:

> Of course, they entered, but it took some time. But you cannot prevent this child from coming to Israel. They [the Israeli authorities, S.V.] would need to change the Citizenship Law to restrict surrogacy babies from entering Israel. Today it says that every child from Israelis is an Israeli by birth. Unless you add a paragraph stating that it doesn't count when the baby is the product of surrogacy in a country that is not acknowledging surrogacy, the Ministry of Foreign Affairs or Justice can do hula-hoops in the air, this is the law. If they don't fix it, then they don't have any argument. If the State of Israel really dislikes transnational surrogacy, then they should just change the Law of Return and add the paragraph on surrogacy, but they are not doing it. Again, because they have this demographic problem, they are afraid. (interview, Tel Aviv, July 15, 2014)

The Law of Return and the Citizenship Law are the legal cornerstones of Zionism's demographic project in Israel/Palestine. The Law of Return provides every Jewish person in the world the right to acquire Israeli citizenship and to settle in Israel. By simultaneously refusing Palestinian refugees the United Nations guaranteed Right to Return to their homeland, the Law of Return also safeguards a demographically Jewish state in Israel/Palestine. One of the important insights from Nahman's work on the oocyte traffic between Israel and Romania is that transnational egg donations are "state-making practices" through which certain imaginaries on citizenship, race, genetics, and the nation are performed. She noticed, for example, how in an Israeli proxy fertility clinic in Bucharest, the sperm and embryo vials of the Israeli recipient couples were all labeled with their Israeli ID number, presupposing that they "somehow already belong to the state" (*Extractions* 60).

She also recalled how at a certain moment, when the Israeli government halted the import of ova from an Israeli proxy clinic in Bucharest, the Israeli couples who had already started their fertilization procedures demanded "their" embryos back, insisting that the embryos had the "right to return" to Israel. Similarly, surrogacy also operates as a demographic frontier through which mostly Jewish Israelis—heterosexual and homosexual alike—but not Palestinians, are encouraged and enabled to reproduce the Jewish nation while "interracial" mixing between Palestinians and Jewish Israelis is actively discouraged.

Surrogacy as a Commodity Frontier: Birthing a Reproductive-Industrial Complex

Surrogacy in Israel/Palestine serves not only as a demographic frontier but also as a commodity frontier powered by a logic of capital accumulation.[8] Similar to what world-ecologist Jason Moore has termed "cheap nature," a capitalist strategy in which use-values such as food, energy, raw material, and labor power are produced with a below-average value composition (53), fertility has become a commodity frontier for the "cheap" (re)production of babies, families, and life in Israel/Palestine and across the rest of the world.[9] The global fertility industry is estimated to become a $40 billion market by 2026, with the United States, China, India, the United Kingdom, and also Israel as important fertility hubs.[10] Indeed, in its selectively pronatalist drive to create and maintain a Jewish state, a burgeoning and innovative "reproductive-industrial complex" has emerged in Israel/Palestine, comprising sectors as diverse as repro-tech and medicine, the stem cell industry, and cross-border fertility tourism, including transnational surrogacy and egg donation services.[11]

In 2008 Tammuz Family was founded, Israel's first transnational surrogacy company with a specialization in surrogacy arrangements for gay couples. Since then around fifteen other surrogacy agencies have been created to fulfill the increasing demand. These agencies coordinate medical, logistical, and legal procedures and broker the demands of commissioning couples and the availability of surrogates and egg cell providers, inside but mostly outside Israel. Only two agencies specialize in domestic surrogacy, while the others focus on transnational arrangements. A recent report on surrogacy by the Knesset Research and Information Center suggested that between 2005 and 2017, 700 babies were born through national surrogacy arrangements in Israel, and 1,513 babies were born through international surrogacy agreements, with a sharp annual increase in the latter.[12] As one surrogacy expert at Israel's Ministry of Health clarified in an interview: "You can see now that the agencies are a lot more interested in working on surrogacy abroad than on domestic surrogacy. There is no bureaucracy, it goes faster, much more money, nobody [is] watching you all the time and checking if everything is exactly according to the law, they can do whatever they want" (Jerusalem, August 3, 2014). Unlike Israel's oocyte provision sector, which is run by fertility doctors, the surrogacy industry is mostly run by lawyers, social workers, and so-called experts through experience, who went through transnational surrogacy procedures themselves and feel confident to guide commissioning parents through the complex surrogacy maze.

While many surrogacy brokers put an effort into concealing the marketized nature of surrogacy under the tropes of help, care, and altruism, it is undoubtedly still a business, as Sharmila Rudrappa and Caitlyn Collins demonstrate. Contrary to Israel's international adoption procedures that are legally required to be implemented by certified nonprofit organizations, Israeli surrogacy agencies are commercial companies that charge between US $9,000 and $12,000 for their services—up to a third of the total cost of international surrogacy. The total cost depends on a broad series of variables, such as the local/nonlocal background of the egg donor, the surrogacy destination, the shipment of frozen sperm, the legal counseling, the inclusion of nonstandard add-on technologies and procedures such as pre-implantation genetic diagnosis or screening (PGD, PGS), and the number of newborns (single baby, twins, or triplets). The agencies use various other marketing strategies to promote their services and cut down on costs, such as "guarantee programs" that offer the promise of a fail-safe cross-border surrogacy procedure resulting in a take-home baby—or "egg cell sharing" deals, whereby two intended parenting couples share the egg cells from one donation cycle.

The principal way in which surrogacy agencies gain profit, however, is by saving money on the reproductive labor costs of surrogates and egg cell providers through subcontracting to the global South/East. In my interview with the founder of Tammuz Family, who himself had two children using an American surrogate, he explained that surrogacy in the United States is of high quality but very costly. In California, the epicenter of the global fertility industry, a surrogacy procedure costs around $150,000 on average, while in Israel, couples often pay up to $70,000. "This is why with Tammuz, we started to think about cheaper routes for surrogacy. In my previous life, I worked in the high-tech industry, where many activities were subcontracted to low-wage countries like India" (interview, Tel Aviv, July 17, 2014).

In India, Nepal, and Mexico—until a few years ago the most popular surrogacy destination for Israelis—surrogacy cost between US$30,000 and $50,000. Indian and Mexican surrogates received between $2,000 and

$8,000 of this. In Georgia, where I conducted my fieldwork, the procedure costs between US$30,000 and $40,000. Georgian surrogates receive US $15,000 in "fees" (not a salary, as gestation and parturition are not viewed as "real" labor). Many of the Georgian surrogates I interviewed mentioned that they would have to work three years in conventional jobs, including laboratory work or waitressing, to make the same amount. Yet surrogates often sign contracts in which they agree to work under questionable health, safety, and psychosocial conditions. In the Republic of Georgia, surrogates are not allowed to decide about the number of embryos transferred to their womb, how to give birth, whether to perform an embryo reduction or abortion, or whether to breastfeed after the birth. The surrogacy contract stipulates that these reproductive decisions are reserved for the intended parents in consultation with the surrogacy agency and the doctors. Furthermore, surrogates in Georgia do not have access to decent postnatal medical care and life insurance. Medical complications due to the pregnancy are therefore never seen or compensated as work accidents but are viewed as ordinary health issues. Moreover, for the duration of the conception and pregnancy, the bodies of surrogates are closely monitored, disciplined, and surveilled: no alcohol, cigarettes, drugs, "excessive" sexual intercourse, or heavy lifting are allowed, while exercise and healthy food are strongly encouraged. Some Israeli parents even request a kosher diet for the surrogate during the pregnancy. Finally, some of the interviewed surrogates struggled with the psychological and emotional stress of having to transfer the baby to the commissioning parents after delivery. One of the main reasons surrogacy subcontracting in Georgia is an exploitative industry is that surrogates refrain from and are dissuaded from identifying as reproductive workers. Despite their undeniable integration into a capitalist export-oriented industry as surplus value producers, surrogates are "housewife-ized," to use Maria Mies's powerful phrase, as "gift-giving mothers" (Mies; Vora; Vertommen and Barbagallo).

The divisions of labor in Israel's transnational surrogacy industry are not only highly gendered but also explicitly racialized. Egg cell providers are recruited based on their presumed "genetic qualities" (such as intelligence, beauty, fitness, race, etc.), while foreign surrogates' genetic makeup is framed as largely irrelevant (Keaney). The latter are recruited "merely" for their gestational capacities. When one Israeli fertility broker was asked in 2014 why egg cells are imported to Israel from Ukraine and not from Georgia—assuming it would be easier to combine egg cell provision and surrogacy in the same country—he replied: "Have you seen Georgian women?," implying that Georgian women are not pretty enough for egg extraction, in comparison to Ukrainian women (interview, Tel Aviv, July 22, 2014). Indeed, Ukrainian egg cells are highly desirable commodities because they are branded as reproducing not only beauty but also "Caucasian whiteness."[13]

As discussed earlier, Palestinian women are not recruited as surrogates in Israel. Scholars in Black, Native, and settler colonial studies have explored how settler colonial formations such as Australia and the United States often opt to import exogenous laborers who can make no sovereign claims to the land (Wolfe, "Settler"; Veracini, *Settler*; King; Shafir; Jackson). Similarly, Israeli surrogacy agencies appear to contract foreign surrogates and oocyte providers instead of using the "cheaper" Indigenous Palestinian surrogates or egg cell providers. Yet, contrary to other types of racialized reproductive work in Israel, such as sex work (which is often performed by Russian, Ukrainian, or Moldovan women from the former Soviet Union) or eldercare work (which is performed by Philippine women), surrogates and egg cell providers are not employed as migrant reproductive workers inside Israel (Bernstein et al.). Instead, they perform the subcontracted work of ovulation, gestation, and parturition outside the borders of the state. Unlike Palestinians who as a surplus Indigenous population are racialized through their exclusion from the assisted reproductive labor force, Georgian surrogates and Ukrainian egg cell providers are racialized through their inclusion. Similar to eldercare workers who, in Hebrew, are often referred to as *filipini* ("my Philippine careworker"), Georgian surrogates and Ukrainian egg cell donors are racialized as Caucasian through the work of gestation and ovulation.[14]

■ ■ ■

Although Israel has a booming domestic reproductive industry, the biggest profits are made when national borders are crossed. In the case of egg donation, the reported "national shortage" of local egg cells in the early 2000s prompted the IVF directors of Israel's major hospitals to start partnerships with proxy fertility clinics abroad in countries like Czech Republic, Ukraine, and Romania (Nahman, *Extractions*). Some of these proxy clinics are certified by Israel's Ministry of Health. The ministry doctor in charge of licensing fertility clinics clarified in an interview:

> There are six official fertility units abroad, in the Ukraine, Czech Republic, and the United States, but there are so many unofficial units that Israeli doctors are working with . . . maybe ten or fifteen units all over: in Cyprus, in Russia, in Kazakhstan. Every day, I hear of another place where Israelis go and make business because the women in these countries are often very poor so they are ready to give their eggs for cheap prices. (Tel Aviv, August 21, 2014)

Depending on the chosen treatment package, a transnational egg donation procedure costs approximately double the amount of a local procedure
and is partially refunded by National Health Insurance.[15] While local Israeli
donors would receive a compensation of approximately US$6,000, foreign
egg cell providers from Eastern Europe and former Soviet countries are paid
between US$600 and $1,000.

Israeli surrogacy agencies also collaborate with local clinics and agencies
abroad. When Nepal was a popular surrogacy destination, Tammuz Family
started its own proxy fertility clinic in Kathmandu, integrating the medical
and logistical services along the surrogacy frontier. Manor Surrogacy, another popular Israeli surrogacy agency, established fertility clinics in Tbilisi
and Kiev, where local physicians perform the medical procedures together
with Israeli doctors "who travel to Tbilisi and Kiev specifically for this purpose."[16] Manor also provides fully furnished apartments where the commissioning parents and surrogacy babies can reside after the birth, while waiting
for the legal documents that need to be approved to return to Israel. Instead
of starting their own proxy clinics abroad, most Israeli transnational surrogacy agencies collaborate with local agencies and clinics. The director of one
famous Israeli surrogacy agency, for instance, travels every month to Tbilisi
with a portable container full of frozen Israeli embryos in their hand luggage
and cooperates with a Georgian surrogacy agency and IVF clinic to which
the recruitment and medical follow-up of the surrogates is outsourced.

Another cross-border trend is that Israeli surrogacy agencies started introducing their "pioneering" surrogacy model to the rest of the world. Tammuz,
for instance, created offices in Brazil, Australia, and the Nordic countries over
the past few years to recruit foreign couples. The director clarified this during our interview: "A year ago, we decided that we wanted to not only focus on
Israel. I mean, until then Israel was our base, but we took a decision to expand
to other destinations. We started to build new offices, like in the Nordic countries and in Brazil, for over a year now. Australia is quite new. So, we now have
representatives in these countries. We now have more intending parents from
outside of Israel" (Tel Aviv, June 21, 2017).

In this sense, Israel's fertility industry, which emerged from the debris
of ongoing histories of settler colonialism and racial capitalism, is expanding into what Bronwyn Parry and Rakhi Ghoshal termed "reproductive
empires."

Frontiers of Reproductive Resistance

Using the frontier trope, I have demonstrated thus far that fertility technologies such as surrogacy operate as both a demographic frontier and a com-

modity frontier in Israel/Palestine. These technologies mobilize the repro-ductivity of settlers, Natives, and racialized reproductive workers in strati-fied yet mutually constitutive ways, depending on their position in the pop-ulation economy. Following the crucial insight by Marxist feminists about social reproduction's "dual characteristic" and by Black feminist scholarship on the crucial role of reproduction in resisting slavery, it is important to note that ARTs operate not only as a colonial-capitalist site of dispossession, extraction, and proletarianization but also as a fertile frontier of resistance (Federici; Weinbaum, "Gendering"). In this last section, I treat the stratified and at times counterintuitive ways in which surrogacy strikes and sperm smuggling have been appropriated as reproductive tools of resistance and sabotage in Israel/Palestine.

The first surrogacy strike was organized by Gays Against Surrogacy, a small anti-Zionist queer collective that opposes the surrogacy industry and Israel's overall pronatalist climate.

> I met Yossi and Yotam, the founding members of the Gays Against Surrogacy collective, on a typically hot July day in South Tel Aviv in 2017. When we were walking to Yotam's house to discuss surrogacy among Israel's gay community, I noticed the No Kidding badge on Yossi's backpack and asked him about it. Yossi laughed and said that these badges were his own creation. He wears and distributes them to critique the consumerist pronatalism in Israeli society, especially among his own gay community (fieldwork notes, Tel Aviv, July 2, 2017).

During our interview Yotam and Yossi pointed at the nuclear family and the army as two of the most powerful institutions for the reproduction of Israel's settler project as they bring forth and reproduce Israelis as settler/citizens and soldiers.

> I see a continuity between the Israeli gay struggle for national belonging by joining the army or by having children. For me, these are the two pillars of Israel's social contract. . . . According to the dominant Israeli discourse you only deserve your citizen rights if you have been in the army and if you have served your country. And if you didn't serve in the army, then you are a hor-rible person. So, I see this struggle to permit gay surrogacy as an attempt by the gay community to prove loyalty and belonging to the state. (Tel Aviv, July 2, 2017)

In 2015 Gays Against Surrogacy joined the Gay Pride parade in Beersheva. Yossi recalled how they carried a huge banner during the parade that said: "We fuck up the ass (which doesn't lead to the birth of soldiers)." In this small act of resistance against Israel's pronatalism, Gays Against Surrogacy explicitly correlated queer sexuality with anticolonialism and antinatalism. Birth strikes are not a recent phenomenon. They have been used throughout colonial history as powerful practices of sabotage. Black feminist scholarship, including many of the contributions in this issue, demonstrated that in the plantation economies of the Caribbean and the United States, enslaved women often refused to reproduce the next generation of property and labor power for the plantation owners (Roberts). Darlene Clark Hine, for example, argued that the insurgency of Black enslaved women in the United States and the Caribbean against sexual and reproductive extraction through sexual abstinence, abortion, and infanticide was crucial in overthrowing the slave economy.[17] Weinbaum, in "Gendering the General Strike," also argued that enslaved women's withdrawal of sexual and reproductive labor (by resisting rape or childbirth) ought to be understood as gendered contributions to the larger general strike against slavery. Gays Against Surrogacy, in their queer reappropriation of the birth strike, provocatively reintroduced the surrogacy strike as a political tool in Israel.

Unsurprisingly, the surrogacy strike as proposed by Gays Against Surrogacy never gained traction in Israeli society. Ironically enough, their call was overruled by a different type of surrogacy strike that was organized in July 2018, when the Israeli Knesset voted against a law that would have allowed surrogacy for gay men. After extending eligibility from heterosexual couples to single women, but not to same-sex couples and single men—the groups undoubtedly most in need of surrogacy—Israel's LGBT community began an unprecedented nationwide strike to protest the government's failure to include gay couples in its surrogacy laws.

The Aguda, Israel's umbrella LGBT organization, announced on its website: "For the first time ever, the gay community will go on a national strike" (*Times of Israel*). And so it happened that in July 2018, in the midst of Israel's deadly incursion against Gaza's March of Return that killed 214 Palestinians and injured 36,100 more, and just a few days before the implementation of the controversial Jewish Nation State Law that allows national self-determination for Jews but not for Palestinians in Israel, hundreds of thousands of Israeli protesters went on strike and blocked the streets of central Tel Aviv to demand equal surrogacy rights for gay men. Moreover, more than forty Israeli companies and branches of multinationals, including Facebook, IBM, and Microsoft, supported the surrogacy strike and encouraged their employees to participate in it. Some companies even committed to financially supporting the international surrogacy arrangements of their gay employees who were forced to look for a foreign surrogate. The Jewish

Agency, in a landmark move, decided to offer an $11,000 loan to its gay employees to cover the costs of surrogacy services abroad. As Isaac Herzog, then chairman of the Jewish Agency, stated in an interview with the *Jerusalem Post*: "The Jewish Agency is one big family, and all its members are equal" (Sharon).[18] The strike was successful in the long run for the organizers. In July 2021 the Israeli Supreme Court ordered the government to lift the ban on surrogacy for same-sex couples and single men within six months, despite the heavy resistance by the Jewish orthodox political parties.

Remarkably, the Israeli surrogacy strike was organized by the relatively privileged (excluded) gay consumers of the reproductive practice, and not by the reproductive workers (egg cell providers and surrogates), as is usually the case during a strike. In this sense, it was a strike *for* surrogacy, rather than a surrogacy strike. These diverging appropriations of the surrogacy strike in Israel/Palestine illustrate the complex articulations of (re)productivity, racialization, and resistance in settler colonial formations. Strikes and withdrawals of labor are usually powerful and effective tools of resistance to obtain more recognition, visibility, or remuneration for the paid and unpaid labor performed by the working class (in its broadest sense). Strikes might be less effective, however, for Indigenous peoples who are deemed surplus populations and whose primary (but not only) value—from the oppressor's point of view—lies in their removal rather than their exploitation. As Gargi Bhattacharyya aptly remarked in her work on racial capitalism and social reproduction: "To be rendered surplus is not to be paid less, it is to be left dying or for dead. Rush too quickly to brush away this ugly distinction and we are in danger of collapsing all racialized economic violence into a claim for equal pay" (20). Or, as Laura Briggs stated in her contribution to this special issue: "We need a stronger account of (post)colonial spaces and reproductive labor."

Throughout its history, Wolfe argued, the Zionist movement has been cautious not to depend too much on Indigenous Palestinian labor. In the early twentieth century, the principle of *avoda ivrit* or Hebrew labor was introduced to encourage Jewish entrepreneurs and company owners in mandate Palestine to hire only Jewish workers at the expense of Palestinian workers, although the former were often more expensive and less skilled than the latter. Since the early 2000s, and especially after the Second Intifada, Israel has given fewer working permits to Palestinians from the West Bank and Gaza to work inside Israel, while increasing the number of migrant workers from Thailand (agriculture) and the Philippines (care work) (Kemp and Raijman; Wolfe, *Traces*). Although Palestinians have effectively used general strikes as a means of resistance against colonial dispossession (for example, during the Great Revolt of 1936, during the First Intifada in the mid-eighties, and in May 2021 during the Israeli onslaught on Sheikh Jarrah and Gaza), as Glen Coulthard argues, from an Indigenous perspective, blockades have been much more effective than strikes in materially dismantling and disrupting colonial relations. In *Red Skin, White Masks* (2014) he explains that blockades and other acts of sabotage constitute a crucial act of negation to processes of colonial extraction, appropriation, and accumulation in settler political economies. Rather than strictly focusing on sabotage as the disruption of so-called productive land (or industry-based infrastructures, technologies, or materialities such as pipelines, powerlines, factories, or power plants), it can also be viewed from a reproductive and embodied perspective (Coulthard).

One act of reproductive sabotage that has been trending in Israel/Palestine is by Palestinian political prisoners who are smuggling their sperm out of Israeli prisons in an attempt to make proxy families (Vertommen, "Babies from behind Bars"). Unlike Jewish Israeli prisoners, Palestinian political prisoners are not allowed physical contact or conjugal visits with their partners. Obviously, these restrictions have far-reaching consequences for Palestinian prisoners and their partners at home who wish to become parents. Thwarting Israel's security policies through their reproductive bodies, Palestinian prisoners started smuggling their sperm out of prisons. The sperm, referred to as "ambassadors of freedom" in Palestinian parlance, is then rushed to fertility clinics in Nablus or Ramallah where the wives of the prisoners attempt pregnancy by means of artificial insemination or IVF (Abumaria).

Salem Abu al-Khaizaran, the leading doctor and spokesperson for the prisoner's project in the Razan Medical Center, estimated during an interview in 2013 that more than sixty-five Palestinian prisoners had succeeded in sneaking their semen out of prison and into the Razan Medical Center for Infertility in Ramallah and Nablus, where it is stored in freezers awaiting fertility procedures. According to "Doctor Salem"—as his patients call him—this had resulted in eighteen pregnancies and six live births, with more deliveries expected in the near future (interview, Nablus, August 3, 2013). Since our interview in August 2013, the sperm-smuggling strategy has gone swimmingly in the West Bank and Gaza, with more than one hundred babies reportedly being born (Murrar).

Although IVF costs around US$3,000 per IVF cycle in the West Bank and Gaza, the Razan Medical Center provides the fertility treatment free of charge to the wives of long-term prisoners as part of their community service. The matter became highly politicized when some prisoners' family members and the Israeli authorities made repeated references to the political tension surrounding this issue in the national and international media. Lydia El-Rimawi, one of the prisoner's wives who gave birth to a boy in 2013 after her husband smuggled his sperm out of Nafha prison, proudly stated during our interview: "The birth of our son Majd is a defeat for the Israelis, and a personal and a political victory for us. Despite all restrictions we managed to find a way" (interview, Beit Rima, August 30, 2014). Dallal Ziben, the first Palestinian woman who got pregnant through the sperm-smuggling strategy, remarked, "This accomplishment is dedicated to the Palestinian people, namely prisoners and their families" (quoted in Sherwood).

Rhoda Kanaaneh and Jacqueline Portuguese both documented how the Palestinian resistance movement has, in similar fashion to the Zionist movement, deployed the ideology of motherhood as a political tool. Portuguese referred to Yasser Arafat's famous speech from the seventies when he compared the Palestinian woman to "a biological bomb threatening to blow up Israel from within" (165). The discourse of reproduction as a form of resistance gathered steam during the intifadas when childbearing was presented as Palestinian women's national duty and a way to replenish those who were martyred as a result of colonial violence. This pronatalist discourse has been criticized by Palestinian feminists and women's organizations as patriarchal, one that restricts women's insurgent capacity to their biological and cultural role as mothers.[19]

In the case of the prisoners' project, Palestinian women are using reproductive technologies as a last resort to comply with the sociocultural traditions and imperatives of motherhood in what is still a patriarchal society. Dallal Ziben, for instance, used pre-implantation genetic diagnosis to select the sex of the embryo, to ensure the birth of a boy, still an important tradition in Palestinian society. Moreover, Doctor Salem informed me that he is keen to help the wives of the prisoners, as they run the risk of "paying a double price." "First, she wastes her life waiting for her husband, and by the time he gets out, his family will start pushing him to get married to another woman, because she will be too old to give him children" (interview, Nablus, August 3, 2013).[20]

Yet assisted reproduction also permeates the political arena as a vexed site through which Palestinians are negotiating and claiming their reproductive-demographic rights as a people, in an act of embodied sabotage against colonial politics of erasure. In her research on Palestinian women giving birth in Occupied Jerusalem, Nadera Shalhoub-Kevorkian concluded that "the willful act of deciding to continue surviving and giving birth is itself perceived as political—as subversion, revolt and agency—by the women themselves" (Birthing 160).

Toward Reproductive Solidarities

In bringing together the intimacies of racial capitalism, settler colonialism, and slavery in this article, commercial surrogacy proved to be an insightful way of making sense of the broader political economy of reproduction in Israel/Palestine. Conversely, Israel/Palestine is an equally fertile lens to understand how reproduction is put to work in settler and racial capitalist formations. While many of the contributions to this issue have a US focus on the intricate relations between transatlantic slavery, "slave breeding," and the racialization of reproductive labor and extraction, my research on the politics of (assisted) reproduction in Israel/Palestine suggests that surrogacy's condition of possibility is as much defined by the colonial episteme and the genocidal elimination and replacement of Indigenous populations. For building a reproductive theory of conquest, it seems crucial to understand the reproductive afterlives of the slave episteme in relation *to* the colonial episteme, and to balance the importance of their variegated reproductive grammars, depending on the historical specificity (in terms of population economy, mode of re/production, divisions of labor) of each racial capitalist formation.

In Israel/Palestine, surrogacy operates as a dialectically interwoven frontier of demographic replacement and capital accumulation, in which the Zionist movement and later the State of Israel capitalized on its colonial impetus to birth and nurture a demographically Jewish state. This biopolitical project materializes at the expense of the lives of Indigenous Palestinians and racialized reproductive workers across the fertility frontier, from Nepal to Georgia and Thailand. However, as Hagar's insurgent surrogacy experience in the opening story illustrates, assisted reproduction constitutes an equally powerful frontier of resistance in Israel/Palestine. From surrogacy strikes to sperm smuggling, different population groups are seizing their means of reproduction. In resisting the state's stratified reproductive policies, solidarities between these different reproductive struggles can be forged. In that sense, Hagar could be viewed as the Georgian surrogate who organizes for better reproductive working conditions, as much as she could be the wife of a Palestinian prisoner who decides to get pregnant using the smuggled sperm of her husband, or the Israeli queer who questions the state's stratified pronatalism. ■

Sigrid Vertommen is assistant professor at the Sociology Department of the University of Amsterdam and senior research fellow at the Centre for Research on Culture and Gender at Ghent University. Her work examines the global politics of (assisted) reproduction at the crossroads of ongoing histories of colonialism, heteropatriarchy, and biocapitalism.

ACKNOWLEDGMENTS

I thank Alys Eve Weinbaum and Jennifer L. Morgan, and the other workshop participants, for their generous and critical feedback on earlier versions of this article. This
work was supported by the Belgian Fund for Scientific Research (FWO, grant no.
1207320N).

NOTES

Certain sections of this article were already included in other published papers and
book chapters. They are listed in the works cited section (Vertommen). This article
was written before the events of October 7, 2023. Since Hamas's attack on Israel, and
Israel's genocidal war on Gaza, it has become even more crucial and urgent to understand how Israel's settler colonial project in Palestine is undergirded by reproductive
grammars of genocide. See, for instance, ReproSist, "Resistance is Fertile—Endorse
our statement for Reproductive Justice for Palestine," December 19, 2023, https://
reprosist.org/2023/12/19/resistance-is-fertile-endorse-our-statement-for-reproductive
-justice-for-palestine/.

1   In 2018 the existing law was modified by allowing single women to obtain surrogacy
    services, while still excluding same-sex couples and single men. July 2021 the Israeli
    Supreme Court ordered the government to lift the surrogacy restrictions for same-
    sex couples and single men.

2   *New World Encyclopedia*, https://www.newworldencyclopedia.org/entry/Hagar
    (accessed April 15, 2022).

3   OECD, 2022, Fertility rates (indicator), https://doi.org/10.1787/8272fb01-en
    (accessed September 21, 2022).

4   Thanks to Daphna Birenbaum-Carmeli for reminding me of this song.

5   According to the most recent data by Israel's Ministry of Health, there were 5,169
    IVF treatment cycles in 1995, resulting in 4.5 cycles per 1,000 women. In 2018 that
    number has risen exponentially to 48,294 IVF cycles or 23.4 cycles per 1,000 women,
    which is over five times the European average and ten times the international aver-
    age. Accordingly, live births via IVF treatment rose from 1.7 percent of Israel's total
    live births in 1995 to 5.1 percent in 2018 (Israel Ministry of Health). See also
    Birenbaum-Carmeli and Dirnfeld.

6   There are some fertility companies that specialize in "Jewish" egg donations. A Jewish
    Blessing, for instance, is an Israel-based agency that recruits American Jewish donors.
    NY LifeSpring is a fertility company launched by an Israeli egg broker, who specializes
    in finding a match between Jewish Israeli donors and couples in the United States.

7   Israel's chief rabbinate has ruled that all surrogacy babies need to be converted if the
    parents want their child to be considered Jewish. If the rabbinical judges of the con-
    version court decide to accept the baby as Jewish, the baby requires immersion in a
    mikve and circumcision if it is a boy.

8   Jason Moore defined commodity frontiers as a capitalist strategy based on the pro-
    gressive appropriation, and often dispossession, of places and people as new and
    cheap reserves of natural resources and labor (Moore).

9   We developed this argument further in Vertommen and Barbagallo.

10 DataBridge Market Research, "Global Fertility Services Market—Industry Trends and Forecast to 2026," https://www.databridgemarketresearch.com/reports/global -fertility-services-market (accessed October 2, 2022).

11 On the reproductive-industrial complex, see Vertommen, "From the Pergonal Project"; Peskin.

12 Knesset Research and Information Centre, "The Surrogacy Procedure in Israel and Abroad and Its Cost Elements in Israel That Are State-Funded," October 7, 2018, https://www.knesset.gov.il/mmm.

13 For more research on the racialization of Caucasian egg donors, see Vlasenko.

14 For more research on the racialization of reproductive labor, see Glenn; Weinbaum, *Afterlife*.

15 In Israel's three largest health funds, there is a standard reimbursement of up to NIS 12.000 for two trials of egg donation abroad, up to one child (Ministry of Health Israel, "Egg Donation," 2015, http://www.health.gov.il/Subjects/fertility/ovum _donation/Pages/default.aspx (accessed October 2, 2022).

16 https://manorsurrogacy.com/our-facilities/ (accessed November 12, 2022).

17 See also the work by Jennifer Morgan, Rhoda Reddock, Alys Weinbaum, and Angela Davis.

18 This section on the surrogacy strikes was included in Vertommen, Parry, and Nahman.

19 While some Palestinian women's and family planning organizations have promoted lower fertility rates and smaller families as a modern model for emancipation against cultural traditions, it seems that large families are at least in part wanted by Palestinian women. Research suggests that in 2006 the family size considered ideal by Palestinian women was around five children, with some differences between the West Bank and Gaza Strip (Wick; Abdul-Rahim).

20 None of the women that I interviewed mentioned this as one of their motivations. Marcia Inhorn has criticized this culturalist trope of "the Arab man" who will separate from his wife if she cannot give him children. She suggests that the new Arab man is actively rethinking patriarchal forms of masculinity (Inhorn).

WORKS CITED

Abdo, Nahla. *Women in Israel: Race, Gender, and Citizenship.* London: Zed, 2011.

Abdul-Rahim, Hanan, Laura Wick, Samia Halileh, Sahar Hassan-Bitar, Hafedh Chekir, Graham Watt, and Marwan Khawaja. "Maternal and Child Health in the Occupied Palestinian Territory." *Lancet* 373, no. 9667 (2009): 967–77.

Abumaria, Dina. "Smuggled Sperm Allows Palestinian Prisoners to Become Fathers." *Media Line*, October 29, 2017. https://themedialine.org/featured/smuggled-sperm -allows-palestinian-prisoners-become-fathers/.

Ben Porat, Guy. "A State of Holiness: Rethinking Israeli Secularism." *Alternatives* 25, no. 2 (2000): 223–45.

Bernstein, Deborah, Hila Shamir, Nomi Levenkron, and Dlila Amir. "Sex Work and Migration: The Case of Tel Aviv and Jaffa, 1918–2010." In *Selling Sex in the City: A Global History of Prostitution, 1600s–2000s*, edited by Magaly Rodríguez García, Lex Heerma van Voss, and Elise van Nederveen Meerkerk, 329–54. Leiden: Brill, 2017.

Bhattacharyya, Gargi. *Rethinking Racial Capitalism: Questions of Reproduction and Survival*. London: Rowman and Littlefield, 2018.

Birenbaum-Carmeli, Daphna, and Yoram S. Carmeli, eds. *Kin, Gene, Community: Reproductive Technologies among Jewish Israelis*. New York: Berghahn, 2010.

Birenbaum-Carmeli, Daphna, and Martha Dirnfeld. "In Vitro Fertilisation Policy in Israel and Women's Perspectives: The More the Better?" *Reproductive Health Matters* 16, no. 31 (2008): 182–91.

Coulthard, Glen Sean. *Red Skin, White Masks: Rejecting the Colonial Politics of Recognition*. Minneapolis: University of Minnesota Press, 2014.

Davis, Angela. "Reflections on the Black Woman's Role in the Community of Slaves." *Massachusetts Review* 13, nos. 1–2 (1972): 81–100.

Davis, Angela. "Surrogates and Outcast Mothers: Racism and Reproductive Politics in the 1990s." In *The Angela Y. Davis Reader*, edited by Joy James, 210–21. London: Blackwell, 1998.

De Sutter, Petra, and Eline Delrue. *De maakbare baby: Een onbegrensd verlangen*. Gent: Academia, 2017.

Efron, Noah. *Judaism and Science: An Historical Introduction*. Westport, CT: Greenwood, 2007.

Federici, Silvia. *Revolution at Point Zero: Housework, Reproduction, and Feminist Struggle*. Oakland, CA: PM, 2012.

Franklin, Sarah. *Dolly Mixtures: The Remaking of Genealogy*. Durham, NC: Duke University Press, 2007.

Ghanim, Honaida. "Thanatopolitics: The Case of the Colonial Occupation in Palestine." In *Thinking Palestine*, edited by Ronit Lentin, 65–81. London: Zed, 2008.

Glenn, Evelyn Nakano. "From Servitude to Service Work: Historical Continuities in the Racial Division of Paid Reproductive Labor." *Signs* 18, no. 1 (1992): 1–43.

Harding, Sandra, ed. *The Postcolonial Science and Technology Studies Reader*. Durham, NC: Duke University Press, 2011.

Hashash, Yali. "Medicine and the State: The Medicalization of Reproduction in Israel." In Birenbaum-Carmeli and Carmeli 271–95.

Hine, Darlene Clark. "Female Slave Resistance: The Economics of Sex." *Western Journal of Black Studies* 3 (1979): 123–27.

Hirsch, Dafna. "Zionist Eugenics, Mixed Marriage, and the Creation of a 'New Jewish Type.'" *Journal of the Royal Anthropological Institute* 15, no. 3 (2009): 592–609.

Inhorn, Marcia. *The New Arab Man: Emergent Masculinities, Technologies, and Islam in the Middle East*. Princeton, NJ: Princeton University Press, 2012.

Israel Ministry of Health. "Report: Statistics on IVF in Israel 1990–2018." 2020. https://www.health.gov.il/UnitsOffice/HD/MTI/info/Pages/IVF.aspx.

Ivry, Tsipy. *Embodying Culture: Pregnancy in Japan and Israel*. New Brunswick, NJ: Rutgers University Press, 2010.

Jabary-Salamanca, Omar, Mezna Qato, Kareem Rabie, and Sobhi Samour. "Past Is Present: Settler Colonialism in Palestine." *Settler Colonial Studies* 2, no. 1 (2012): 1–8.

Jackson, Shoana. *Creole Indigeneity: Between Myth and Nation in the Caribbean*. Minneapolis: University of Minnesota Press, 2012.

Jacobs, Margaret. *White Mother to a Dark Race: Settler Colonialism, Maternalism, and the Removal of Indigenous Children in the American West and Australia, 1880–1940*. Lincoln: University of Nebraska Press, 2009.

Kahn, Susan Martha. *Reproducing Jews: A Cultural Account of Assisted Conception in Israel.* Durham, NC: Duke University Press, 2000.

Kanaaneh, Rhoda. *Birthing the Nation: Strategies of Palestinian Women in Israel.* Berkeley: University of California Press, 2002.

Keaney, Jaya. "The Racializing Womb: Surrogacy and Epigenetic Kinship." *Science, Technology, and Human Values* 47, no. 6 (2021): 1157–79. https://doi.org/10.1177/016224 3921105228.

Kemp, Adriana, and Rebeca Raijman. *Migrants and Workers: The Political Economy of Labor Migration in Israel.* Jerusalem: Van Leer Institute and Hakibbutz Hameuchad, 2008.

King, Tiffany Lethabo. *The Black Shoals: Offshore Formations of Black and Native Studies.* Durham, NC: Duke University Press, 2019.

Lentin, Ronit. *Traces of Exception: Racializing Israeli Settler Colonialism.* London: Bloomsbury Academic, 2018.

Lowe, Lisa. *The Intimacies of Four Continents.* Durham, NC: Duke University Press, 2015.

Massad, Joseph. "The Persistence of the Palestinian Question." *Cultural Critique* 59, no. 1 (2005): 1–23.

Mies, Maria. *Patriarchy and Accumulation on a World Scale: Women in the International Division of Labor.* London: Zed, 2014.

Moore, Jason. *Capitalism in the Web of Life: Ecology and the Accumulation of Capital.* London: Verso, 2015.

Moreno, Adi. "Crossing Borders: Remaking Gay Fatherhood in the Global Market." PhD diss., University of Manchester, 2016.

Morgan, Jennifer L. *Laboring Women: Reproduction and Gender in New World Slavery.* Philadelphia: University of Pennsylvania Press, 2004.

Morgenson, Scott Lauria. "Theorizing Gender, Sexuality, and Settler Colonialism: An Introduction." *Settler Colonial Studies* 2, no. 2 (2012): 2–22.

Murrar, Alaa. "Palestine: With 'Liberated' Sperm, the Impossible Becomes Possible." Mediterranean Network for Feminist Information, January 9, 2023. https://med feminiswiya.net/2023/01/09/palestine-with-liberated-sperm-the-impossible-becomes -possible/?lang=en.

Nahman, Michal. *Extractions: An Ethnography of Reproductive Tourism.* Hampshire, UK: Palgrave Macmillan, 2013.

Nahman, Michal. "Materializing Israeliness: Difference and Mixture in Transnational Ova Donation." *Science as Culture* 15, no. 3 (2006): 199–213.

Neumann, Boaz. *Land and Desire in Early Zionism.* Waltham, MA: Brandeis University Press, 2011.

Parry, Bronwyn, and Rakhi Ghoshal. "Reproductive Empires and Perverse Markets: Unpacking the Paradoxical Dynamics of ART Market Expansion in Non-urban India and Beyond." *Catalyst: Feminism, Theory, Technoscience* 8, no. 1 (2022): 1–26.

Peskin, Doron. "Israeli Tech Companies Take Fertility Treatments to Next Level." *Al-Monitor,* July 5, 2022. https://www.al-monitor.com/originals/2022/07/israeli-tech -companies-take-fertility-treatments-next-level.

Portuguese, Jacqueline. *Fertility Policy in Israel: The Politics of Religion, Gender, and Nation.* Westport, CT: Praeger, 1998.

Reddock, Rhoda. "Women and Slavery in the Caribbean: A Feminist Perspective." In "Latin America's Colonial History," edited by Steve J. Stern. Special issue, *Latin American Perspectives* 12, no. 1 (1985): 63–80.

Roberts, Dorothy E. *Killing the Black Body: Race, Reproduction, and the Meaning of Liberty.* New York: Vintage, 1997.

Rudrappa, Sharmila, and Caitlyn Collins. "Altruistic Agencies and Compassionate Consumers: Moral Framing of Transnational Surrogacy." *Gender and Society* 29, no. 6 (2015): 937–59.

Schuz, Rhona. "The Developing Right to Parenthood in Israeli Law." *International Survey of Family Law,* 2013: 197–225.

Shafir, Gershon. *Land, Labor, and the Origins of the Israeli-Palestinian Conflict, 1882–1914.* Oakland: University of California Press, 1996.

Shalhoub-Kevorkian, Nadera. *Birthing in Occupied East Jerusalem: Palestinian Women's Experience of Pregnancy and Delivery.* Jerusalem: YWCA, 2012.

Shalhoub-Kevorkian, Nadera. *Security Theology, Surveillance, and the Politics of Fear.* Cambridge: Cambridge University Press, 2015.

Sharon, Jeremy. "Jewish Agency to Help Gay Employees with Surrogacy Costs." *Jerusalem Post,* March 3, 2019. https://www.jpost.com/israel-news/jewish-agency-to-help-gay -employees-with-surrogacy-costs-582342.

Sherwood, Harriet. "Gaza's First 'Prison Baby' on Way after Jailed Palestinian Smuggles out Sperm." *Guardian,* October 13, 2013. http://www.theguardian.com/world/2013 /oct/13/gaza-first-prison-baby-palestinian-smuggles-sperm.

Smith, Andrea. *Conquest: Sexual Violence and American Indian Genocide.* Durham, NC: Duke University Press, 2015.

Spillers, Hortense J. "Mama's Baby, Papa's Maybe: An American Grammar Book." *Diacritics* 17, no. 2 (1987): 64–81.

TallBear, Kim. "Making Love and Relations beyond Settler Sex and Family." In *Making Kin Not Population: Reconceiving Generations,* edited by Adele E. Clarke and Donna Haraway, 145–64. Chicago: Prickly Paradigm, 2018.

Taub Center for Social Policy Studies in Israel. "Why Are There So Many Children in Israel?" February 2019. https://www.taubcenter.org.il/en/research/why-are-there -so-many-children-in-israel/.

Teman, Elly. *Birthing a Mother: The Surrogate Body and the Pregnant Self.* Berkeley: University of California Press, 2010.

Times of Israel. "Thousands to Join Day-Long Strike Sunday by LGBT Community over Surrogacy Law." July 21, 2018. https://www.timesofisrael.com/israel-gears-up-for -strike-protests-by-lgbt-community-over-new-surrogacy-law/.

Turner, Frederick Jackson. *The Significance of the Frontier in American History.* Chicago Annual Report of the American Historical Association, 1893: 197–227.

Veracini, Lorenzo. *Israel and Settler Society.* London: Pluto, 2006.

Veracini, Lorenzo. *Settler Colonialism: A Theoretical Overview.* Hampshire, UK: Palgrave Macmillan, 2010.

Vertommen, Sigrid. "Babies from Behind Bars: Stratified Assisted Reproduction in Palestine/Israel." In *Assisted Reproduction across Borders: Feminist Perspectives on Normalizations, Disruptions, and Transmissions,* edited by Merete Lie and Nina Lykke, 207–18. New York: Routledge, 2018.

Vertommen, Sigrid. "From the Pergonal Project to Kadimastem. A Genealogy of Israel's Reproductive-Industrial Complex." *Biosocieties* 12, no. 2 (2017): 282–306.

Vertommen, Sigrid. "Towards a Political Economy of Egg Donations: 'Doing It the Israel Way.'" In *Critical Kinship Studies: Kinship (Trans)formed*, edited by Charlotte Kroløkke, Stine Willum Adrian, Lene Myong, and Tine Tjørnhøj-Thomsen, 169–84. London: Rowman and Littlefield International, 2017.

Vertommen, Sigrid, and Camille Barbagallo. "The Invisible Wombs of the Market: Waged and Unwaged Reproductive Labor in the Global Surrogacy Industry." *Review of International Political Economy* 29, no. 6 (2021): 1945–66.

Vertommen, Sigrid, Bronwyn Parry, and Michal Nahman. "Assisted Reproductive Technology's Colonial Present: Colonial Lineages of Global Fertility Chains." *Catalyst: Feminism, Theory, Technoscience* 8, no. 1 (2022): 1–16.

Vlasenko, Polina. "Desirable Bodies/Precarious Laborers: Ukrainian Egg Donors in Context of Transnational Fertility." In *(In)Fertile Citizens: Anthropological and Legal Challenges of Assisted Reproduction Technologies*, edited by Venetia Kantsa, Giulia Zanini, and Lina Papadopoulou, 197–216. Athens: InFERCIT, 2015.

Vora, Kalindi. "After the Housewife: Surrogacy, Labour, and Human Reproduction." *Radical Philosophy* 2, no. 4 (2019): 42–46. https://www.radicalphilosophy.com/article/after-the-housewife.

Weinbaum, Alys Eve. *The Afterlife of Reproductive Slavery: Biocapitalism and Black Feminism's Philosophy of History*. Durham, NC: Duke University Press, 2019.

Weinbaum, Alys Eve. "The Afterlife of Slavery and the Problem of Reproductive Freedom." *Social Text* 31, no. 2 (2013): 49–68.

Weinbaum, Alys Eve. "Gendering the General Strike: W. E. B. Du Bois's Black Reconstruction and Black Feminism's 'Propaganda of History.'" *South Atlantic Quarterly* 112, no. 3 (2013): 437–63.

Weiss, Meira. *The Chosen Body: The Politics of the Body in Israeli Society*. Stanford, CA: Stanford University Press, 2002.

Wick, Livia. "Building the Infrastructure, Modeling the Nation: The Case of Birth in Palestine." *Culture, Medicine, and Psychiatry* 32 (2008): 328–57.

Wilderson, Frank B. III. *Red, White, and Black: Cinema and the Structure of US Antagonisms*. Durham, NC: Duke University Press, 2010.

Williams, Dolores S. *Sisters in the Wilderness: The Challenge of Womanist God-Talk*. New York: Orbis, 1993.

Wolfe, Patrick. "Palestine, Project Europe, and the (Un-)Making of the New Jew: In Memory of Edward W. Said." In *Edward Said: The Legacy of a Public Intellectual*, edited by Ned Curthoys and Debjani Ganguly, 313–37. Carlton, Australia: Melbourne University Press, 2007.

Wolfe, Patrick. "Settler Colonialism and the Elimination of the Native." *Journal of Genocide Research* 8, no. 4 (2006): 387–409.

Wolfe, Patrick. *Traces of History: Elementary Structures of Race*. London: Verso, 2016.

Wynter, Sylvia. "1492: A New World View." In *Race, Discourse, and the Origin of the Americas: A New World View*, edited by Vera Lawrence Hyatt and Rex M. Nettleford, 5–57. Washington, DC: Smithsonian Institution, 1996.

Yuval-Davis, Nira, and Daiva Stasiulis. *Unsettling Settler Societies: Articulations of Gender, Race, Ethnicity, and Class*. London: Sage, 1995.

Halle-Mackenzie Ashby and Jessica Marie Johnson

Injury and Value
Black Mothering in Slavery and Its Afterlife

ABSTRACT This essay explores two historical subjects, Catharina, an enslaved woman living and working in eighteenth-century New Orleans, and Ruth, a free field laborer in post-emancipation Barbados. Through a careful reading of their different but overlapping legal petitions against the planters who worked to control their labor, this essay seeks to distill a shared battle around Black mothering and to reconsider what it means to mother in the eighteenth- and nineteenth-century Atlantic world, respectively. In so doing, this essay contributes to scholarship that analyzes reproductive racial slavery's afterlife, particularly how slavery's matrilineal principle shaped the meaning of Black motherhood in bondage and in freedom. Exploring violent confrontations with empire in moments of profound change, the stories of Catharina and Ruth each offer new definitions of labor and value and hint at how Black women theorized a world beyond racial capitalism.

KEYWORDS reproduction, injury, value, slavery, emancipation

In June of 1773 a thirty-five-year-old woman named Catharina made a request for freedom. Catharina did not simply request manumission papers. Writing to Spanish Louisiana governor Luis de Unzaga, she requested that she, as a "mulata esclaba" and slave of the deceased planter Sieur Jean Baptiste Destrehan, receive an "estimation of her value" from Sieur Etienne de Boré, the administrator of the Destrehan estate.[1] Catharina had found "certain persons" who, in return for her services and good work, promised to pay her purchase price and that of her five-year-old daughter Felicité. As justification for her request, Catharina described being sick at work from "certain accidents" that had befallen her. In May 1876, a century after Catharina petitioned for her freedom, a pregnant mother named Ruth Sealy petitioned for restitution before the Bridgetown Petty Debt Court in Barbados.[2] Ruth did not pursue manumission from slavery; rather, she fought to make her freedom meaningful by mobilizing her rights as a free laborer. Ruth submitted a

HISTORY of the PRESENT ▪ A Journal of Critical History ▪ 14:1 ▪ April 2024
DOI 10.1215/21599785-10898385 © 2024 Duke University Press

claim to Judge Fleming, clerk of the court, against William Burgess, guardian of the Lears' sugar estate, for assault and battery while at work. In response to her perceived recalcitrance, Burgess trampled her with his horse, "mashed me into a cane hole and stood over me." As a result of this assault, Ruth sustained several injuries and her pregnancy was threatened. She demanded £10 as restitution ("Bridgetown").

Ruth's and Catharina's respective injuries became the grounds upon which they renegotiated the terms of their value as mothers and laborers. This article presents injury and value as necessary categories of analysis that offer insight into the meaning of reproduction and racial capitalism in slavery and its afterlife. Injury names the entanglement of productive and reproductive labor as it meets the physical demands on and limits of the body. Injury, while experienced by all Black people, becomes specific to the "Black female condition" as it enters the realm of the spectacular and unredressed (Hartman 167). Value names the economic calculus placed on Black bodies and labor that created the possibility for racial capital, credit, and wealth to be exchanged. Value, which Jennifer Morgan describes as constructed in the seventeenth century by bifurcating African culture and life from emergent European thinking around numeracy and demography, helped Europeans delegitimize African sovereignty and market knowledge (*Reckoning* 6, 75). Each woman discussed here engaged in different kinds of self-valuation. Catharina was engaged in self-valuation through negotiating her freedom, while Ruth was engaged in self-valuation as a legal claim for monetary restitution. Reading these two theorizations of value together and placing them into dialogue with reproduction demonstrate how value and its attending accounting practices structured racial capitalism. It also allows us to examine how value shifts and fluctuates across time and space, chronology and empires.

Comparing Ruth's and Catharina's stories challenges the distinction between slavery and freedom. It allows us to contend with overlap across claims made before and after emancipation. Black women grappled with challenging, surviving, and taking advantage of the economic and symbolic labor demanded of their wombs, care work, kinship networks, service, and the value (or lack thereof) of their offspring. Their strategies shifted in distinct yet overlapping ways across space and time. This article takes up Saidiya Hartman's contention that "facile notions of progress . . . erect unequivocal distinctions between bondage and liberty" (304) and turns to Ruth and Catharina to explore how Black women's experiences cohere and fracture on either side of emancipation. Both women, we argue, were "economic thinkers" (Morgan, *Reckoning* 30), who understood the stakes and limits of valuing their labor and their motherhood. They challenged white landowners to recognize the range of their labor on their own terms and to offer restitution (manumission documents and wages). In sum, their experiences demonstrate the ways Black women's wombs, offspring, and service to owners and employers took on distinct and overlapping meanings and values across time and place. We highlight the importance of focusing on Black motherhood as a space of potential injury that Black women sought to heal in complex ways as they sought to preserve forms of autonomy and care that could not be easily quantified within racial capitalism.

Catharina's Value: Injury and Mothering in Spanish Louisiana

Catharina made her request at a propitious time. Seven years earlier, her owner Destrehan had passed away, leaving behind a massive estate, several offspring of French and African descent, and dozens of enslaved Africans. He died in the middle of a major imperial transition. In 1762 the King of France transferred the colony of Louisiana to Spain in the secret Treaty of Tordesillas. Between 1762 and 1771, the transition from French to Spanish control threw the francophone colonial elite into chaos. They refused to work with the first Spanish governor, Don Antonio de Ulloa, causing him to retreat from the Gulf Coast to Spanish Cuba. An armed revolt of white francophone elites was met with the arrival of the Spanish armada led by the new governor, Alejandro O'Reilly. In 1769 O'Reilly established formal Spanish rule in the form of a cabildo (Spanish colonial governing council) and executed the rebels. When the Spanish arrived, the Destrehans were among a land- and slave-owning cohort of white French, Louisianan, and Canadian-born officials who controlled resources, land, and political appointments along the Gulf Coast. But in 1765, when Destrehan père passed away, he left no adult male heirs. In 1771 his eldest daughter Jeanne Marguerite Marie Destrehan des Tours married Étienne de Boré, and Boré was named guardian of the estate.

For enslaved people, the death of an owner often meant devastating changes. Mothers were taken from their children, and kinship networks were ruptured when enslaved property was redistributed among heirs and creditors. Imperial shifts added to the distress, uncertainty, and confusion. Changing imperial structures, in this instance, brought the new legal codes and customs from across the Spanish empire into Louisiana. Under French rule manumission required slave owners to be of a certain age and receive the approval of the Superior Council, the governor, and the intendant (Johnson, chap. 4). The Spanish brought a manumission system called *coartación* to Louisiana, which for Catharina, along with Destrehan's death, also created an opportunity.

Coartación allowed enslaved people to demand self-purchase from their owners, force their appraisal, and become *coartado*—literally "cut" from slavery (de la Fuente and Gross 104–5). By petitioning the *regidores* (the cabildo's governing councilmembers), men, women, and children held in bondage could request and receive an estimation of their value, then set about paying their owner, either through their earnings or with third-party assistance (Hanger 14). *Coartación* could even occur despite slave owner protest. Though united in status, race, and property with slave owners, Spanish imperial officials did not immediately side with owners or prevent *coartación*. Appraisers considered enslaved peoples' race, gender, age, skills, and service to their former owners when they heard *coartación* petitions. Enslaved petitioners could contest valuations issued by their owners and their owners' evaluators, or request reappraisals by third parties chosen by themselves or the *regidores*.

Enslaved people in the Spanish-speaking Americas insisted on their right to *coartación*, taking advantage of tensions between royal and local officials. As Bianca Premo notes, the number of eighteenth-century litigations initiated by enslaved Africans increased in numerous Spanish colonies, and the demographic of litigants trended toward urban enslaved populations and women, especially enslaved street vendors, wet nurses, and artisans (9). Enslaved people made *coartación* real by taking conscious and deliberate advantage of it as a resource for securing freedom (Chira 133–34). They banded together to share information about the *coartación* process and pooled resources to fund self-purchase. They cultivated white and free people of African descent as their co-conspirators. They justified their petitions by describing their good habits, reputation, and service to their owners and the community at large. They used their economic knowledge of their value to demand appraisals and reappraisals. In the 1770s *coartación* arrived in Louisiana, riding this "common wind" of Black resistance to enslavement (Scott). It did not take long for enslaved people in Louisiana to use *coartación* and push for revaluations of their labor that moved from bonded work owed to their masters as sovereign patriarchs to domestic labor having a market value worth investing in and trading for manumission (Hanger 26).

Enslaved women took center stage in *coartación*. As Kimberly S. Hanger has demonstrated, female bondspeople outnumbered males in manumission cases and petitions almost two to one. Before Catharina, another woman enslaved to the Destrehan estate initiated the first documented case in the Spanish era. In 1771 Juana Catalina claimed that she did "special services" for her owner and his wife, and so deserved to be released from bondage. Juana Catalina was appraised, based on the inventory of the estate at Destrehan's passing, alongside her son at nine hundred pesos. However, Juana Catalina requested a *carta* only for herself, bringing the appraisal estimate down to three hundred pesos. She paid the sum and received her freedom (Spear 116). When Catharina brought her suit to Boré two years later, she may have learned how to do so from those who went before. The slaves owned by Jean Baptiste Honoré Destrehan and his heirs constituted a plantation-based "slave community" (Blassingame). In other words, what we might think of as a curriculum of manumission and its value likely circulated among the enslaved, in courtyards, gossiped over fences, and whispered about in the streets, squares, and markets of the city. In 1771 the census count of free people of African descent in the colony of Louisiana comprised just over 3 percent of the population (Hanger 17). By 1805 it comprised 19 percent. Use of *coartación* shifted access to and the meaning of freedom along the Gulf Coast.

Black women contested their value to their owners and colonial authorities. As laborers and economic thinkers, they understood how value could be indexed by several factors, including their current and future progeny, their sexual availability, phenotype, age, known skills, and kinship networks. To put it another way, enslaved women knew that their monetary value could not be separated from the many other categories used to commodify and quantify their lives, including their reproductive capabilities and future increase. Juana Catalina, for example, chose to secure her freedom separately from her son. There are a number of reasons she would have made this decision. There is a possibility her son could not be freed. He may have been hired out and out of contact. He may have been owned by another owner and beyond the boundaries of her appeal to Boré and the Destrehan heirs. She may not have been able to secure funds to meet his purchase price. Or she simply might not have wanted to free him, as difficult as this may be to understand.

Two years after Juana Catalina, Catharina likewise fought to control the terms of her value, her motherhood and, therefore, her route to freedom. By the time Catharina stood before the cabildo, Boré had been guardian of the heirs of the Destrehan estate for two years, and it was he who fought her freedom claim. At first, he ignored it. After Catharina submitted her petition, she heard nothing for months. She repeated her request, reiterating her desire for Boré to draw up an estimate of her price. She affirmed that she had the cash on hand, "which she would promptly give" for her freedom and that of her daughter. Boré still did not respond. He may not have received the notices of her petition, or he may have again chosen to ignore them. He was certainly busy expanding the plantation dominion he'd married into.

In 1773 Boré had also purchased a sugar mill and hired a Saint-Domingue engineer to lead the transition from indigo to sugar on property about six miles from the main town of New Orleans (Powell 159). Whatever the reason, only after Don Almonester y Rojas, then a notary in the colony, proffered documentation confirming Boré as the executor of the estate and requiring him to respond did Boré issue a response to Catharina's petition.

Boré's disdain for Catharina bleeds through the manuscript page. Speaking through a translator, Don Francisco Broutin, Boré responded to the cabildo that "in no manner will he consent to giving her [Catharina] freedom." His reasoning was specific: "her bad conduct, wickedness, the dissimulation she has made [in] becoming sick in order to be appraised for a very low price, and the embargo placed in favor of Your Christian Majesty on the liquidation of the inventory of the minor heirs [of the estate]" (*Catharina v. Destrehan*, fol. 11). Boré, in his response, unleashed an explosion of seemingly unnecessary vitriol against Catharina as a person, laborer, and supplicant. Slavery's archive, as is often the case, does not make specific mention of why Boré so impugned Catharina's character. Certainly, his remarks tapped into a broader lexicon of Black womanhood as illicit and degraded. But Boré revealed more than this in his charge of bad conduct, wickedness, and dissimulation. He conceded that Catharina possessed a market knowledge about the value of her labor and body, a knowledge keen enough to potentially "dissimulate" her infirmities. His attack also revealed the value he placed on good conduct. Which is to say, by challenging her character, he revealed his own awareness of enslaved Black women's value as inclusive of the good and agreeable services they provided their owners, the affective and intimate labor they performed for their *Amo* (master). Boré finished by requesting that Catharina's petition be dismissed and that she be asked to pay all court costs.

Catharina refused Boré's portrayal of her and defended her right to an estimation of her value, once again revealing enslaved women's economic and juridical knowledge. Like Black women across the Spanish colonies, she claimed the customary rights and practices of *coartación* as her own. She knew Destrehan's passing opened the door for her to secure an estimate of her value. She knew notaries created inventories of estates when owners passed away and argued, "The appraisal already completed by named experts and the estimate given [about] me authorizes my freedom." She also knew that enslaved people had access to the newly instituted *coartación* process and that "this privilege [*beneficio*]; that some charitable persons may offer the money, may intervene at some time; [and] that I may collect together [the money]; what I am experiencing, thus, is a grave prejudice and there is not a single reason to contravene my cause [*fundada*] in this and for justice" (*Catharina v. Destrehan*, fol. 13). A connection between Juana Catalina and Catharina is untraceable in the archive, but the parallels are striking. Enslaved women understood how to read their worth using the tools available at the time.

Catharina further justified her manumission request by describing the value of her domestic and affective labor to her owners, in particular, a lifetime of caregiving. She made clear that she had done her time, having "been a slave of this estate all of her life" (*Catharina v. Destrehan*, fol. 13). She also stressed that she "had served all of the children of my master Destrehan, most of whom are now married." Catharina positioned the marriages and majority (adult age) of those children as the culmination of her service. The Destrehan heirs no longer needed her if they were managing households (as wives) or heading households (as husbands). She had, in other words, mothered them into adulthood, reproducing another slaveholding generation, who, with enslaved and free servants of their own, presumably no longer needed her. As Adriana Chira points out in her discussion of Cuban manumissions, enslaved people understood that "there is a market logic in domestic slavery" (164). Slave owners, she writes, preferred to see affective and intimate labor in a "separate sphere of exchange" or rather "a domestic and affective realm in which an enslaved person's emotional labor for the enslaver was supposed to transcend transactional thinking by being akin to the self-giving labor of a family member" (164). In contrast, enslaved people viewed their intimate and affective labor, including care work and sex work, as deserving compensation and having a market value. For Catharina, the market value of her lifetime of service to the Destrehan family was her freedom.

Catharina also rejected Boré's claims of her bad conduct, painting a picture of her caregiving services that wove together loyalty and the toll loyalty had taken on her body. She stated that she "had served with fidelity and intention until she fell ill with the habitual infirmity [*enfermedad*] which I suffer from and took me out of service" (*Catharina v. Destrehan*, fols. 13–14). In turning to her injury, Catharina gestured toward "certain accidents" that had taken a toll on her physical health and abilities. This toll existed alongside the caregiving services she'd already performed. It didn't make sense, Catharina pointed out, for Boré to retain the services of "an enslaved female who has the contingency of dying from her habitual infirmities any given day." Not when it was possible for him "to buy with the profit [from her self-purchase] a Negro *mozo* [a young, enslaved boy] servant who would be much more useful to the estate to work." Catharina described her labor, including her service work for her owners, point by point, each as an item for market that could be assigned a value by an outside party. More than that, she bargained for a purchase price she could meet herself and which would also replace her labor in the form of a male slave young enough to train and old enough to learn.

While Catharina offers an enumeration of her caregiving, service, and fidelity to the Destrehan estate as deserving of freedom, she keeps the mothering of her own child in half shadow. She does not describe her care of Felicité, her five-year-old daughter, as part of the merit of her request. Having placed her in the petition and requested that she be part of the appraisal, Catharina's silence around Felicité and her mothering of her cannot be regarded as an accident. There is no reason to suggest Catharina would have held back any fact that might have leveraged her petition in her own favor. Catharina's silence about Felicité therefore emerges as a strategy and a critique and offers provocative suggestions for the ways enslaved people did or did not leverage Black motherhood. Catharina deftly articulated the legal and market knowledges that distilled her affective, intimate, and domestic care for the white family for whom she labored into concrete terms, revising, as Chira noted, what was seen by owners as customary labor into labor having a market value. But a parallel for that same labor between herself and her own progeny did not exist or did not yet exist in these early years of *coartación*. Perhaps the best case she could make for herself and Felicité was no case at all. Whatever interpretation is made of her silence, Catharina's decision to include Felicité in her request for manumission but keep the mothering of her own children out of focus is deliberate and demonstrates enslaved women's economic knowledge about the value (or lack thereof) of Black progeny, fertility, and care under racial capitalism.

More instructive, Boré also offered no rationale for retaining Catharina's reproductive labor, though the gesture to do so is there. In a document registered on October 6, 1773, he called her a liar. He declared that her claims of service to the Destrehans were "very false" and that she could not have been laboring all her life, "since she would have been just a girl and the deceased Destrehan did not lack from other servant girls [*criadas*]" (*Catharina v. Destrehan*, fol. 17). He claimed that a declaration from Don Francisco Le Beau, a doctor in the city, would confirm that she fabricated her injury. He further implicated her propriety, purity, and virtue when he named the cause of her infirmity. Mobilizing an array of Atlantic-wide stereotypes of sexualized Black womanhood, he stated, "If she has any indisposition it comes from her great debauchery [*libertinage*] in this city." However, her supposed licentiousness and dishonesty did not stop him from wanting to maintain her as his slave. In fact, Boré was clear that he valued her for much more than her ability to tell the truth or maintain her moral purity. Boré stated that it was her skilled labor that he required, "in consideration that she is a Mulata who knows how to sew and wash very well" (*Catharina v. Destrehan*, fol. 18).

Felicité was not Catharina's only child. In 1771 Catharina appeared in a Destrehan estate inventory with three children: Carlota, Manon, and Felicité. However, Catharina did not include Carlota and Manon in her petition for self-purchase. When Boré's appraiser determined too high a value for Catharina and Felicité, a flurry of exchanges between Governor Unzaga, Boré, and Catharina ensued, with each arguing the relative accuracy of two slaves' value versus four. In an echo of Juana Catalina's case, Unzaga ordered Boré to name an appraiser who could adjust Catharina and Felicité's price to exclude the value of her other two children. Don Antonio Thomassin served as Boré's proxy and adjusted the value of the enslaved mother and child to 450 pesos from the original 600. Catharina contested his estimation, arguing she'd been appraised with two additional children at five hundred pesos. "It is to be inferred that Mr. Thomassin proceeded without full knowledge to make this price and without taking her infirmity into consideration" (*Catharina v. Destrehan*, fol. 24). Catharina ordered a reappraisal, to be completed by someone who "knows her health, habitual infirmities" and the service that she had performed for her owners (fol. 24). Unzaga agreed, and the new appraiser cut the estimate nearly in half. Five months after her first petition, on November 6, 1773, Boré was forced to allow Catharina and Felicité to purchase their freedom for the price of 320 pesos (*Catharina v. Destrehan*, fol. 32).

Catharina bore at least three living children but secured freedom for only one. Here we argue that she did so deliberately. She appeared before the cabildo with a dollar figure in mind, investment through a third party, and the tenacity to contest her owners. When Catharina brought her request to the Spanish cabildo, her awareness of her value extended to a broader market of slaveholding and labor, but also to a global struggle over the terms of slavery and what freedom would mean. Catharina's attempt to secure freedom encourages scholars to question how enslaved women lived in the wake of the changing systems of valuation, in which, as Morgan has argued, "travelers described women as sexual favors, as sellers of goods, and as chaotic and unaffected parents" (*Reckoning* 111). Catharina took advantage of the imperial transition in Louisiana, a moment when systems of French valuation of enslaved labor were still changing, when colonial conceptions of mastery were being interceded on by differing Spanish conventions. She argued for an expanded rubric of enslaved valuation, one that included caregiving for her owners as a commodity, service and fidelity as for exchange, and injury, or the toll taken on the body, as having a price that should be paid by owners in the form of freedom. Catharina's case illuminates how enslaved women's economic knowledge required them to understand their owners' licit and licentious evaluations of their bodies and physical ability, their everyday lives, and intimate practices.

Ruth's Injury: Valuing Reproduction in Post-emancipation Barbados

Ruth suffered after Burgess, the estate manager, brutalized her. Accommodated by a chair owing to her sustained injury, she told the judge assessing her case, "I am laborer there [on the Lears Estate], where I worked for 30 cents a day." On the day of the assault, a mule-led cane cart overturned. Before Ruth could assist in righting it, Burgess sped by her on horseback and spouted "ill words towards her." As she testified, he threatened "to mash me and my g—ts out," and "before his final words were out his horse's head had me down. The horse mashed me into a cane hole and stood over me." As a result of this assault, Ruth sustained injury and her pregnancy was threatened. She demanded £10 as restitution ("Bridgetown"). After his attack, Ruth had to wait an hour before Rebecca Quarles, her neighbor, could assist her home. When Rebecca found Ruth, her limp and bruised body was wrapped in trash. "I cannot say what part of her body got crushed," Rebecca testified later, "but I heard her cry out, Oh God! Oh God!" ("Bridgetown").

At first, it wasn't clear that Ruth's pregnancy would survive. Following the assault, Ruth's mother took her to see Dr. Rogers, the medical practitioner for St. George's parish. When he examined her, though there were no external marks of violence on her body, "she complained of great pain on being pressed on the right side of the abdomen," and "she appeared to have received a great shock to her nervous system." He judged Ruth to be about four months pregnant, which did not bode well for her being able to carry the pregnancy to term. He testified later that "such shocks as being extremely dangerous to a person in her condition; they are invariably followed by unfavorable circumstances. Such a shock sustained by a woman in the early stages of pregnancy are always attended with danger of abortion, causing great pain and loss of labor to the sufferer" ("Bridgetown"). Ruth returned to the doctor about two weeks later. When Rogers examined her again, she still appeared "very weak, and her general health had suffered in consequence of the shock," but "she had not aborted, nor [did Rogers] now think her in danger of doing so" ("Bridgetown"). Ruth's pregnancy survived, perhaps just barely, the violent caprice of her employer.

Burgess, for his part, blamed the entire affair on Ruth's bad conduct and refusal to obey him. When the cart fell over, Burgess stated, she was one of only two women who did not come to its aid, although "they knew it was their business to come." Burgess's testimony is replete with frustration at Ruth's slow pace, never mind that her pace may have been slower because of her pregnant status. "I called to them several times to come and assist the mules," he stated, "and after some delay they started to come, but walked so slowly that when they came to the cart I told them it appears as if they did not care whether the mules were killed or not, and I desired them to leave the field" ("Bridgetown"). Burgess then claimed he dismissed them from the field. Moreover, he would not admit attacking Ruth. While Rebecca went to leave, Burgess claimed that when Ruth "fell immediately down before the horse, and I did not think she had been touched by it. She did say something, but I don't know what it was, nor whether or not it was said in pain" ("Bridgetown"). Ruth's refusal sparked a spectacular level of violence from Burgess, violence against which she had little recourse except to petition for redress and attempt to heal.

Ruth's case is an example of the ways pregnant Black women and their children came to be valued differently in the years after slavery's end. In 1834 the British empire abolished slavery across all its colonies. Following a four-year "apprenticeship" period of forced labor, former slaves became legally freed from bondage and the property claims of their owners. Denied ownership of freed Black women's offspring, Barbadian planters collectively divested from Black women's reproductive care. No longer slave owners, but still plantation or "estate" owners, white masters closed plantation hospitals, denied pregnant women laborers the right of lying-in confinement when they reached the end of their pregnancies, and rejected requests for time off before or after childbirth. The revision of formal laws and customary practices related to childrearing left Black women laborers both liable and subject to reproductive violence and economic insecurity. For example, pregnant Black women who took any time away from their employers after childbirth to recover, even those who contracted postpartum illnesses, were required to repay that time and/or labor (Paton, "Struggles" 254; Paugh 180). Ruth's seeking medical care with her mother's assistance became a commonplace occurrence, as the responsibility for medical care shifted from plantation owners to individuals. Elderly and infirm laborers, the ones who had previously provided necessary reproductive and childcare, began to be expelled from estates for being unproductive laborers (Inniss 257). Abolition restructured the overall function and labor organization of plantation labor, introducing a new set of challenges to female estate workers, such as Ruth, as they sought to protect themselves and their pregnancies and to raise their children. In other words, despite the difference in status between enslaved and "freed" women, the reduced economic interest in Black women's reproduction in the post-emancipation era ensured they would face continued constraints around their motherhood.

After abolition, the revised calculus around reproduction reintroduced a discourse around Black mothers' alleged bad conduct, immorality, and licentiousness. For example, as a district doctor, Rogers believed he understood the ways reproductive violence, infant mortality, and injury animated post-emancipation life for Black female laborers in Barbados. Appointed by the local legislature, Rogers would manage the health of Black Barbados laborers for over thirty years. He reported examining, on average, over a thousand people per year, many of them infirm Black women with sickly young children. By the 1870s imperial and local government officials began to express deep concern over the overwhelming rates of infant mortality occurring across the island. Prompted by the legislature to account for the high rates of infant mortality, Rogers stated that he had "known of deaths from want of food, children being the chief sufferers. It is a common circumstance for fathers to refuse to support their illegitimate children; others emigrate leaving them in a state of destitution, their mothers thus having to attend to them and being prevented from making a livelihood." In other words, while planter brutality, poor access to food and medical care, and low wages damaged maternal and fetal health in post-emancipation Barbados, elite white men like Rogers made moral, not economic, judgments about the health of Black families on the island. They described Black single motherhood and absentee fathers as the root of the problem, because both prevented Black women from performing their primary function of "making a livelihood."[3]

Ruth's case exposes the failure of emancipation to protect Black women from injury, despite its promises. For decades, abolitionists argued that ending slavery would liberate Black women into the private and protected sphere of the domestic (Lightfoot; Hall; Brown; Newton). Under the apprenticeship system, however, Black women were subject to heightened forms of physical abuse and injury and frequent family separation (Altink; Beckles; Boa; Holt; Inniss). After apprenticeship ended, colonial institutions continued to prioritize controlling Black labor and white estate owner investments over Black women's health, their pregnancies, or their children. The medical establishment transformed structural divestment of resources into moral quandaries, pathologizing Black mothers and assisting in the creation and revision of a new racial calculus around Black reproduction and mothering

(Cooper Owens; Barclay; Ivy). Planters, like William Burgess, demanded subservience and accused laborers of bad conduct to obscure the many ways the reproductive violence and exploitation inherent within slavery's labor relations extended and remade itself in the post-emancipation labor system. The refusal on the part of planters, the colonial office, and abolitionists to attend to forms of reproductive violence that stretched from slavery into freedom ultimately created the conditions possible for Burgess to trample Ruth, without regard for her pregnancy, nearly forty years after the formal abolition of slavery. Pregnant, injured, and destitute, Ruth embodied the compounding oppressions that remained endemic to Black womanhood even in slavery's wake.

Ruth's petition also demonstrates the limits of legal and financial forms of restitution for injury. Despite Ruth's success in court, the payment she was ultimately rewarded would do little to ease the financial hardship Burgess's act of brutality placed on her family. Ruth's mother, as her primary caregiver, would become responsible for protecting Ruth and their family from eviction (Carter 728). If Ruth later miscarried, she would require both the physical and emotional support of the women within her community to recover from the pain of this loss. In other words, financial redress could not undo the racial capitalist system which left Black women exposed to ungendered and reproductive violence. The legal system undergirded, rather than uprooted, estate owners' right to brutalize laborers. The court, by individualizing the physical and reproductive violence of the plantation, did not ease the debilitating pace of sugar production but rather failed to mitigate the unrestrained authority plantation owners held over the laborers in their employment. All of this would continue to leave mothers like Ruth vulnerable to violence and injury.

Black Mothering across Time and Space

Bringing Catharina's and Ruth's stories together challenges us to consider what it means to mother under varied states of unfreedom. Ruth was born into her freedom, yet she still encountered systems and structures that governed her ability to mother. The system of contract labor that emerged in slavery's wake kept intact the plantation logics that devalued Black women's reproductive labor and kinship rights in favor of the property and economic interests of racial capitalism. Catharina's and Ruth's legal battles unsettle the neat boundaries between slavery and freedom. Because they span time, space, and even empire, each of Catharina's and Ruth's injuries offers instructive windows into how reproduction, value, and labor operated together in the Atlantic market economy.

While both Ruth and Catharina were injured, their reproductive values differed by status, forcing them to position their claims for restitution in particular ways. As an enslaved domestic, Catharina could argue her injury diminished her value because her injured body would be unable to perform the around-the-clock care demanded of her by Boré and others. Through careful accounting of her own value, Catharina not only recognized this, but she also leveraged her injury to set a purchase price that responded to a broader market system. Catharina's own children, however, owing to their inherent value, posed a potential challenge to her bid for freedom. By contrast, Ruth's injury would ultimately devalue her as a free laborer, but her pregnancy was without value to Burgess. Catharina's and Ruth's differentiated values would ultimately shape how they negotiated their motherhood. Catharina's petitions drew attention away from her motherhood and reproduction, to safeguard her own freedom and her child's. Ruth, on the other hand, worked to make her reproduction matter. Ruth drew attention to her body as being *so* injured that she risked miscarriage. Ruth, in other words, claimed her reproductive body as a body that should have been protected from terrorizing violence, and herself as deserving of financial restitution.

Both women also demonstrate the ways Black women's economic and imperial knowledge shaped the kinds of claims they made about their value and their injuries. Ruth, like Catharina, positioned her claim within the language of labor and capital. She itemized each expense incurred by her injury: five dollars to see Dr. Rogers, two shillings for brandy to soothe her pain, and three shillings to support her and her mother's transportation to the Bridgetown court. She then juxtaposed these expenses with that of her daily wage of thirty cents a day.[4] She brought her claim to court through an understanding of the British colonial legal system and Judge Fleming's responsibility as a representative of the authority of the Crown. She knew he would work to uphold the power of the law over the individualized power of the planter to discipline and punish (Paton, *Bond* 55). In the end, Judge Fleming awarded £10 to be paid to her by William Burgess ("Bridgetown"). Catharina, likewise, understood the *coartación* process well enough to argue for her value as an obedient worker with years of loyalty to her owners, and to advocate for herself when her self-purchase price was set too high. Catharina and Ruth are both examples of how necessary it was for Black women, enslaved or freed, to understand the structures around them and the ways their productive and reproductive bodies fit into them.

Finally, Ruth's and Catharina's examples demonstrate the ways white landowners used accusations of bad conduct, deviance, *libertinage*, and recalcitrance to justify their control over Black labor. As Sarah Haley has argued, claims of Black women's immorality fall into a larger pattern of colonial representations of Black womanhood (Haley 20). Planters attempted to undermine the legitimacy of Black women's demands for redress by blaming Black women's immoral behavior for their lot. As we see in the case of Catharina, Boré claimed superior and intimate knowledge over the extent of her injury. Likewise, Burgess's comment, that "they [the women in the field] knew it was their business to come," reflected the web of social and servile expectations Black women navigated ("Bridgetown"). Plantation owners used their contractual authority over women's labor to demarcate the limits around where and how Black women should be using their bodies on the estates they worked. To protect his property rights in her, Boré impugned Catharina's character and rejected her attempts to negotiate her own value, claiming superior knowledge of her body and her skills. Likewise, Burgess blamed Ruth for her injury by claiming superior authority over her laboring body and an entitlement to her obedience and subservience as a laborer on his estate.

Conclusion

Ruth's and Catharina's experiences with both injury and value, the similarities and differences in slavery and freedom, suggest the complicated links between Black mothering and racial capitalism. The Atlantic system of reproductive slavery, which mandated that two of Catharina's three children remain chattel, even as she gained her legal freedom, also structured the post-emancipation system of free wage labor that empowered planters to ignore whether Ruth's unborn child lived or died. Gendered racial capitalism required Black mothers to be savvy and careful with how they valued their reproductive labor. When enslaved women like Catharina battled to secure freedom for themselves and others, self-conscious, rational, and precise debates over their value to their owners (as indexed by services provided, conduct, and reproduction) occurred (Hanger 17). Catharina's petition for freedom and response to it foreshadows the ways emancipation, as Natasha Lightfoot has argued, "especially failed to free Black women" because of freed women's role as productive and reproductive laborers (8). The gender-specific failures of the emancipation project come into focus through Ruth's experience as a pregnant field laborer attached to Lears' estate in post-emancipation Barbados. In a post-emancipation society, planters like Burgess recognized that Black women's offspring no longer promised an extension of property, and Black women's reproduction ultimately detracted from, rather than enhanced, planter power. This comparative treatment of the cases of Catharina and Ruth—two Black women on either side of

emancipation—allows for a reading of injury, value, mothering, and reproduction across time and space.

Black women grappled with ways racial capitalism's crushing logic impacted their ability to make claims as mothers. Though a century apart, Catharina and Ruth demonstrate how Black women built economic and legal
knowledge to protect themselves. They demonstrate the ways the value of
Black women's reproductive capacity could differ in slave versus post-
emancipation societies. But they also demonstrate the limits of claims
of Black motherhood, limits that forced Black women to be creative
with their own self-valuations and aware of the imperial and economic
structures they lived under. The physical and emotional demands of providing caregiving service to men, women, and children; the physical and
emotional demands of labor; and the threat of injurious violence—these
all shaped how Black women mothered. More important, those demands
shaped how, where, when, and whether Black women would claim to be
mothers. These two cases reveal the synergies not just of the imperial legal
system, which could be capricious as well as implacable, but also the
important role fissures, tensions, and shifts in legal and economic regimes
played in the lived reality of Black women as mothers. ■

Halle-Mackenzie Ashby is a PhD candidate in the Department of History at Johns Hopkins
University. She writes on the history of gender, slavery, and emancipation in the Caribbean. She is the current African American History Mellon Dissertation Scholar at the Library Company of Philadelphia.

Jessica Marie Johnson is associate professor in the Department of History at Johns Hopkins University. She is author of *Wicked Flesh: Black Women, Intimacy, and Freedom in the
Atlantic World* (2020) and founding director and editor of *Keywords for Black Louisiana*
(keywordsforblacklouisiana.org).

ACKNOWLEDGMENTS

This collaborative piece would not have been possible without the Reproducing Racial
Capitalism workshops organized over the past several months. We are grateful to all
participants for their thoughtful and attentive feedback and would like to issue our grat-
itude to Jennifer Morgan, Alys Eve Weinbaum, and Lila Chambers for cultivating and
convening such a generative intellectual space. We would like to extend a huge thank you
for the care, support, and patience provided by Alys Weinbaum and Jennifer Morgan
throughout the publication process, as well as the editors and anonymous reviewers of
History of the Present. Finally, we are thankful to the participants and conveners of
Johns Hopkins Black World Seminar, as well as the Latin American and Caribbean Studies
seminar for providing feedback on earlier versions of this piece. A special thank you to Dr.
Nathan Connolly's work in progress on the history of Atlantic history, which inspired the
first drafts of this article.

1 Catharina vs. Destrehan, Louisiana Historical Center, 1773-06-25-01. Hereafter *Catharina v. Destrehan* with corresponding folio numbers. This case is being transcribed for a forthcoming digital edition, "Kinship and Belonging in Louisiana," vol. 142 of *Scholarly Editing* edited by Olivia Barnard, Emma Bilski, Leila Blackbird, Ellie Palazzolo, and Jessica Marie Johnson. It is also included in *Keywords for Black Louisiana*, a National Historical Publications and Records Program digital documentary edition project directed by Jessica Marie Johnson (keywordsforblacklouisiana.org). All Spanish translations are by Johnson in consultation with Emma Bilski, Leila Blackbird, Kaillee Coleman, Guadalupe Garcia, and Christina Villarreal. All mistakes are Johnson's alone.

2 Hereafter, "Ruth" to maintain consistency between both historical actors, as Catharina as an enslaved woman does not possess a surname.

3 BS 39a, "Report of the Commission on Poor Relief 1875-1877," August 28, 1875, Barbados Department of Archives.

4 During this period Barbados was using different kinds of currency, including shillings, pounds, and dollars.

WORKS CITED

Altink, Henrice. "Slavery by Another Name: Apprenticed Women in Jamaican Workhouses in the Period 1834-8." *Social History* 26, no. 1 (2001): 40-59.

Barclay, Jenifer L. "Mothering the 'Useless': Black Motherhood, Disability, and Slavery." *Women, Gender, and Families of Color* 2, no. 2 (2014): 115-40.

Beckles, Hilary. *Great House Rules: Landless Emancipation and Workers Protest in Barbados, 1838-1938*. Kingston, Jamaica: Ian Randle, 2004.

Blassingame, John W. *The Slave Community: Plantation Life in the Antebellum South*. New York: Oxford University Press, 1979.

Boa, Sheena. "Experiences of Women Estate Workers during the Apprenticeship Period in St Vincent, 1834-38: The Transition from Slavery to Freedom." *Women's History Review* 10, no. 3 (2001). https://doi.org/10.1080/09612020100200291.

"Bridgetown Petty Debt Court: Ruth Sealy v. W.C Burgess." *Barbados Times*, May 20, 1876.

Brown, Christopher Leslie. *Moral Capital: Foundations of British Abolitionism*. Chapel Hill: Published for the Omohundro Institute of Early American History and Culture, Williamsburg, Virginia, by the University of North Carolina Press, 2006.

Carter, Henderson. *Labour Pains: Resistance and Protest in Barbados, 1838-1904*. Kingston, Jamaica: Ian Randle, 2012. Kindle.

Chira, Adriana. *Patchwork Freedoms: Law, Slavery, and Race beyond Cuba's Plantations*. Cambridge: Cambridge University Press, 2022.

Cooper Owens, Deirdre. *Medical Bondage: Race, Gender, and the Origins of American Gynecology*. Athens: University of Georgia Press, 2017.

Fuente, Alejandro de la, and Ariela Gross. *Becoming Free, Becoming Black: Race, Freedom, and Law in Cuba, Virginia, and Louisiana*. Cambridge: Cambridge University Press, 2020.

Haley, Sarah. *No Mercy Here: Gender, Punishment, and the Making of Jim Crow Modernity*. Chapel Hill: University of North Carolina Press, 2016.

Hall, Catherine, *Civilising Subjects: Metropole and Colony in the English Imagination, 1830-1867*. Oxford: Polity, 2002.

Hanger, Kimberly S. *Bounded Lives, Bounded Places: Free Black Society in Colonial New Orleans, 1769-1803*. Durham, NC: Duke University Press, 1997.

Hartman, Saidiya. *Scenes of Subjection: Terror, Slavery, and Self-Making in Nineteenth-Century America*. New York: Oxford University Press, 1997.

Holt, Thomas C. *The Problem of Freedom: Race, Labor, and Politics in Jamaica and Britain, 1832-1938*. Baltimore, MD: Johns Hopkins University Press, 1992.

Inniss, Tara A. "From Slavery to Freedom: Children's Health in Barbados, 1823-1838." *Slavery and Abolition* 27, no. 2 (2011): 251-60.

Ivy, Nicole. "Bodies of Work: A Meditation on Medical Imaginaries and Enslaved Women." *Souls* 18, no. 1 (2016): 11-31.

Johnson, Jessica Marie. *Wicked Flesh: Black Women, Intimacy, and Freedom in the Atlantic World*. Philadelphia: University of Pennsylvania Press, 2020.

Lightfoot, Natasha. *Troubling Freedom: Antigua and the Aftermath of British Emancipation*. Durham, NC: Duke University Press, 2015.

Morgan, Jennifer L. *Reckoning with Slavery: Gender, Kinship, and Capitalism in the Early Black Atlantic*. Durham, NC: Duke University Press Books, 2021.

Mustakeem, Sowande' M. *Slavery at Sea: Terror, Sex, and Sickness in the Middle Passage*. Urbana: University of Illinois Press, 2016.

Newton, Melanie. *The Children of Africa in the Colonies: Free People of Color in Barbados in the Age of Emancipation. Antislavery, Abolition, and the Atlantic World*. Baton Rouge: Louisiana State University Press, 2008.

Paton, Diana. "Maternal Struggles and the Politics of Childlessness under Pronatalist Caribbean Slavery." *Slavery and Abolition* 38, no. 2 (2017): 251-68.

Paton, Diana. *No Bond but the Law: Punishment, Race, and Gender in Jamaican State Formation, 1780-1870*. Durham, NC: Duke University Press, 2004.

Paugh, Katherine. *The Politics of Reproduction: Race, Medicine, and Fertility in the Age of Abolition*. Oxford: Oxford University Press, 2017.

Powell, Lawrence N. *The Accidental City: Improvising New Orleans*. Cambridge, MA: Harvard University Press, 2013.

Premo, Bianca. *The Enlightenment on Trial: Ordinary Litigants and Colonialism in the Spanish Empire*. New York: Oxford University Press, 2017.

Scott, Julius. *A Common Wind: Afro-American Organization in the Revolution against Slavery*. New York: Verso, 2018.

Spear, Jennifer M. *Race, Sex, and Social Order in Early New Orleans*. Baltimore, MD: Johns Hopkins University Press, 2009.

SJ Zhang

What Cecilia Knew
Reading Reproduction and Marronage in Records
of Recapture

ABSTRACT This article explores how, in 1784 New Orleans, Cecilia Conway—a recaptured maroon woman—asserted that she was pregnant and thereby leveraged the power of her reproductive labor. Her claims about her body briefly slowed down the system of capital punishment activated in response to her *marronage* by altering the trajectory of the state-sanctioned sexual violence inflicted on her. The conversations between Cecilia and the prison's authorities that this article unearths constitute an original archive of Cecilia's assertions while accounting for their heavily mediated and yet remarkable presence. By centering the details of Cecilia's life, this article helps recast the threat of *marronage* in colonial Louisiana from simply one of male-led armed rebellion to one of reproduction, thorny kinship networks, and a potential maroon society.

KEYWORDS marronage, reproduction, prison, pregnancy, Louisiana

In October 1784 in Spanish New Orleans, the actions of a recaptured maroon woman named Cecilia triggered the creation of four documents about her body. In these documents, the colonial administrator Francisco María de Reggio returned to Cecilia's case four months after he first postponed her execution. Her death was delayed then because she told officials when she was recaptured in June that she was pregnant. When in October she asserted that she was *"preñada de nuevo"* (pregnant again), Reggio ordered two doctors to reexamine Cecilia. In their report, they said they could neither confirm nor deny that Cecilia was pregnant, that *"sus artes no les daban bastantes luces para reconocer una preñez de esta naturalesa"* (their arts do not shed sufficient light so as to recognize a pregnancy of this nature). They instead reported Cecilia's own claims for how she knew she was with child. The documents wrestle with what to do about what is essentially Cecilia's counterclaim. She stated that she knows she is pregnant because she stopped menstruating and

HISTORY of the PRESENT ▪ A Journal of Critical History ▪ 14:1 ▪ April 2024
DOI 10.1215/21599785-10898396 © 2024 Duke University Press

because she previously had sex with male prisoners. Reggio's subsequent missive brims with frustration, and the series of documents ends with his order to postpone Cecilia's execution for two additional months. The last lines consist of a directive to the warden that Cecilia not be allowed to have further sexual relations with any person in the jail. In Cecilia's case, the archive's fragmentation makes it impossible to know for certain whether she was pregnant a first time, a second time, or ever. Certainty on this point appears essential to the story, but in many ways the uncertainty *is* the story. Cecilia's choices to leverage that uncertainty create the record. Cecilia made claims that had to be noted down and addressed by the "powerful men recording the lives and actions of those whom they subordinated" (Cooper 105). Her actions turn on the recorder and are the only reason we can today read her story, a simultaneously novel and quotidian maroon narrative.

Cecilia's arrest and incarceration occurred during a dragnet military campaign described at the time as *la expedición contra los negros cimarrones*, in which the Spanish authorities, then in control of Louisiana, sought to eliminate the "maroon problem" they worried threatened the stability of the colony. Scores of maroons escaped from the city of New Orleans and nearby plantations into the surrounding cypress forests and swamps, often called *el monte*. Reggio, a Frenchman, was at this time the *alcalde ordinario de primer voto* and acting civil governor in Governor Miró's absence. The *alcaldes ordinarios*, "besides acting as judges . . . were expected to patrol the city and investigate crimes. They enjoyed the assistance of the *alguacil mayor* (chief constable), his lieutenants, the *Cabildo escribano* (colonial council scribe), and, if necessary, citizens or troops" (Din and Harkins 107). Despite being empowered to act as both law and order by the Spanish royal authorities, Reggio's efforts to eliminate the growing maroon community were mostly unsuccessful before 1783.

In response to the failed attempts, officials, planters, and other members of the public debated the best course of action. Planters (mostly French) resented and blamed the more "lenient" Spanish slave code for increased marronage but did not want to pay taxes to fund the slave-catching missions they demanded (Din, "Cimarrones" 241). The fears and the increasing level of alarm of the planters is documented in transcribed cabildo sessions, petitions, and Spanish government correspondence (McConnell 22–23).[1] The protracted *expedición* of the 1780s created a notable paper trail of who engaged maroons in conflict and when. These documents are examples of what Kathryn Joy McKnight and Leo J. Garofalo call "Ibero-Atlantic documentary genres," those printed materials that remain archival and were not published for broad perusal, enjoyment, or consultation (xix). The archive of marronage in Louisiana is scattered across a variety of these genres from the Spanish, French, and American periods. The documents concerning Cecilia's case are found at the end of a long series of witness testimonies and transcribed court proceedings concerning a trial of two maroons named Carlos and Jasmin from the previous year, 1783.[2] Like the trial records, her documents offer rare details of what recapture meant for those who went maroon in Louisiana.

When Michel Foucault theorized the fragmented archives of "infamous men," he argued that we come to know them only because a confrontation with the state "snatched them from darkness. . . . [W]ithout that collision, it's very unlikely that any word would be there to recall their fleeting trajectory" (284). True, the archive of Cecilia's experience "snatches" her from the darkness. But it is not simply a collision with those in power that gives us a fleeting glimpse of her life. Cecilia triggered this archive because of what *she* did after that collision with power. In the documents, we can read for how she negotiated her body, her pregnancy(ies), her relationships with certain men, and her position as a prisoner returned to New Orleans. In so doing, she compels a record of her actions and arguments, all of which she makes of her own volition, according to the text. Yes, her archive is a site of violence and oppression. It can also be read, despite itself, for Cecilia's account of her experiences. From the documents, one can glimpse how she might have understood the import of her various relations and the political weight of her pregnant body in her historical moment.

Reading for Cecilia's knowledge is a practice of navigating texts of recapture as they were created in alarmed response to the juncture of marronage and reproduction. Many women escaped to the swamps and cypress forests outside New Orleans to join or start families. When some were recaptured in 1783, they were interrogated for information about their survival strategies and their "family ties" (Hall 218). They described their flight in relational terms, mapping a community defined by kinship networks.[3] Roseta, Maria, Catiche, and others said that they went maroon to join a spouse or reconnect with children and other family. These women's responses form the larger archival context in which Cecilia's particular story can be read. They are the women Cecilia knew, and they too asserted kinship in response to the state's probing questions.

Cecilia's attempts to undermine her death sentence underscore recapture as another context in which racial capital was reproduced. In a world that depended on a binary of free and unfree, the reproductive labor of a woman who lives as a maroon signifies a departure, an outlier.[4] Nevertheless, the state must reckon with Cecilia; it attempted, through physical examination and official discussion, to reconcile her outlying body with its various bina-ries: slave/free, pregnant/not pregnant, fugitive/captured. Despite the vio-lent attention of its actors, the state finds Cecilia's pregnancy is difficult to "see" (this is the vision-oriented language of the archive) and thus Cecilia's assertions momentarily confound the cooperating plantation and carceral systems. Her assertions stand in contradiction with the colonial archive that contains them. They evince what she knew: her own ability to impact the system (however minimally and temporarily).

In the first part of this article, "*Ir Simarrona*," I contextualize the archival documents concerning Cecilia in terms of the gendered histories of slavery that "unsee" enslaved and maroon women. Jessica Marie Johnson describes the way the "null values" of absent bodies "surfac[e] silence in the empirical, imperial archive," thus "imbu[ing] absence with disruption and possibility" (134–35). In this case, it is scholarship more than the archive that ignores the women in this Louisiana maroon community. In the case of Cecilia and the other maroon women recaptured in 1783 and 1784, the "silences" and the "absence" are produced in the retellings of this period, the historiogra-phy, some of which I briefly address here. Following a Black feminist method of attention, my close readings center Cecilia and her assertions of her preg-nancy and argue for the ways in which her voice is present in the text. The details of her records suggest Cecilia might have made a move in line with many other enslaved defendants in colonial Louisiana who, as Sophie White argues, often used the moment of testimony to "redirect[t] the court's focus away from the crimes at hand" (4).

In the second part of the article, "Leveraging Uncertainty," I argue that Cecilia's pregnancies pose a twofold problem for a state that is unprepared to legislate a case in which a formerly enslaved woman becomes pregnant while living in a maroon community and again while in prison. Cecilia's assertions lay bare an internal conflict within this slave society between mandates for punishment and the promotion of slave "increase" (Morgan, *Laboring* 82–83). Beyond "null value," the "problem" of marronage where it meets the repro-duction of racial capital underscores the *uncertain* value of someone like Ce-cilia who maintained a life adjacent to the colonial plantation-carceral sys-tem. By asserting more than once that she was pregnant, Cecilia added an additional layer of uncertainty to the state's racial capital calculus. In Ceci-lia's case (and that of other women in similar positions), giving birth must precede punishment or death. As a result, the questions of her pregnancy and the timing of the birth become the state's business, even as the planter who would benefit from her "increase" is presumably looking over the state's shoulder, if not yelling in its ear.

The interests of men in power in whether Cecilia was truthful about her reproductive labor is not simply a response to how her fraught status as an enslaved prisoner revealed the conflicting aims of the colonial authorities and the planter class. Holding these records up to the light, a watermark becomes visible. It is the sign of the implied maroon child. Cecilia and other maroon women created and maintained blood and chosen family in *el monte*. They made possible a generation born, not in or after, but apart from slavery. Cecilia's assertions reveal how such children, even just their potential, troubled the accounting that reproduced racial capitalism. While I will not discuss the maroon child at length in these pages, I want to flag how their specter signified a radical future yet to be born. The amount of ink spilled over the question of whether Cecilia was with child can only be fully explained by what she knew: the uncertainty around her pregnancy and future child stood in for the possibility of a multigenerational maroon community. Her actions begged the question: who can claim the child born into marronage?

Ir Simarrona: Gender and Marronage in Louisiana

In step with a lamentably persistent historiography in which "slave" equals "man" is an account of the past in which "maroon" also equals "man." Many women in the Atlantic world escaped slavery as fugitives headed to so-called free states, but a larger number of women escaped to live as maroons, often while pregnant or with their children. They did so by living within the bounds of the slave state in clandestine communities big and small, sustained by subsistence agriculture, human networks, and illicit economies.[5] They formed, at minimum, a quarter of maroon communities in every slave society (Morgan, *Reckoning* 231). As Jennifer L. Morgan details, historiography has consistently "unseen" women in maroon communities, dismissing them as part of contraband, as "plunder" stolen from plantations, or as passive members of "harems" of the men living as maroons (Morgan, *Reckoning* 217). She writes of those attempting to narrate insurrection: "At best, white colonists would have understood Maroon women as providing the food and shelter that nurtured the rebels" (228). Discourses of armed resistance and insurrection often find such rebellions incompatible with family and motherhood.

The existence of women living as maroons and taking prominent positions in maroon communities has been thoroughly documented by scholars across many fields (Bilby; Davis; Gottlieb; Diouf; Price). These scholars emphasize the transhistorical import and meaning of the decisions that women made to escape and live as maroons. Of course, there are some women well known for having gone maroon, including Solitude, who was officially named a Guadeloupean national hero; Queen Nanny, leader of the Cockpit Maroons in Jamaica; or La Virreina Juana in New Granada, for example. These individuals, though, are often figured as anomalous. Present-day maroon communities, descendants of communities that lived in proximate separation from historical plantations, preserve the histories of these women in stories, songs, and traditional practices. In many instances, members of these communities have informed the scholarship referenced above, offering more insights than the fragmented archive can ever spit up.

■ ■ ■

Cecilia and San Malo were captured on the same day in June 1784. He appears first on the list of thirty-two maroons taken from La Tierra Gayarre and is described as "San Maló de Mr. Darensbourg." Cecilia, on the next line, is described as "Cecilia à Mr. Canuet su mujer."[6] The modifications to her name, in the indexical and possessive form, indicate, according to the colonial recorder, that she belongs prepositionally to Mauricio Conway, she belongs *to* or is *of* his things, while also belonging relationally to San Malo, as *his* wife. Though no other maroons from this community described Cecilia as San Malo's wife, despite detailing many other husband-wife relationships, Spanish officials insisted on this connection. Cecilia is described as San Malo's "inseparable companion in all his exploits" in a description of her arrest (Hall 232). Unlike the men with whom she was meant to be executed, Cecilia was not accused of murder, and yet she received the death sentence. Even officials at the time sought an explanation for what seemed like an excessive punishment based on their perceived relationship. Her proximity to San Malo in the eyes of the state is not seen to reflect a possible leadership role; their relationship is interpreted by the state (and only the state) as that of a man and "his wife" (Morgan, *Reckoning* 236). Below I discuss additional letters between officials concerned with her connection to Conway as his property and their feared conflicts of interest. It is these relationships to men that both doomed Cecilia in life and preserved her in the archive.

Of the thirty-two maroons captured that day, including Cecilia and San Malo, at least eleven were women. They were called Theresa, Janeton, Charlota, Margarita, Rosete, "una negra." These women were labeled "*simarronas*," declared guilty and sentenced to be taken out of prison with a rope around their neck and branded on their left cheek with *M* for *marron* (a vestige of the previous French regime). Theirs and Cecilia's plots, that is, their own plotting and strategy, do not feature in the typical account of marronage. Their absence is a matter of attention, not a result of an archive too fragmented to assess. Cecilia's archive allows us to read the scenes of the plot without the need to fully fabulate them (Hartman, "Venus" 11; "Plot"). The scenes from this brief period of her life are preserved in the mediation itself. Peeking through the squiggles and flourishes in the signatures of self-aggrandizing men are representations of Cecilia's actions and her account of her life and her body in the prison. The result is an additional history of what it meant *ir simarrona* (to go maroon) in the late eighteenth century.

The archive created around Cecilia must be understood in the context of a historical continuum of the plantation and carceral systems—the collaboration of state and planter in the shackling of Black and Native "runaways." Scholars have also noted seemingly counterintuitive "uses" of early carceral spaces, like enslaved people "escaping" to prisons to avoid cruel punishments on plantations (Manion 27). Flight to a jail or slave owners' using prisons as a form of punishment is a reminder of the continuum between bondage and captivity, and how unfreedom was a spectrum that people navigated strategically. Christopher R. Adamson's work underscores the paradox of the enslaved prisoner: the "very idea of imprisonment as punishment for crimes committed by slaves was a contradiction. The African slave was already a prisoner" (557). Marronage pushes further on this formulation. The African slave is better understood as a captive (Spillers 67–68). When Cecilia, or Janeton, or Maria escaped the plantation, joined a maroon community but was later caught and imprisoned for the crime of being a maroon, they experienced *recapture*. They were taken from the land and families they nurtured in *el monte*.

For the incarcerated enslaved person, there is no neat analogy between being on "the outside" and "freedom" and being on "the inside" and "unfreedom" because "the outside" was most likely the plantation. Again, marronage complicates this picture. Someone incarcerated for living as a maroon would have also experienced the "outside" as some kind of freedom, some world apart. The maroon women jailed after being recaptured had a fundamentally different experience than the English soldier imprisoned for assault or the enslaved person arrested for theft. I agree with Diana Paton that "it is much harder to get at the point of view of enslaved and free people who spent time in prisons"; the record of their presence is of a quantitative and categorical nature and "reduce[s] the complex humanity of the people it seeks to represent" (39). The archive is dehumanizing in this way. Still, the details of the records concerning Cecilia (explored below) demand we not lose sight of the particular kinds of knowledge someone might acquire in their experience of recapture, and how they might use it to respond to the trauma of separation from their community. In addition to revealing Cecilia's strategies, her assertions urge us to consider the plantation-carceral regime of colonial New Orleans as one that, despite itself, revolved around Cecilia and her body.

The "problem" of what to do with a recaptured maroon woman, temporarily property of the state as a prisoner, is compounded by her pregnancy and doubled when she gives birth. When an imprisoned free-born woman is or becomes pregnant, leading to a reduction or stay of her execution, it is called "pleading the belly" and was common beginning in Medieval Europe (Butler, "More"). The pregnant prisoner becomes more troublesome for authorities who must consider the rights of her future free-born child, and suspicion of her claim was a common response of the court (Butler, "Pleading" 132). But when an enslaved woman becomes pregnant while imprisoned, the penal system struggles to concede conception beyond the boundaries of the plantation and that the child is in part a product of the state's prison system. Diana Paton recounts a hypothetical as proscribed by Jamaican legislation in 1831:

> Legislators invented elaborate means to ensure that the process of incarceration did not end with a slave's being released without a master. What was to happen, for instance, to the unborn child of an enslaved woman who was pregnant when she was sentenced to execution, transportation or life imprisonment (the woman would not be executed or transported until her child was born)? The owners of such a slave would be entitled to compensation for her value. Theoretically, then, her child became the property of the state, because it had effectively purchased her. While state authorities had no desire to maintain enslaved children in the prisons, it was imperative that a child in these anomalous circumstances did not become free. The 1830 slave code legislated for this anomaly, proposing that the child should be kept in the workhouse for the first five years of life and then sold at public auction. This clause was amended on the grounds that it was inhumane to expose a young child to public sale; instead, he or she was to become the property of his or her mother's former master. (48)

Of course, the irony of the legislation's conclusion, that the "inhumane" feature of this situation is the *public* nature of the sale, was probably not lost on some of the historical actors involved. The state's role, via the prison, as de facto slave owner reveals the prison's original dehumanizing role and previews its subsequent absorption of chattel slavery and the plantation system of labor extracted from unfree individuals.

Cecilia's story is not hypothetical, and it further underscores the reality that a woman imprisoned in a slave society was likely to be imprisoned while pregnant or to become pregnant while in prison. Cecilia, like so many others, was punished for committing one of the many "offenses that by definition could only be committed by slaves," that is, she stole herself (Paton 34). In this case, the law must further contort itself in response to the pregnant prisoner. Cecilia asserted pregnancy on two different occasions, forcing officials to confront conception within a growing and extremely proximate maroon community as well as within the prison newly crowded with maroons. For this imprisoned woman who lived as a maroon, reproduction meant *delayed* punishment, a frustration of the system. The contrived logic of chattel slavery reveals a tension between the interests of the state and those of the private planter class. The former wants death to those it views as conspirators; the latter wants "social death" that, most importantly, can be reproduced (Patterson).

Cecilia's experience in the *royal carcel* is both disturbing and familiar. A woman of color in custody of the state is pregnant, and the white men who control that "state" find that her body, as it grows a second person, interferes with her imprisonment and punishment. Her body becomes what Sasha Turner has called a "contested site" (9). In this instance, Cecilia's knowledge of her person is deemed less reliable than the state's tracking of her sexual activities and menstrual cycle. Cecilia's experience in jail is, of course, part of a long history of the state ordering "medically unnecessary pelvic examinations" while shackling pregnant incarcerated women.[7] Nevertheless, enslaved women took impressive control of their bodies, given the literal restraints they faced; their inherent and inherited knowledge and practices enabled their choices about when to become or not to become a mother. The scholarship of historians, including Barbara Bush, Jennifer L. Morgan, Marisa Fuentes, and Sasha Turner, details the ways in which enslaved women's bodies were sites of contest, competition, and conflict. Even more urgently, their work shows how these women asserted control over their bodies in contested circumstances. When plantation medical practices took forms that today would be called imprisonment and torture (though many persist or resurface in practice today with the increased rolling back of reproductive rights), and when doctors aided enslavers and did the medical/punitive bidding of the state, all while trying to maintain "scientific methods" in pursuit of objective truths, women still managed to sometimes control their reproductive labor.

Cecilia's assertion that she had sex with other prisoners evokes numerous questions about Cecilia's experience inside the jail, including questions of safety and consent, and also curiosity about how much contact and communication was possible for her and the others imprisoned in the *royal carcel*. The original jail was constructed by the French from 1729 to 1730, then reconstructed and expanded in 1753. After transfer of the colony to the Spanish, fires in the cabildo led to repairs of the jail in 1788, not long after Cecilia was held there. Sophie White describes the jail during the French years to include a structure of two buildings connected by a courtyard, the *chambre criminelle* for interrogations, and four upper-level "communal cells." There appear to have been four additional *cachots* or solitary confinement cells and the *chambre de consierge* (15). The prison at the time of Cecilia's confinement was crowded with maroons captured during the *expedicíon* (Din and Harkins 166). Following Paton's logic, it seems that "it would be remarkable if the prisoners had not told one another stories of how they came to be in prison and, in doing so, exchanged information about techniques of resistance" (42). Additional difficult questions concern: How would Reggio's final proscription have been carried out? How would they prevent sexual intercourse, consensual or nonconsensual, inside the jail? Through solitary confinement? With a personal guard? Of course, in all this speculation, no answer is good for Cecilia.

Twentieth-century scholars have been primarily interested in Cecilia's case as a brief mystery within the tragic rise and fall of San Malo. Historians have also asked why she wasn't executed with the others, and their shared answer is that she faked a pregnancy. Gwendolyn Midlo Hall (1992) and Sylviane A. Diouf (2014) agree that Cecilia lied, and they offer miscarriage as a possible explanation for the second pregnancy: "Cecilia was not really pregnant, or else she miscarried, because on October 25, 1784, her execution was suspended when she claimed again to be in the early stages of pregnancy" (Hall 232–33). Diouf writes, "On October 25, Cecilia, who should have delivered a child by then, was reexamined. She said she was pregnant again. The physicians, stating it was too early to make a determination, asked to see her two months later. Playing on a pregnancy that seemed as fabricated as the first—unless she had miscarried—Cecilia escaped death a second time and nothing is known of what ultimately happened to her" (182). Hall's and Diouf's assessments characterize Cecilia's assertions as "claims" and "fabrications," as acts of "playing on a pregnancy." In their writing, Cecilia's potential miscarriage falls between two commas and two dashes; it is destined for grammatical interstices. In this construction, the authors suggest that one can read the sentence *without* the miscarriage and it still makes sense: "Cecilia was not really pregnant . . . because on October 25, 1784, her execution was suspended when she claimed again to be in the early stages of pregnancy"; "Playing on a pregnancy that seemed as fabricated as the first, . . . Cecilia escaped death a second time." Of course, a miscarriage would have been very likely. Given the stress and deprivations of her imprisonment, the trauma of facing execution, and the loss of her community outside the prison walls, it may have been especially difficult in her first five months in jail for Cecilia to carry a pregnancy to term. It seems equally possible that Cecilia did choose to lie strategically about one or both of her pregnancies. If there was local precedent, she perhaps already knew that becoming pregnant could produce a delay in her execution. That history would be the kind of urgent knowledge shared among enslaved and maroon women. She might have learned this information while imprisoned. Perhaps she knew a good deal about Conway's position in the planter political class, or she thought she could leverage her relation to San Malo and the state's obsession with him.

Leveraging Uncertainty: What Cecilia Told Them

Like many colonial documents, the records concerning Cecilia's pregnancy and incarceration serve to relay information between officials; but they also offer a glimpse of an unrecorded conversation between Cecilia and the doctors. What the scribe Fernando Rodriguez depicts in his documents are really two conversations, one of which he did not witness: the doctors tell Rodriguez that Cecilia told them she is pregnant. Contained within the doctor's report is the conversation they had with Cecilia in which she declares herself pregnant, that she believes she is pregnant again (*"se creía preñada de nuevo"*) because her menstruation has stopped (*"respecto a ser suprimido sus reglas"*) and that she came to be pregnant as a result of relations she had with male prisoners (*"provenia esta preñez de la comunicacion que tenia con los hombres que estaban presos"*). The echoes of what they said to each other leave a strikingly different impression than the controlled mediated testimonies of other maroons in the jail recorded elsewhere by the colonial scribe. In the odd turns of phrase and unexpected vocabulary of Cecilia's documents, we get a sense of the translation of the conversation, the parts Rodriguez could paraphrase and those that, perhaps, he could only transcribe. The uneven description, especially as compared to other documents produced by Rodriguez, suggests that some of the language might have survived the journey from ear to paper taken by the private conversations.

The following passage is my translation of the first half of the document written by Rodriguez in which the relayed conversations are evident, and referred to somewhat directly:

> In the city of New Orleans, on the aforesaid day month and year, I attest that Don Jph Montegut and Dn Roberto Dow, surgeons of the King, appeared before me, the public notary, and said that, according to that which was mandated by the previous order, they examined the *negra* Cecilia imprisoned in the public jail—they have declared she told them that, considering her menstruation has

stopped she believes herself to be pregnant again and that she came to be pregnant as a result of relations she had with male prisoners.

Cecilia knows how pregnancies happen. The missing period(s) is the "symptom" or sign of pregnancy, but she tells the doctors the cause is that she had
sex with other prisoners. She came to be pregnant by having sex. Cecilia
asserts her own diagnoses produced by what she knows about her body,
and the doctors are obliged to convey them for reasons discussed below.
The text contains echoes of how Cecilia spelled out for the doctors the
ways in which a person becomes pregnant. The silence, too, is loud around
questions of consent. Reference to the "male prisoners" also evokes their empowered foil, the "male guards." Cecilia was certainly strategic in *relaying*
that she had sex with other prisoners to the doctors. It is not at all out of
the question that the sex itself was strategic, even if that was unimaginable
to the doctors.[8] She forces their attention onto the conditions of the prison
and alerts us to the proximity of prisoners of all sexes, that "*la comunicacion*"
was possible. It does not seem likely that she would have claimed the ability
to have sex with other prisoners if it were not physically (in terms of the space
and the protocols) possible somewhere in the *royal carcel*. This detail of her
assertions is not disputed by any of the authorities in this exchange; it is, in
fact, spitefully recognized by Reggio.

After Rodriguez notes Cecilia's claims as they are described by the surgeons, he elaborates in the same report on how the surgeons describe their
relation to Cecilia's self-diagnosis.

> According to that which the aforementioned surgeons told me, that they could
> not certify more than what she said and that they are obligated to refer to that
> which she said, that their arts do not shed sufficient light so as to recognize a
> pregnancy of this nature, they requested I make a report of this. I attest that
> they signed it.
> Jph Montegut
> Robert Dow
> Appear before me
> Fernando Rodriguez

Rodriguez underscores the extent to which the doctors defer to Cecilia's account; he is careful to tell Reggio that, in fact, Cecilia remains the authority
on her own case. The surgeons' knowledge is limited, and they are all for the
time being obligated to refer and defer to what she said. The surgeons' failure
to offer their own interpretation of Cecilia's womb is couched in an inability
to see ("*sus artes no les daban bastantes luces*") and a dehumanizing language of

animal husbandry and discourse of the "natural" (*"para reconocer una preñez de esta naturalesa"*). They put distance between her body and the "nature of things" that can be known. They turn to metaphor in explanation of their *artes* that fail them, those arts being the recently male-controlled modern gynecological discourse.

In his final official missive concerning Cecilia, Reggio acknowledges the doctors' examination "concerning the pregnancy" of Cecilia: "Given that the examination completed by the doctors Don Roberto Day and Surgeon Don Joseph Motegui, concerning the pregnancy of the free black woman Cecilia,[9] is inconclusive of whether or not it is such a pregnancy and consists only of the declaration of the aforesaid, suspend for a period of two months the death penalty pronounced against her." Reggio deems it inconclusive because their report "consists only of the declaration of the aforesaid." For that reason, he decides to suspend Cecilia's execution for two months. Cecilia's conclusive argument for why she knows she is pregnant is deemed "inconclusive," and, predictably, her authority is not honored in this municipal criminal context. She cannot be a credible witness to her own body. Despite the dialogue with Cecilia and the limited deferral to her glimpsed in the previous document, this order reveals the ways in which Reggio also has no interest in being in conversation with Cecilia.

Reggio underscores his distrust and dismissal of Cecilia in the final lines of the documents: "It is understood that at the end of the said two months it will proceed even without an examination; so that they will make the warden of the jail aware, do not let the aforementioned have relations with any person." The state will try, then, a strategy of imposed birth control, so as to ensure that Cecilia will never again be *"preñada a nuevo"* while in custody, that she not have sex with anyone else. The colonial regime here stands bare in its violent intentions. As Marisa J. Fuentes has noted, such glimpses at the explicit sexual violence of the plantation regime are rare (126). In his response to the "declarations of the aforesaid," Reggio has no time for euphemisms and does not talk around sex and rape or use enlightenment and biological metaphors to convey the situation. He does not want to hear for a third time that Cecilia is pregnant. Rather than promote "slave increase" or delay the punishment so that the "future slave" could be born, the state wants to ensure that Cecilia does not get pregnant again. Though the record holds no explicit explanation of Reggio's perplexing two-month delay, his intent is clear: he wields the ultimate state control over a person's body and orders her killed.

I have yet to find a conclusive explanation of Reggio's final order. The two-month delay may refer to a policy or precedent I am unaware of; it may be a typo or a poorly recorded statement; it may be that he was acting irrationally out of his documented hatred of maroons. It is, however, recorded that his prosecution of the maroons and specifically his treatment of Cecilia's case were at that time under scrutiny as excessive and unauthorized. On October 1, 1784, Governor Miró (who was away "at Indian congresses in Pensacola and Mobile") wrote the Count of Gálvez with concern that Cecilia's punishment was excessive. He asked for advice on the case and noted that he hesitated to act because he was related by marriage to Mauricio Conway, the man who claimed ownership of Cecilia. The letter's quick turn to the personal exemplifies the tight kinship networks between planters and politicians, but also that Cecilia was one relationship removed from the governor of the colony. That *she* posed a potential conflict of interest for Miró (standing in for the state) is something she might have known, if, say, Conway's brother-in-law, the governor, had on occasion visited the Conway plantation for family gatherings (Din and Harkins 166).[10]

Cecilia's potential to produce another enslaved person, another laborer, is exactly the power that she can wield briefly, that which she can assert to doctors, that which gets her words passed on by men who hold all the power. Her reproductive labor obligates them to delay her punishment and discuss her situation. As the documents show, Cecilia's speech and actions shape the narrative, even control it, if momentarily. Rather than continue as an "essential cog in the machine of profit," Cecilia slowed down, if only for a few months, the machine in its morbid work (Fuentes 129). She gummed up the gears, jamming the levers in a way that a commoditized body—no longer a person—should not have. Importantly, she did so with the aspect of her body that had the potential to be most exploited by the chattel slavery system—her reproductive body.

There are many unanswered questions about the end of Cecilia's life that are arguably more significant than whether she lied to colonial authorities about her body. They include but are not limited to: Was she ever executed? Was her sentence reduced to correspond to that received by the other maroons who did not kill anyone? Was she forced to return to the Conway plantation and later have her baby? Did she escape again? Was the community too disrupted for her personally to try escaping again? Despite these unknowns, the work of many Black feminist historians and critical archive scholars demonstrates that there are many ways to tell a story like hers, to talk about a life that "defies coherence and representability" (Fuentes 1).

Her voice is noted, and though heavily mediated, it stands in contradiction with the archival account that contains it. It calls into question at the time the record is made the claims of the document and its authors. It strains the text from within. This is another way of saying that the text not only needs to be read against the grain for the counterargument or anti-colonial logic. The suppressed, subaltern position can be heard because Cecilia's straining "hangs in the balance" with ours, those of us "straining against the limits of the archive" to tell impossible stories of lives dismissed in these archives (Hartman, "Venus" 14). Cecilia stands in disagreement with the colonial authorities and asserts herself according to the text. The men who meant her so much harm note it down. And so, oddly, disturbingly, to write about Cecilia, is not to write about a woman who is totally silenced. Her voice in the text is precarious, heavily mediated—not necessarily something to celebrate as a powerful exception to the violent tendencies of the archive (though it is that). Cecilia's own account and her ways of refusing her scheduled state-sanctioned murder refute the reductive narrative of a lying licentious woman.

To reconsider the period of increased marronage in 1780s New Orleans by centering the experiences of Cecilia and the other women in the maroon community underscores the role of the carceral in this example of North American marronage, and also demands a consideration of how reproductive labor shaped the persistent flight of women who escaped enslavement along the Mississippi River. Cecilia's response to her recapture is not neatly categorized as "resistance" or "reproduction" or even as reproduction as resistance. Like many women who formed chosen families in small ephemeral maroon communities, Cecilia "fell in the space between" those heuristics and categories, in her time and ours (Morgan, *Reckoning* 223). Refracting the archive through Cecilia's actions recasts the threat of marronage from simply one of male-led armed rebellion, violence against whites, or pillaging plantations, to one of embodiment, thorny kinship networks, and a potential maroon society. ▪

SJ Zhang is assistant professor of English at the University of Chicago. Their current project, *Going Maroon and Other Forms of Family*, considers how reproduction and carceral forces shaped the decisions and triggered the archives of four women who went maroon in North America and the Caribbean between 1781 and 1820. Zhang's work is published in *William and Mary Quarterly*, *Small Axe*, *Representations*, and *Women and Performance*.

ACKNOWLEDGMENTS

Thank you to the editors of *History of the Present* and to Jennifer L. Morgan and Alys Eve Weinbaum, editors of this special issue. I am lucky to have received feedback from all the amazing contributors to this issue at the outset of this process. Many thanks also to those who discussed the original Spanish with me and gave feedback on my transcriptions and translations: Guillaume Beaudin, Alyssa Brewer Garcia, Tania Islas, Agnes Lugo-Ortiz, and Kathryn McKnight. I am grateful to Janet Dees for bringing my attention to an additional set of questions around the prisoners and the guards. Invaluable workshop feedback on this material came from many folks in the Chicago Native American and Indigenous Studies Working Group, the Omohundro Institute, and the University of Chicago Institute on the Formation of Knowledge. Finally, I am eternally grateful to the librarians and archivists at the Historic New Orleans Collection and the Louisiana Historical Center. Thanks for the scans. You did not have to.

NOTES

1   See also Acts and Deliberations of the Cabildo of New Orleans, Spanish Transcription, 5 vols., Louisiana Collection, New Orleans Public Library. September 27, 1782, vol. 2, 136–37; May 28, 1784, vol. 2, 209.

2   "Criminales que se siguen de oficio contra les simarrones," Colonial Documents Collection (CDC), Louisiana Historical Center, New Orleans Jazz Museum, in the Old U.S. Mint. SCDIB #10–11; 806 Sp. file #3330.

3   "Criminales que se siguen de oficio contra les simarrones," Colonial Documents Collection (CDC), Louisiana Historical Center, New Orleans Jazz Museum, in the Old U.S. Mint. SCDIB #10–11; 806 Sp. file #3330.

4   *Outlyer* was an early English term used to describe a Native, Black, or White enslaved laborer who fled from the colonial settlement. Those outlandish outlyers posed a consistent threat to the early development of the colonies by "stealing" the labor force (themselves) on which early subsistence settlement and small plantations desperately depended to survive each winter (Robinson; Diouf).

5   For a very extensive bibliography of Atlantic World maroon studies as of 2020, see Nevius.

6   "Lista des Los Cimarrones que se hallan en la banda de Sn Malo," in letter from Acting Governor Francisco Bouligny to Governor Miró (away in Florida) June 3, 1784, Archivo General de Indias (AGI), Papeles de Cuba (PC), legajo 10, Historical New Orleans Collection, New Orleans, Louisiana.

7   I borrow this phrase from a 2019 order by the Missouri state legislature that required the *then* last remaining health care provider that performed abortions, Planned Parenthood of the St. Louis Region, give patients an additional pelvic exam before they were allowed to get the procedure. One doctor at the clinic described the forced exam as "inhumane" (Fieldstadt).

8   My thanks to Alys Eve Weinbaum for asking me to think more about the possibility of Cecilia's use of strategic sex.

9   There are discrepancies in the race and bondage terms used to describe Cecilia. While I disagree with Diouf that these inconsistencies indicate Cecilia's status as a freewoman, I think it might be possible to find out more relevant information.

10   Miró to the Count of Gálvez, no. 135, New Orleans, October 1, 1784, AGI, PC, leg. 3A, Historical New Orleans Collection, New Orleans, Louisiana.

WORKS CITED

Adamson, Christopher R. "Punishment after Slavery: Southern State Penal Systems, 1865–1890." *Social Problems* 30, no. 5 (1983): 555–69.

Bilby, Kenneth M. *True-Born Maroons*. Gainesville: University Press of Florida, 2005.

Butler, Sara M. "More than Mothers: Juries of Matrons and Pleas of the Belly in Medieval England." *Law and History Review* 37, no. 2 (2019): 353–96.

Butler, Sara M. "Pleading the Belly: A Sparing Plea? Pregnant Convicts and the Courts in Medieval England." In *Crossing Borders: Boundaries and Margins in Medieval and Early Modern Britain: Essays in Honour of Cynthia J. Neville*, edited by Sara M. Butler and K. J. Kesselring, 131–52. Leiden: Brill, 2018.

Cooper, Afua. *The Hanging of Angélique: The Untold Story of Canadian Slavery and the Burning of Old Montréal*. Toronto: HarperCollins, 2006.

Davis, Angela Y. "Reflections on the Black Woman's Role in the Community of Slaves." *Massachusetts Review* 13, nos. 1–2 (1972): 81–100.

Din, Gilbert C. "Cimarrones and the San Malo Band in Spanish Louisiana," *Louisiana History* 21, no. 3 (1980): 237–62.

Din, Gilbert C., and John E. Harkins. *The New Orleans Cabildo: Colonial Louisiana's First City Government, 1769–1803*. Baton Rouge: Louisiana State University Press, 1996.

Diouf, Sylviane A. *Slavery's Exiles: The Story of the American Maroons*. New York: New York University Press, 2014.

Fieldstadt, Elisha. "Missouri's Last Abortion Clinic Will Defy an 'Inhumane' State Mandate as It Battles to Stay Open." *NBC News*, June 20, 2019. https://www.nbcnews.com/news/us-news/missouri-s-last-abortion-clinic-will-defy-inhumane-state-mandate-n1019616.

Foucault, Michel. "Lives of Infamous Men." In *The Essential Foucault*, edited by Paul Rabinow and Nikolas Rose, 279–93. New York: New Press, 2003.

Fuentes, Marisa J. *Dispossessed Lives: Enslaved Women, Violence, and the Archive*. Philadelphia: University of Pennsylvania Press, 2016.

Gottlieb, Karla. *The Mother of Us All: A History of Queen Nanny, Leader of the Windward Jamaican Maroons*. Trenton, NJ: Africa World, 2000.

Hall, Gwendolyn Midlo. *Africans in Colonial Louisiana: The Development of Afro-Creole Culture in the Eighteenth Century*. Baton Rouge: Louisiana State University Press, 1992.

Hartman, Saidiya. "The Plot of Her Undoing." Feminist Art Coalition, 2019. https://feministartcoalition.org/essays-list/saidiya-hartman.

Hartman, Saidiya. "Venus in Two Acts." *Small Axe* 12, no. 2 (2008): 1–14.

Johnson, Jessica Marie. *Wicked Flesh: Black Women, Intimacy, and Freedom in the Atlantic World*. Philadelphia: University of Pennsylvania Press, 2020.

Manion, Jen. *Liberty's Prisoners: Carceral Culture in Early America*. Philadelphia: University of Pennsylvania Press, 2015.

McConnell, Roland C. *Negro Troops of Antebellum Louisiana: A History of the Battalion of Free Men of Color*. Baton Rouge: Louisiana State University Press, 1968.

McKnight, Kathryn Joy, and Leo J. Garofalo. *Afro-Latino Voices: Narratives from the Early Modern Ibero-Atlantic World, 1550–1812*. Indianapolis: Hackett, 2009.

Morgan, Jennifer L. *Laboring Women: Reproduction and Gender in New World Slavery*. Philadelphia: University of Pennsylvania Press, 2004.

Morgan, Jennifer L. *Reckoning with Slavery: Gender, Kinship, and Capitalism in the Early Black Atlantic*. Durham, NC: Duke University Press, 2021.

Nevius, Marcus P. "New Histories of Marronage in the Anglo-Atlantic World and Early North America." *History Compass* 18, no. 5 (2020): 1–14.

Paton, Diana. *No Bond but the Law: Punishment, Race, and Gender in Jamaican State Formation, 1780–1870.* Durham, NC: Duke University Press, 2004.

Patterson, Orlando. *Slavery and Social Death: A Comparative Study.* Cambridge, MA: Harvard University Press, 1982.

Price, Richard. *Maroon Societies: Rebel Slave Communities in the Americas.* Garden City, NY: Anchor Books, 1973.

Robinson, Cedric J. *Black Marxism: The Making of the Black Radical Tradition.* Rev. and updated 3rd ed. Chapel Hill: University of North Carolina Press, 2020.

Spillers, Hortense. "Mama's Baby, Papa's Maybe: An American Grammar Book." *Diacritics* 17, no. 2 (1987): 65–81.

Turner, Sasha. *Contested Bodies: Pregnancy, Childrearing, and Slavery in Jamaica.* Philadelphia: University of Pennsylvania Press, 2017.

White, Sophie. *Voices of the Enslaved: Love, Labor, and Longing in French Louisiana.* Williamsburg, VA: Omohundro Institute of Early American History and Culture, 2019.

Rickie Solinger

My Debt to Slavery

White Sex, White Pregnancy, White Maternity

ABSTRACT This autobiographical essay sets up a white middle-class young woman's emergence as a rights-bearing, choice-making exemplar of sexual freedom and as a holder of intimate racial capital in the 1970s. At the same time, elites and various professional authorities were re-stamping this young woman's Black peers with slavery- and Jim Crow-era tropes, as sexual criminals, bad choice-makers, producers of worthless and expensive children, not citizens. The essay considers the roles played by *Roe v. Wade*, the availability of contraception, "modern" midwifery services, the "sexual revolution," welfare policy, public rhetoric, and public policies in locking in new iterations of racism and racial difference in the post–civil rights era, and the importance of female sexuality, pregnancy, and maternity in constructing arenas for deploying these developments.

KEYWORDS racial reproduction, sexual citizenship, racialized sex system, white sexual supremacy, 1970s sexual/reproductive public policy

In the 1960s and 1970s the civil rights movement and the so-called sexual revolution competed for my attention: I noticed that it was okay if a white girl took up new sexual entitlements. But then, I couldn't miss the voices of white backlash insisting that Black girls and women had no claim to the sexual and reproductive rights that people like me were appropriating for ourselves.

As a white girl—in particular, a white girl from a middle-class family—my white body had become in those years a deserving, rights-bearing site of pleasure and choice. My mildly rebellious sexual adventures showed that I could flout middle-class dicta—and had the guts to keep at it—at least in part because I sensed the valuable race protections that I could count on, living as I did in my middle-class white body in New York. Surely, I felt this protection as I walked around in my white body, sensing my possession of the hard specie that constituted racial capital. My white-embodied sexual adventures

HISTORY of the PRESENT ▪ A Journal of Critical History ▪ 14:1 ▪ April 2024
DOI 10.1215/21599785-10898407 © 2024 Duke University Press

were part of what *Time* magazine and other media ballyhooed then as the "Sexual Revolution," an uprising that was, it looked like, for white girls alone.

Before the revolution, my white-girl status would have required obedience to the sexual norms my mother insisted on, or at least a slew of high-quality, artful obfuscations. When one of us white girls was found to be straying, parents and community imposed a mean raft of punishments. Now, the sexual revolution permitted girls like me to thumb our noses at the old rules, mostly with astonishing impunity.

Back then, white people responded to "civil rights" with a kind of brutal ambivalence. Many romantically embraced the social justice claims of the 1963 March on Washington and decried the brutality of Birmingham attack dogs and Bloody Sunday on the Edmund Pettus Bridge. But plenty also supported policies that gave new life to slavery-era distinctions between the sexuality, pregnancy, and maternity of people like me—and the sexuality, pregnancy, and maternity of my peers whose ancestors had been enslaved. In this way, many white people resisted the racial blurring that the civil rights movement stood for.

White middle-class parents in the 1960s and 1970s hated when their daughters openly pursued sex but also said "No!" to shotgun weddings, maternity homes, and secret relinquishments of "illegitimate" babies. Some sought out clandestine, criminal abortion. Or became single mothers. Just like Blacks. The public spotlight on the sexuality of white girls (together with reports of their eager use of the pill and then legal abortion) was a threat to a key marker of race difference, one can say, a threat to *white supremacy.*

Election results and public opinion polls in the 1970s showed that a majority of white Americans (definitely those over thirty) found these developments intolerable and responded by redrawing the distinctions between white-girl and black-girl sex. In fact, my status as an independent, white sexual revolutionary, tempered after 1973 by my status as a choice-maker and a natural-birthing nurturer, transformed my white body. It was no longer a mere body, helpless and vulnerable to sex and its consequences. I had become a white "social being" with sexual prerogatives (Roberts 303).

Throughout the 1960s and forward (and backward), politicians and policymakers had effectively marked the Black male body as criminal. Now law and policy cast Black female bodies, their mere bodies, as equally threatening to the body politic. My Black peers weren't typically locked up in prison then. But they were re-marked, as targets for tough sexual and reproductive regulation.

My body stood for the necessary obverse, as good defines evil. The sexual and reproductive status that white girls inherited and then reinvented in the

1970s amounted to a race gift: a cascading, recirculating accumulation of racial capital. Now, many middle-class white girls like me could do just about whatever they wanted to do, sexually and, to an extent, reproductively, without harming their white-girl identity.

My white body, especially given its class-inflected diction, crypto-hippie clothes, and particular frames of reference, guaranteed me race-based dispensations as I pursued sex, pregnancy, and maternity in those days. I picked up—from my college textbooks, from my therapist, from the *New York Times*—that I was not like Black girls. In my case, sexual pursuits were not the result of inbred, biologically determined wantonness but, rather, expressions of complex psychological syndromes, like "neuroses," my own and my mother's.

I learned that being burdened by such syndromes was a noble mark of a complex mind, even if neurosis always seemed to lead me to the threshold of trouble. Years later, as a scholar, I read books by white experts from that era, including one by an influential expert on unwed pregnancy who described my Black peers as *lacking* psyche, as having "no personality structure," and no "standards," as dwelling in the "psychological wastebasket" (Young 80).

My relationship to sexuality was also an important aspect of my relationship to *freedom*, a term I, like all Americans, had become familiar with in the 1960s as a race word. My white body was propped up by my white education, my access to jobs, and by my ownership of the means of reproductive control. Unlike Black girls, maybe Diane Nash and Angela Davis, I didn't have to struggle for this freedom, I could just lie back and try to enjoy it.

In 1975 I got pregnant and I was not married. So I found a justice of the peace who walked with us into the north woods of Vermont late that summer, with about a dozen friends and family. I stood beneath the pines in a long batik dress and said my vows so as to allay everybody's anxiety or family shame or, more fundamentally, to pledge allegiance to my white culture.

Following the ceremony, I appeared to be a responsible young woman, in contrast to those marked Black, who had not gone looking for a wedding officiant. What's more, I could sense my new status as an exemplary white citizen and an emergent "republican mother." I was going to give birth to a white child, a child who my family, my community, the whole entire country would value as a noble, contributing, free white citizen, himself. Nobody raised the possibility that I had no business being a mother, as, in fact, I had almost no money at all when the baby was born.

Altogether, my white sexuality, white pregnancy, and white maternity gave me opportunities to show I *owned* my own life. As a middle-class white girl, by definition, I possessed a complex intelligence. I possessed the capacity to embrace my own personal freedom. I was animated by a socially productive sense of responsibility. In short, my whiteness meant I owned the qualifications for generative citizenship. And, to be sure, I possessed the capacity for maternal love and care. These were the very characteristics that public policies and white public opinion, revitalizing founding tropes, specifically and emphatically denied to my Black peers, to my everlasting benefit.

The Binary Sex System

I was the iconic white girl learning to move freely, even boldly, in a climate of privacy and choices. The other iconic girl, the legatee of enslaved ancestors, was scorched now, in the post–civil rights era, by a resurrected climate of fearmongering, hate, and degradation. She had to dodge a white polity that harped on her sexuality and reproduction and seemed daily to cook up mid-twentieth-century-style tactics of control. I was a dubious and genteel revolutionary, but free. She was targeted for varieties of corporal punishment deemed appropriate to her Blackness. In retrospect and to a significant extent, she existed to make me free.

In 1970s New York, city leaders and many of their white constituents, facing plunging tax revenues, the evaporation of working-class jobs, and white flight, supported policies that amounted to a ramped-up disinvestment in Black lives. This was a harsh position: since Black lives no longer directly *enhanced* white wealth, they *drained* it. Public rhetoric marked the value—now, the *valuelessness*—of Black lives in economic terms, as under the slavery regime. Politicians and policymakers enacted programs giving new life to slavery-era and Jim Crow practices, inventing strategies for policing Black bodies, constraining reproduction, stripping away supports such as welfare provision, regulating family relations and domestic arrangements, hardening residential and educational segregation.

At the same time that politicians cut capital investments in programs serving low-income people—schools, day care programs, hospitals, libraries, housing, and welfare—public officials went after the sexual and reproductive bodies of women of color with vigor. They defined this group as a "population" undeserving of the "privacy" that I enjoyed, as a bunch of unsuitable, bad choice-makers. Congress crafted the Hyde Amendment in 1976, prohibiting Medicaid funding for abortion, thereby legally canceling "privacy" and "choice" for poor women and making "reproductive freedom" into a commodity for purchase by people who had enough money to buy it, people who understood that sex itself was a class-and-race privilege.

Now public policies, together with everyday white opinion, defined Black reproduction as a crime, sometimes punishable by sterilization. Consistent with nineteenth-century racial eugenics, the Black woman's womb was still a debased manufactory, but now it produced worthless, possibly deadly products. Politicians and policymakers defined her pregnancy-and-motherhood-while-poor as the Welfare Queen's acts of *prostitution*: having a baby simply to get her thieving hands on public money in the form of welfare benefits.

The Black baby wasn't an economic investment for slaveholders anymore. Now, this baby was an emblem of "overpopulation" and "population explosion." White public rhetoric cast the little Black child who cost white taxpayers too much as an agent of destruction: a dangerous, scary emblem of unregulated Blackness, a homunculus-criminal, a certain threat to the white social order. In the wake of the civil rights movement, official America was brutally chasing my Black peer out of the public sphere.

On the contrary, I was passively earning my secure public identity as a free sexual person possessing valuable reproductive capacities—and a future—that belonged to me. I became, anew, the necessary and defining contrast to my Black peer. The supremacist intentions of whites who resisted the Black citizenship claims of the civil rights movement made me into a respectable young woman—and their political asset.

In this context, the sexual revolution enhanced my freedom: my right to legitimate, dignified free sex, free love, free choice, a full menu of freedoms based on my white race. My body became a new political body, an updated advertisement for superior whiteness. Within the racialized, class-inflected regime of sex, I always, ultimately, looked like chastity. I always held that pricey ticket.

Clearly, that ticket bought me negative rights that carried very positive benefits.[1] I was able to procure contraception, for example, without ever having been part of a coercive or medically risky experiment testing the pill's effectiveness and safety. My sex life didn't enrage white taxpayers. My sexual freedom never stimulated a public official or a physician to offer me abortion access in exchange for tubal ligation. I was never officially required to name the boys I had sex with.[2] Authorities never labeled me a prostitute or monetized my sexuality or its consequences, even though I received public benefits, like unemployment checks and tax deductions as a result of becoming a mother. Neither public officials nor psychologists condemned my white sex life and near-illegitimate maternity as racially determined.

And there was more. I became a member of a vaunted "generation," not a reviled "population." If my exercise of sexual freedom produced a pregnancy and a baby, that child would never be defined as a statistic in the population explosion or a contributor to environmental degradation, or a potential criminal, or an agent of assault on the eugenic health of white society. As a member of my *generation*, I was an upstanding choice-maker.

Indeed, I was exempt from being labeled "risky" and from prevention-training programs, and I was not damned as a member of an emergent "white matriarchy." I was not surveilled. If I had secrets, they were mine to keep to myself. *Newsweek* and TV talk shows imagined my sexuality as a vibrant, if nettlesome, expression of white-girl freedom.

It is worth saying, though, that freedom did not mean guiltlessness regarding sex. But, really, thank god for guilt, the proof that my mind was working, in fact, working overtime. Guilt was proof of my whiteness radiating outward from my most important organ, that engine of freedom: my white brain.

While I was living this free life, I ignored the elements that protected me. I didn't question the racialized sex system that operated right in front of my eyes, elevating and dignifying me at the expense of my Black peer. I took what I could get.

White Pregnancy: Responsibility and Citizenship

I behaved as if my sexual and reproductive decisions expressed my rights, were valid expressions of my rightly freedom.

My sources of information told the opposite story about the reproductive decisions of my Black peers. I learned that their decisions were not even decisions. White journalists, sociologists, and politicians explained that the sex of Black females expressed their *enslavement* to lust and to criminality in the form of welfare-prostitution.

Joining these experts were US Representative Henry Hyde of Illinois and presidential counselor Daniel Moynihan, all of whom (along with many others) narrated Black-woman irresponsibility for the edification of the white public, in order to define Black people as distinct from whites. For example, at a Senate Finance Committee hearing in 1967, Senator Russell B. Long of Louisiana described a group of African American women who protested in front of the Capitol against reduced social provision as "female broodmares who were here yesterday" (*Social Security Amendments* 1647). Recapitulating the dicta of the slavery regime, politicians crafted laws and policies committed to updating the codes and processes that would affix race, sex, and reproduction to every aspect of modern freedom and unfreedom.

Enforcement was harsh. In Senator Long's state, the legislature persisted in denying Black people the citizenship status of voter. Their go-to tactic was excluding Black voters on grounds of sexuality and reproduction, passing laws requiring Black men to report any children they fathered with women to whom they were not married and barring any Black woman from the franchise if she had a child while unmarried. In Newburgh, New York, an infamously anti-Black city manager, underscoring the criminality of Black reproduction and mothering, required all welfare recipients to collect their Aid to Dependent Children checks at the police station (Pope 295, 307).

I, on the other hand, walked around in a sufficiently responsible body that gave me the right to represent myself. I understood that using contraception was a marker of responsible maturity for people like me. I knew that seeking either an illegal or a legal abortion (pre– or post–*Roe v. Wade*) was the same kind of marker. Alternately, so was getting married if there was a baby coming, and I was willing to have it. And probably owning a copy of *Our Bodies, Ourselves*, first published by the Boston Women's Health Book Collective in 1973, fit into that category, another sign of modern, white-girl responsibility.

Roe v. Wade was a big help in this regard. The 1973 Supreme Court decision marked me for the whole duration of my fertile period as a choice-maker, a good, *white* choice-maker. Whichever choice I made, I had my reasons, and those reasons were my business. Possessing this individual *right to choice* distracted me from thinking about the obstacles to *free choice* that others might face. For example, many girls and women might have felt that they were too poor or too racially reviled or too lacking in access to medical services or safe housing and educational opportunities to choose motherhood, or to purchase "choice" at all.

The white public regularly assessed the "behavior" of my Black peers: they don't even know their own bodies; in that sense, one could say they don't even *own* their own bodies. I took it for granted that I knew my own body. I was perfectly aware that *Roe* was convenient, liberating, and defining, for me.

As an obsessively distracted young woman in the dawn of *Roe*, I was simply too busy to pay sustained attention to the brilliant political voices of my Black and Brown peers, founders of the National Welfare Rights Organization and the Combahee River Collective, among others, who were claiming extraordinary, if constrained, spaces in the public square. I lost track of the charges against Medicaid as a racially oppressive regime and also of the emergent shards of information about rampant sterilizations of Native American, Mexican American, Puerto Rican, and Black women across the United States. I was the blinded witness and the beneficiary of disasters that I did not see.

My dim vision was in line with the opinions of the knowledge purveyors, in particular, their ideas about how, when a Black girl assumed sexual and reproductive latitude for herself, "we" saw what happened when the wrong people got rights. These public voices still treated the reproductive capacity of Black girls and women as a cost-benefit issue, not an issue of reproductive liberty. In contrast, I simply possessed my au courant white right to sexual and reproductive freedom, in whatever way white, male legislators and judges defined that freedom. In this way, my ownership of my own narrative and my own body was affirmed. I was credible, a "property-owning" citizen.

Overlooking: The Core Practice of Genteel White Supremacy

When the Supreme Court designated me a legitimate choice-maker, I simply universalized that marker. That's what we needed and what we won. I overlooked the ways that the lived experiences of many people met obstacles to exercising this so-called choice. In 1973, and even in 1977, when the Hyde Amendment kicked in, I largely overlooked the ways that choice became a privilege and also a strategy for defining and protecting white supremacy. The courts, naturalizing and invisibilizing the "legal rhetoric of race," went beyond *privilege* as they cut the material of choice to fit the bodies of white women and only white women (Ross 21). Courts, of course, denied any racism, underscoring the judiciary's innocence and the innocence of its deserving beneficiaries. These maneuvers were particularly easy to overlook.

I think I largely overlooked the ways that many white people characterized the thank-god-that's-over end of the civil rights movement: the government has done enough. Now the ball's in their court. And there better not be any more mayhem in the overpopulated streets.

I'm afraid that I didn't really understand the pornographic human rights violations at the heart of the "welfare queen" trope that coronated the "queen" as ruler of "the underclass," and the queen-mother of "the culture of poverty," while training the white eye on her sexuality and recruiting the white mind to pronounce on her sex-induced poverty. Maybe I disapproved of the characterization but still failed to understand quite how valuable it was to many white people, me included, as a substitute for old-fashioned expressions of race hatred.

Having taken history courses in college, I could have understood the connection between the strategies of white backlash in these years and the white backlash of the post–Civil War period in the 1870s. But I had been raised and continued to make myself as, in effect, a racial separatist, so it was the most natural thing in the world to overlook this business.

When I read "poverty porn" by, say, anthropologist Oscar Lewis or journalist Susan Sheehan, I overlooked—that is, I didn't make counterarguments to myself about the relevance of US imperialism and deindustrialization; the rise of low-wage, no-benefit service jobs; the lack of a national day care policy; the burgeoning foster care system; the disinvestment in educational and employment opportunities for poor people; inadequate laws enforcing child support; and welfare policies that mandated poor people be destitute and stay destitute to establish eligibility for almost all forms of public support.

I overlooked criminalization of the reproductive behavior of women of color. I did not know a story like this one, about a welfare recipient with two small children, who described herself as "desperate" for money, in such straits that she would have "gone out and sold my body if I knew how—or thought I could get anything for it." Instead, she didn't tell her welfare worker about a little bit of income she had earned. The court gave her a stiffer sentence as a first offender than the judge handed out to an armed robber, a man who had committed an assault with a deadly weapon, a drunk driver who had hit and nearly killed a ten-year-old, and a fifth-time offender pimp.[3]

Most profoundly, I overlooked the ways that law, policy, and public rhetoric drew on and repurposed elements of the slavery regime in order to make racial difference hyper-distinct, again, especially the ways that law and policy targeted Black women's bodies and created dangerous crises for Black women, their families and communities. I largely overlooked elites calculating the gap between the value of white children against the valuelessness of Black children, then funding and defunding programs, educational institutions, and other initiatives accordingly.

I didn't see that the Hyde Amendment was printed on a parchment remnant saved from the slavery era, a document directing the government to use poor women's bodies to merge the interests of church and state, degrading women (iconically Black), using them as simple tools of reaction. The amendment denied poor women, symbolically Black, the human consideration that *Roe v. Wade* had guaranteed women who had the money to pay for their civic dignity and safety. The Hyde Amendment and *Harris v. McRae*, the Supreme Court decision that constitutionalized Hyde, spelled out the government's right to balance the choices of one group against the choicelessness of the other.

Roe v. Wade marked a revival of one more foundational slavery-era distinction. Many celebrated this decision as the achievement of reproductive liberty, the affirmation of the linkage of *freedom* and the right to control reproduction. But the *Roe* decision degraded notions of "liberty," privileging *my right* not to be pregnant while ignoring the dangers to millions of poor girls and women (iconically Black) who stayed pregnant and became mothers, while living in a harsh, punitive, and parsimonious society.

In all these ways white policymakers, jurists, and others emphasized that this "population" did not own their own bodies. The heavy hands of legislators and the courts pressed down on them, denied them legitimate choices, and left me *Roe*-enabled, free, in contrast.

There were still more old/new coercions. Numerous hospitals did not discourage attending physicians from performing unsought sterilizations on poor women, disproportionately Black and Brown. Doctors sometimes said they performed these operations because "these women" should not have (more) children. Doctors sterilized them with legal impunity and without asking the woman for consent (Rothman).

Nial Ruth Cox, whose sterilization at eighteen by a North Carolina physician in 1965 became an infamous act, said that the doctor had treated her like "an animal" and as "retarded." Providing an echo of another slavery-era trope, one that expressed her thin claim to ownership of her own body, Cox added, "When you're black and poor, you have to forget what you want and do what the rich, white people say." In 1973 the ACLU lawyer filing suit against the state of North Carolina said, "This girl was sterilized because she was black, a member of a welfare family and, at the time of the operation, a minor," while Cox provided her own view of causation: "They want to stop the black population" (Hudson).

To that end, some judges encouraged poor women to accept birth control in exchange for time in prison or a public assistance grant (Waldron). The ones who were incarcerated might be coercively sterilized in New York City and elsewhere, even if locked up for a minor drug charge.[4]

Roe did redress the reproductively degraded status of some girls and women. But the poorest among us remained degraded, coming and going. Whether they were punished by the welfare office for reproducing or constrained by the law from forestalling reproduction, the public, racialized messaging was identical: "these people" are not legitimate decision-makers; they are degraded persons. In this way, too, *Roe v. Wade* refreshed and reinforced meanings of racial difference.

About the time I rented my own apartment, the Supreme Court determined that welfare offices should cease the "midnight raid," the practice of welfare-office staff barging into a client's home at night, as if it were a public space lacking privacy protections and residents' privilege of self-protection. The aim was to find evidence—a man in the house—proving that the client was both collecting benefits and having sex, a combination banned by welfare departments.

But even after this practice was outlawed, the welfare system found other legal methods for regulating or criminalizing poor pregnant women and mothers, often via the foster care system and the Medicaid program, using agency policies to justify surveillance, supervision, and disciplinary actions such as child removal.

Policymakers and urban bureaucrats forced poor mothers into the labor force, often speaking out about their worthlessness as mothers. Amendments to the Social Security Act of 1967 mandated this requirement, in part because the number of mothers in the labor force was nearly equal to the number staying home to (incompetently) take care of children, so why not? Then the first group got larger than the second, and the pressure mounted. Women forced by the new rules to leave their babies for pitiful wages saw the connection between slavery-era practices and their own lives. They spoke of "forced work," "slave labor," and "slave-wage employers" and of the problem of children without child care. They spoke out for their authority *as mothers*, with rights to make decisions about their children's care. One woman fiercely articulated what she saw as the issue: "Welfare officials want to break up our families. . . . We refuse to be separated from our children one by one" (Solinger 172).

Brutal disrespect for Black family relations was a hallmark of public policies repurposing slavery-era distinctions. Speaking in 1963 for an unknown number of white people, the infamous Sheriff Jim Clark of Selma, Alabama, spat out this answer to a question about a Black woman's marital status: "She is a nigger woman and she hasn't got a Miss or a Mrs. in front of her name."[5]

Daniel Patrick Moynihan, still much honored in the twenty-first century, reviled absent Black fathers in the twentieth century as part of his broader attack on Black families. He taunted "these men" (forbidden by welfare policies to contact their families) for succumbing to the "attractions" of "freedom of movement" when they "disappeared." Unselfconsciously using slavery-era ideas (such as invoking the "runaway") and slavery-era diction, Moynihan advised presidents, crafted legislation, and issued influential public pronouncements.

While Moynihan and I overlooked so much, Black women organized and deployed their hard-won public voices to speak out against the dangers welfare policy and white supremacy created for their reproductive and laboring bodies. They pointed to "slave wage employers" and public policies that forced women into "slave labor jobs" that separated mothers from their children (Kornbluh 156; Solinger 156–57). They drew attention to officials and bosses who limited Black women's freedom and cursed them on the grounds of sex and reproduction in order to lift up white bodies, again. All this at the same time I was exploring the capacious contours of my own freedom.

White Maternity: Love

My explorations, as I prepared to become a mother, were shaped by the fact that I hardly had enough money to pay the rent and was walking around with a near "illegitimate" pregnancy and soon-to-be-born child. Nevertheless I did not see my options as constrained. Any irregularities I had created did not undermine my citizenship status, rooted as it always was in my white, middle-class body, and in the generally imputed sense of maternal responsibility and value that my body carried.

After a cold encounter with a bossy male obstetrician on Central Park West, I read, on page 12 of the September 15, 1975, edition of the *New York Times*, an article by young Jane Brody describing a birthing facility opening soon in New York. Brody emphasized the center's "home-like" atmosphere, its "oriental carpets" and "spiral staircase," the "flowery curtains and house-plants," the garden, and the sitting room in the townhouse just off Fifth Avenue at Ninety Second Street. There, the fifty-eight-year-old Maternity Center Association, historically an educational and obstetric service for New York's poor and immigrant communities, was launching a renovated midwifery service for modern times, the Childbearing Center (CBC) (Brody).

I was always looking for a home, especially a lovely home. What's more, I thought, this could be a place where I could be a kind of activist, spurning cold, male obstetricians and their conventional, medicalized pregnancy care. I could pursue political and aesthetic goals as a consumer of alternative obstetric services. I would be treated respectfully. I would be making the healthiest and most caring choices possible for my child.

Reading Brody's *New York Times* article, I also noticed that the center eschewed enemas during labor, as well as pubic shaves, episiotomies, and general anesthesia, all routine hospital practices then, and midwives facilitated births. (Finally, in 1971 the American College of Obstetricians had approved traditional female-centered midwifery, ruling that under a physician's supervision, "midwives may assume responsibility for the complete care and management of uncomplicated maternity patients.") And the CBC was cheaper than the obstetrician on Central Park West.

I was the third pregnant woman to enroll in the CBC program, and I was thrilled—to be accepted and to be so cool. The garden was lovely, the rugs were beautiful, and the staff was warm and, indeed, respectful. My visits to the center were pleasant and fulfilling. I wasn't worried about my pregnancy, so I could focus on assessing how successfully the center met my political and aesthetic concerns.

Around this time, a woman in California explained her similar choice of venue: "We are a group . . . who have taken our birthright—freedom, and decided for ourselves what our rituals of birth will be" (Arms 212). Indeed, the center was yet another expression of the freedom I believed I was born and raised to possess. According to a CBC survey, I was similar to most center clients: I felt my freedom-birthright included the unfettered right to be "in control," not dominated by others, including obstetricians (Sacks and Donnenfeld 472).

My acceptance into the program meant the staff believed that, under a nurse-midwife's supervision, I could learn how to take my own blood pressure, test my urine, measure the fundal height, estimate the fetal position, and record the fetal heart rate. I must have possessed another CBC criteria, a "high level of personal autonomy and confidence," since they let me into the program. The staff invited me to be a "member of the decision-making team" (Lubic, "Barriers" 73–74). In that setting, I was not just another body in the maternity department of a public hospital. I was anointed by the CBC, I was important; my white body was my precious asset. It vouched for me.

I was one of the "knowledgeable young people" and the kind of citizen-*consumer* the new program sought, one part of a "well-educated [couple who has] done their own reading and investigation on pregnancy and childbirth . . . [intending] to limit their families to one or two children, [planning] to arrange their childbearing experience to satisfy their own needs and standards" (94).

The center staff and I were rewriting the meaning of modern childbirth. Their ideal clients showed up in magazine spreads and local newspapers, exemplifying "a particular version of postwar femininity—white, heterosexual, companionately married: the new 'domestic ideal.'" We reimagined the "ignorant, superstitious, uneducated [read: Black] midwife" of old. In partnership with us, the midwife became new again, too: whitely modern (Doughty 168).

Now that I was pregnant and going to be a mother soon, I wanted to be on the Margaret Mead team, the teams of the British obstetrician Grantly Dick-Read, the American obstetrician Robert Bradley, La Leche League, and all the other teams that proclaimed my heroic, natural capacity as a birthing woman. Never having been great at protesting in the streets, I wanted to be part of what some folks were calling an "unarmed revolution" in the delivery room (Lubic, "Developing" 1687). I wanted to be a class rebel, mastering labor pains as against the helpless whimpers and yelps of the "more cultured races of the earth" (Arms 134). I wanted the process to remake me, as a rebel-parent with a Baby X, a mother who loved her baby—and the world—so much as to make an indelible mark.[6]

Yet I didn't recognize the CBC as a "racializing institution." Today, adapting anthropologist Khiara Bridges's construct, I see that the CBC marked its patients as possessing power and privilege by virtue of their status as patients of the institution. Moreover, when that possession was read within a racializing logic, the patients were produced as possessing racialized power and privilege—that is, the patients were produced in that setting as white/congruent with the CBC's aims (Bridges 236). An early study of the CBC's clientele found that nineteen out of twenty women in the program were "Caucasian," all in their mid- to late twenties. I fit in (Sacks and Donnenfeld 470).

Fitting in established me as "modern," an urban, white, middle-class, hip young woman, in large part because of the out-of-hospital, midwife connection. At the same time, authorities claimed the "non-white" woman's ignorance of modern practices of childbirth was proof of *her* degraded status (Doughty 200n83). (Articles about childbirth in mass media largely ignored the poor standard of care in underfunded public hospitals, and the paucity of options available to women with few financial resources.) Identifying midwifery, an ancient tradition, and a vibrant one still, especially in rural African American communities, with *white modernity* was brutal.

In addition to attracting people like me in 1975, the center had plans to open two other childbirthing centers, in the South Bronx and East New York in Brooklyn, both poor, Puerto Rican and African American neighborhoods. Its proof-of-concept site was the one I went to, on the upper-crust Upper East Side. I'm guessing CBC staff felt confident that the pregnant women who chose that site would possess characteristics the program valued and *needed* in order to meet state-mandated statistics required for the CBC to evolve from an experiment into a permanent program.

My sense today of the CBC as a "racializing institution" is necessarily entangled with the center's decision to rely on my white body for proving its concept to a hostile, conservative medical establishment worried about protecting its turf. Women in the Bronx and Brooklyn—the center's historical constituency—would benefit, after I went first. This is an interesting idea. My body, never a guinea pig for pharmaceutical companies producing risky contraceptives, never target of dubious experiments or punitive operations, was in fact the testing ground for the Childbearing Center.

But in 1975, inside the lovely spaces of the CBC, I was colorblind. As were the CBC's ideas about midwifery. One expert, championing the excellence of new, professionally trained urban midwives, explained that the future required midwives, not physicians, because "today it is rare for a woman to die in childbirth, and infant mortality is down to 16.5 per one thousand live births" (Steinmann 34). The expert overlooked the fact that in the thirty years after World War II, 1972 was the only year that the Black maternal mortality rate was less than three times greater than the white rate. In about one-third of those years, the Black rate was four times greater. The maternal mortality rate of Black women in 1973 was equal to the rate for white women in 1955 (Lee 261–62). As for the babies, in the 1970s, the white infant mortality rate per 1,000 live births was 17.8; for black babies, the rate was almost twice as high, 32.6 (CDC).

Consistent with effacement of information about maternal and infant mortality, white administrators of programs serving African American communities also committed violent erasure by simple condescension. The director of a birthing center serving poor communities in Philadelphia, for example, congratulated her own program: "We help [our client] build confidence in herself and her ability to do things—which I think is essential for motherhood." She didn't explain what she meant by "confidence base" and "the ability to do things." Perhaps the head of this other racializing institution in the 1970s wished her "population" could become more like the CBC imagined me, even though I was a young woman with no history of infant care or, really, much care at all (Lubic, "Developing" 1688).

Back in New York, the Maternity Center faced ongoing attacks. Between March 1975 and March 1978, New York City, under intense pressure from medical associations, refused to issue a Medicaid vendor number to the CBC, a strategy that would certainly cripple its program plans in the Bronx and Brooklyn.

Like US Representative Henry Hyde, the New York powerbrokers downtown used the bodies of poor women to achieve political goals. That is, Congress designed the Hyde Amendment to Medicaid to block poor women's access to abortion because of some politicians' religious preferences. In New York the politicos used Medicaid to block poor women's access to midwifery services at the CBC because obstetricians wanted to maintain control over childbirth. The truth was, the center could use me to test its concept, but even if the concept was proven, so what, if women in the South Bronx and East New York were denied access to Medicaid and so, to the birthing centers, a conundrum that deepened the travesty of "choice."

Ultimately, after three months of lovely prenatal visits at the CBC, and only eight weeks before my due date, a nice staff member whose face I can't remember came into the examining room where I was sitting, waiting. He told me that in reviewing my medical records, the staff had (finally) noticed that twelve years before, in the early 1960s, I had experienced an unexplained seizure. He said I would have to leave the CBC program because prior seizures were associated with seizures during labor, and the center couldn't afford to have a patient with a history that might require medical intervention: a poor statistic.

I understood that my job had involved proving the CBC concept. But I had become a guinea pig for poor women and was found wanting. My cool wiped away, my glory as a birthing pioneer with bragging rights gone. I can imagine I skulked out of the Childbirthing Center in a body that no longer felt like a source of ennobled white dignity but rather felt more like a source of humiliation and rejection. As if I'd just had a sharp, glancing encounter with the limits of my white superiority.

It's just a thought, forty-eight years later. Just a thought. Because before I left the building, I figured out a way to operationalize my anger and disappointment, imperiously requiring the staff member to make up for kicking me out of the program by arranging for the people over at the new midwifery program at Roosevelt Hospital, unencumbered by the medical implications of an ancient seizure, to take me in, with just eight weeks to go.

In this way, I met my baby boy in a public hospital with no lovely appurtenances, none necessary. ▪

Rickie Solinger is a historian and a curator, the author or editor of a dozen books about reproductive politics and satellite issues and the organizer of exhibitions that have traveled to 150 college and university galleries in the United States.

NOTES

1   In *Killing the Black Body*, the author succinctly defines "negative rights" and "positive rights": "The Constitution protects only an individual's 'negative' right to be free from unjustified intrusion, rather than the 'positive' right to be free to lead a free life" (Roberts 229).

2   New York City required mothers applying for public assistance "for their children born out of wedlock" to sign the following affidavit: "I had relations with the above-named father at or about the period of conception preceding the birth of said child, and I did not have relations with any other male person during such period of conception" (Mink and Solinger 430).

3   I collected this story from a legitimate source in about 2000, using it in my book *Beggars and Choosers: How the Politics of Choice Shapes Adoption, Abortion, and Welfare in the United States* (Solinger 174n164) with an incomplete citation that neither I nor the copy editors caught. It remains a striking story, although I can't find the source.

4   The Committee to End Sterilization Abuse (CESA) organized against such practices in New York in the mid-1970s; committee member Frances M. Beal called these operations "surgical genocide" (Beal).

5   "Dear Friend Letter," March 1963, Alabama Governor's Administrative Assistants Files, 1963–1966, SCLC, SG 19972, folder 24, Alabama State Archives, Montgomery.

6   Baby X was the protagonist of an amazing fable, "X: A Fabulous Child's Story," by Lois Gould, published in the sixth issue of *Ms.* magazine, December 1972, about a couple who refused to identify the gender of their child, first discomfiting everyone and then changing everyone and everything (Gould).

WORKS CITED

Arms, Suzanne. *Immaculate Deception: A New Look at Women and Children in America*. Boston: Houghton Mifflin, 1975.

Beal, Frances M. "Double Jeopardy: To Be Black and Female." In *The Black Woman: An Anthology*, edited by Toni Cade Bambara, 109–122. New York: New American Library, 1970.

Bridges, Khiara. *Reproducing Race: An Ethnography of Pregnancy as a Site of Racialization*. Berkeley: University of California Press, 2008.

Brody, Jane. "Center for Childbirth a Home-Like Setting." *New York Times*, September 15, 1975. https://www.nytimes.com/1975/09/15/archives/center-for-childbirth-a-home like-setting.html.

CDC (Centers for Disease Control and Prevention). "Health, United States, 2014, Trend Tables. Table 12. Infant Mortality Rates, By Race: United States, Selected Years 1950–2013." https://www.cdc.gov/nchs/data/hus/2014/012.pdf (accessed June 12, 2023).

Doughty, Dierdre Gae. "Having a Baby the Natural Way: Primitive Bodies, Modern Women, and Childbirth in Mid-century America." PhD diss., University of Texas at Austin, 2013.

Gould, Lois. "X: A Fabulous Child's Story." *Ms.* 1, no. 6 (1972): 74–76, 105–6.

Hudson, Edward. "Suit Seeks to Void Sterilization Law." *New York Times*, July 13, 1973. https://www.nytimes.com/1973/07/13/archives/suit-seeks-to-void-sterilization-law -aclu-asks-1million-for-north.html.

Kornbluh, Felicia. *The Battle for Welfare Rights: Politics and Poverty in Modern America*. Philadelphia: University of Pennsylvania Press, 2007.

Lee, Anne S. "Maternal Mortality in the United States." *Phylon* 38, no. 3 (1977): 259–66.

Lubic, Ruth W. "Barriers and Conflict in Maternity Care and Innovation," PhD diss., Teachers College Columbia University, 1979.

Lubic, Ruth W. "Developing Maternity Services Women Will Trust." *American Journal of Nursing* 75, no. 10 (1975): 1685–88.

Mink, Gwendolyn, and Rickie Solinger, eds. *Welfare: A Documentary History of US Policy and Politics*. New York: New York University Press, 2003.

Pope, Andrew. "Making Motherhood a Felony: African American Women's Welfare Rights Activism in New Orleans and the End of Suitable Home Laws, 1959–1962." *Journal of American History* 105, no. 2 (2018): 291–310.

Roberts, Dorothy. *Killing the Black Body: Race, Reproduction, and the Meaning of Liberty*. New York: Random House, 1997.

Ross, Thomas. *Just Stories: How the Law Embodies Racism and Bias*. Boston: Beacon, 1997.

Rothman, Sheila M. "Funding Sterilization and Abortion for the Poor." *New York Times*, February 22, 1975. https://www.nytimes.com/1975/02/22/archives/funding -sterilization-and-abortion-for-the-poor.html.

Sacks, Susan Riemer, and Penny B. Donnenfeld. "Parental Choice of Alternative Birth Environments and Attitudes toward Childrearing Philosophy." *Journal of Marriage and Family* 46, no. 2 (1984): 469–75.

Social Security Amendments of 1967. Part 3: Hearings on H.R. 12080 Before the Senate Comm. on Finance, 90th Cong., 1st session, on September 20–22, 26, 1967 (statement of Senator

Russell B. Long of Louisiana). https://www.google.com/books/edition/Social_
Security_Amendments_of_1967/IWtqAAAAMAAJ?hl.

Solinger, Rickie. *Beggars and Choosers: How the Politics of Choice Shapes Adoption, Abortion, and Welfare in the United States.* New York: Hill and Wang, 2002.

Steinmann, Marion. "Parent and Child: The New Old Way of Delivering Babies." *New York Times Magazine,* November 23, 1975. https://www.nytimes.com/1975/11/23/archives/parent-and-child-the-new-old-way-of-delivering-babies-now-the.html.

Waldron, Martin. "Birth Control Urged to Cut Relief Costs." *New York Times,* March 11, 1979. https://www.nytimes.com/1979/03/11/archives/new-jersey-weekly-birth-control-urged-to-cut-relief-costs-birth.html.

Young, Leontine. *Out of Wedlock.* New York: McGraw Hill, 1954.

Keep up to date on new scholarship

Issue alerts are a great way to stay current on all the cutting-edge scholarship from your favorite Duke University Press journals. This free service delivers tables of contents directly to your inbox, informing you of the latest groundbreaking work as soon as it is published.

To sign up for issue alerts:

1. Visit **dukeu.press/register** and register for an account. You do not need to provide a customer number.

2. After registering, visit **dukeu.press/alerts**.

3. Go to "Latest Issue Alerts" and click on "Add Alerts."

4. Select as many publications as you would like from the pop-up window and click "Add Alerts."

read.dukepress.edu/journals

Agricultural History

The official journal of the Agricultural History Society

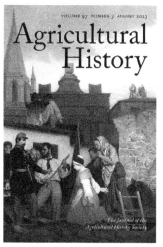

Albert Way, editor

Agricultural History is the journal of record in its field. As such, it publishes articles that explore agriculture and rural life over time, in all geographies and among all people. Articles in *Agricultural History* use a wide range of methodologies to illuminate the history of farming, food, agricultural science and technology, the environment, rural life, and beyond.

Sign up for new issue alerts at dukeu.press/alerts.

Subscribe today.

Quarterly. Subscription included with membership in the Agricultural History Society. To subscribe, visit aghistorysociety.org.

dukeupress.edu/agricultural-history

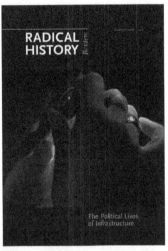

Printed and bound by CPI Group (UK) Ltd, Croydon, CR0 4YY

25/03/2025

14647324-0003